The book discusses the inevitable stress, frustration, anger, and pain parents feel when they learn their child is using drugs. Brief vignettes depict typical parental reactions—effective and ineffective—and suggest where and to whom parents can turn for help. Experts give advice to parents on how to listen actively, sensitively, and constructively to their teenagers; how to avoid problems related to either indulging or punishing the teenager; and how to be a more self-assured, secure, and relaxed parent of a teenager.

The contributors emphasize the importance of secondary prevention methods, designed to prevent novice drug users from becoming hard-core ones. Specific illustrations of school-based secondary prevention programs are given. They also suggest how to organize, implement, and evaluate secondary prevention programs.

George M. Beschner is chief of the Technology Transfer Branch of the National Institute of Drug Abuse.
Alfred S. Friedman is director of research at the Philadelphia Psychiatric Center.

Teen Drug Use

Teen Drug Use

edited by

George Beschner
Department of Health and
Human Services

Alfred S. Friedman
Philadelphia Psychiatric
Center

Lexington Books
D.C. Heath and Company/Lexington, Massachusetts/Toronto

Library of Congress Cataloging-in-Publication Data
Main entry under title:

Teen drug use.

Includes index.
1. Youth—United States—Drug use—Addresses,
essays, lectures. 2. Marihuana—Addresses,
essays, lectures. 3. Drugs—Physiological
effect—Addresses, essays, lectures. 4. Narcotic laws—United States—Addresses, essays,
lectures. I. Beschner, George M. II. Friedman, Alfred S.

HV5824.Y68T44   1985   362.2'93'088055   85–45378
ISBN 0–669–11602–5 (alk. paper)
ISBN 0–669–13834–7 (pbk.: alk. paper)

Published simultaneously in Canada
Printed in the United States of America
Casebound International Standard Book Number: 0–669–11602–5
Paperbound International Standard Book Number: 0–669–13834–7
Library of Congress Catalog Card Number: 85–45378

The paper used in this publication meets the minimum requirements of American National
Standard for Information Sciences—Permanence of Paper for Printed Library Materials,
ANSI Z39.48–1984. ∞™

The last numbers on the right below indicate the number and date of printing.

10 9 8 7

95 94 93 92 91 90

Contents

Preface and Acknowledgments

What makes this book different from others written about adolescent drug use? First, it offers a different perspective on the subject. Most books focus on the problems posed for society by adolescent drug abuse. They generally include information on the prevalence of drugs used, the sociocultural and demographic breakdowns, theories on the causes of drug abuse, and the relationship between drug abuse and criminality and delinquency. This book goes one step further and also looks at adolescent drug use from the perspective of young drug users and their parents. It distinguishes between drug use and drug abuse. It explores the reasons why some users have serious problems while others do not. It reviews the ways patterns of adolescent drug use have changed over time. It includes information on the effects that different drugs have on adolescent users, and about drug dealing (how marijuana is sold by and to adolescents). It provides information on the legal consequences that can result from illicit drug use and how families, caught in these situations, can find help. It describes the predicaments in which parents of drug users find themselves and presents information about the types and availability of treatment services. It discusses how secondary prevention methods can be applied when youngsters are already using drugs.

This book is written not only about adolescent drug abusers, it is also written *for* them and their families and for people who are interested in learning more about youngsters who use drugs. It should be of interest also to educators, judges, probation officers, recreational workers, physicians, and others who have contact with adolescents. The writing is, for the most part, basic and nontechnical. Where appropriate, the chapters include research findings to document the ideas and concepts presented and the conclusions drawn. These findings are expressed in nontechnical language.

The information in this book is based on extensive research and the application of a variety of research methods and techniques at different levels (national, state, and local studies). Data were obtained from studies of adolescents in treatment, surveys, ethnographic studies (youngsters observed over time in their natural communities), independent studies of adolescents who are in or out of treatment, interviews with treatment program staff, interviews with young drug users, and newspaper reports.

The editors have been conducting national and local studies of adolescent drug abuse for more than ten years and both have had many years of clinical experience in treating young substance abusers and their families. The chapter authors are recognized as experts in the subject areas about which they have written.

In chapter 1, George Beschner provides an overview of teen drug use, including the different types of drug users, the drugs used, the steps that can be taken once drug use is detected, and the types of treatment services available. Interviews with adolescent drug abusers from different parts of the country are presented to show how knowledgeable youngsters are about drugs and the role that drug taking plays in their lifestyles.

In chapter 2, Jerry Mandel and Harvey Feldman present a social history of adolescent drug use and abuse in the United States, including a detailed description of events, trends, and social-political factors. Also included is a history of the government's policies for controlling drug use, enforcing anti-drug laws, and providing treatment resources for drug users.

In chapter 3, Kenneth Schonberg and Sidney Schnoll report on the physical and psychological consequences and effects on youth of drug use: amphetamines, cocaine, sedatives and barbiturates, heroin, hallucinogens, inhalants, intoxicants (marijuana and alcohol), and multiple drug use. This chapter also explains, in nontechnical language, the basic principles of how drugs act on the body, and the five steps involved in this process: absorption, distribution, action, metabolism, and excretion.

James Inciardi, in chapter 4, discusses the legal ramifications of adolescent drug use and abuse. The need for the information provided in this chapter is underscored by the fact that teenagers pay little attention to the potential legal consequences of using illicit drugs although these consequences can be very serious. Inciardi provides a detailed description of the juvenile justice system procedures when an adolescent is picked up by the police for illicit drug use, drug possession, or drug sales. Among other questions addressed are: What are the current laws regarding illegal drug use? How are these laws enforced in different localities? What are the penalties for breaking these laws? What is the potential for getting arrested? If arrested, what is likely to happen? What happens in the juvenile court? Do adolescents have any legal rights? Where does someone turn for help? What if someone cannot afford a lawyer?

Chapter 5, by Allen Fields, is based on an ethnographic study of young black males who sell marijuana. Fields points out how changes in the marijuana laws have created a niche for street-level marijuana dealers in some cities. Black youths involved in "weedslinging" (selling marijuana) have few legitimate job opportunities and tend to approach marijuana selling in the same spirit as the small scale entrepreneur approaches a legitimate enterprise. They think of it as a successful achievement in a competitive sphere of activity.

Based on another ethnographic study, Barry Glassner, Cheryl Carpenter, and Bruce Berg report on the role that marijuana and other drugs play in the lives of adolescents (chapter 6). Liberal use of verbatim transcripts of interviews with adolescents provides a realistic, lifelike picture of the behavior and attitudes of youngsters who use drugs. The differences (family characteristics, friendship patterns, and so on) between daily users of marijuana and weekend or casual users are discussed.

In chapter 7, Stanley Kusnetz describes the various types of resources, services, treatment programs, and settings that are available for adolescent drug abusers and their families in many communities. The chapter identifies the sources of information available to parents and describes how parents should go about finding the most appropriate treatment program for their son or daughter. Kusnetz also includes the procedures to be used by parents when applying for treatment, and what they should expect to learn during the diagnostic phase of treatment. Nine treatment programs, classified as good by state authorities, are described in terms of their philosophies, program activities, treatment methods, and the clients they are qualified to treat.

Jerome Carroll presents a pragmatic approach to the prevention of substance abuse among adolescents (chapter 8). He describes secondary prevention methods that have proven to be effective in preventing novice users from becoming more seriously involved with drugs. Specific illustrations of school-based secondary prevention programs are given. In addition, suggestions are offered on how to organize, implement, and evaluate secondary prevention programs.

"The parent's predicament" is addressed in chapter 9. Leslie H. Daroff, S.J. Marks, and Alfred S. Friedman direct this chapter primarily to parents faced with the problem of having a child or adolescent involved in using drugs. They describe the challenging, stressful, and frustrating situation in which parents are caught. The authors give examples of questions most frequently asked by parents regarding teenage drug use and suggest ways parents can respond to the problem. Brief case vignettes illustrate the problems and the family situations discussed. The various types of emotional reactions that parents may have to their drug-abusing youngster are highlighted. Suggestions and instructions are given for parents: (1) on listening "actively," sensitively, and constructively to their youngster; (2) on problems related to either indulging or punishing the youngster; and (3) on how to be a more self-assured, secure, and relaxed parent.

Chapter 10, "The Family Scene," describes the severe and sometimes destructive impact on the family, particularly on the parents, when a teenage member is regularly involved in drug abuse or becomes addicted. One of the methods used in this chapter to convey the picture of the impact of adolescent drug abuse on a family and of the family interactions and dynamics as they relate to the substance abuse, is the presentation of three case vignettes of adolescents and their families applying for treatment at a drug abuse clinic. The case vignettes show how the parents might have unwittingly contributed to the maintenance of the adolescent's drug abuse problem and how their efforts to deal with it are ineffective or counterproductive. There is also a brief presentation in this chapter of the rationale for family therapy as a method to help the family get relief from the problem and to learn how to cope with the problem more effectively.

This book could not have been completed without the conscientious and competent editorial support and technical assistance of Francine Silverman of Philadelphia Psychiatric Center during the preparation of the manuscript, and the editorial assistance and preparation of manuscript drafts by Debbie Brown and Estelle Goldman, National Institute on Drug Abuse.

1
Understanding Teenage Drug Use

George Beschner

T he compulsive use of drugs and alcohol by teenagers is one of the most perplexing and challenging problems facing society today. This problem exacts tremendous societal costs; the most important are paid by young people. They do not reach their potential in the formative years and, as a result, forfeit their futures. Society pays an enormous, albeit unknown, price because of the association between drug abuse, drug dealing, and crime, particularly organized crime. In addition, millions of dollars are spent to treat drug crises in hospitals and special drug treatment programs.

How can a country that sends astronauts to the moon fail to conquer this problem? Why isn't more being done? Why are present drug treatment programs having so little effect on the total problem? Why is it that some young people develop serious problems after experimenting with drugs and others do not? Sadly, most parents, treatment providers, and researchers simply do not know enough about adolescent substance abuse to answer these questions.

This chapter will examine the teenage drug use issue, focusing on the kinds of youngsters who use drugs, the drugs they use, the parents' predicament, the steps that can be taken once a child's drug problem is detected, and the kinds of resources and services that might be available.

Magnitude of the Problem

Almost all young people in the United States are exposed to illicit drugs, and a high percentage experiment with them during early adolescence. By seventh grade, about half of all students feel pressure to try marijuana (Borton 1983). By twelfth grade, more than half (57 percent) have succumbed to this pressure (Johnston et al. 1984) and 5.5 percent use marijuana daily. Marijuana experimentation and abuse is only one element of the problem. Among high school seniors surveyed in 1983, for example,

93 percent had used alcohol at some time during their lives

27 percent had used stimulants

16 percent had used cocaine

15 percent had used hallucinogens, including LSD and PCP

14 percent had used sedatives or barbiturates, and an equal percentage had used inhalants

13 percent had used tranquilizers

10 percent had used opiates other than heroin

9 percent had used LSD

8 percent had used amyl and butyl nitrites

Surveys generally do not include dropouts, who are even more likely to have experimented with and abused drugs and therefore would increase the percentages quoted.

It may be reassuring to know that the daily use of marijuana among high school seniors declined from 10.7 percent in 1978 to 5.5 percent in 1983, but it is not clear what these statistics really mean. Are the drug use patterns of high school seniors less serious, or have students shifted to other possibly more dangerous drugs such as cocaine? Surveys indicate that, although drug use among junior and senior high school students has declined in recent years, students are using a wider variety of drugs. The full meaning of this multiple drug use phenomenon and the impact of various intoxicants on the health and overall development of adolescents are just now beginning to be investigated by researchers.

The magnitude of adolescent drug use is frightening to most adults, particularly to parents, who realize that their children probably will be exposed to drugs at a very young age. Most parents feel ineffective in trying to convince their children that drug use is hazardous and in protecting them from its dangers. Part of this inability is the result of a lack of information and understanding about drugs and their effects. By high school, most children know more about illicit drugs than their parents. Few parents have the time or capability necessary to study the available literature or analyze research findings. Most rely on public information booklets and, unfortunately, on television as their principal source of education. The media tend to dramatize, even glamorize, drug use in pursuit of newsworthy stories or high ratings. Reporters often highlight isolated statistics without capturing their full meaning, thus presenting atypical examples of youthful drug users.

Even some of the most well-informed adults, the so-called experts, have trouble understanding the adolescent drug abuse phenomenon. For over twenty years, drug abuse researchers have gathered and studied data from household and school surveys, using information provided by clients in treatment and ethnographic studies. Although surveys help identify which drugs are being used over time, they are limited; considerable care must be taken in interpreting and comparing survey findings. The type of sampling strategy utilized for the survey determines whether generalizations can be made from the data. Moreover, self-report data are difficult to verify. Even if based on sophisticated epidemiological approaches, such data are often questionable.

Survey statistics do not adequately tell the whole story. For example, household and high school surveys conducted in the mid-1970s showed high prevalence rates of marijuana use, which, in turn, led other researchers to focus additional attention on marijuana use. Since then, many millions of dollars have been invested in marijuana research, although marijuana is not necessarily the most serious adolescent drug problem.

Most young substance abusers begin using marijuana in junior high school. Some might share a joint daily, each taking a few drags as part of a ritual or social activity. Surveys might report this as chronic marijuana abuse, even though users may experience very little if any effect from the marijuana. These rituals often involve low potency, "homegrown" marijuana. In contrast, the same adolescents might go on periodic alcohol binges. If one simply compiled statistics on the frequency of use of these two substances, the abuse of alcohol might appear as less of a problem, even though the alcohol binges are more serious and more potentially damaging.

Because the media have portrayed marijuana as being more serious than alcohol under most circumstances, parents tend to be more concerned about marijuana use. They are more familiar with alcohol and its effects, but know relatively little about marijuana. Does this mean that marijuana use among adolescents is *not* a serious problem? Of course not. All chemical substances can be harmful and can contribute to a youngster's drug problem.

Recently, ethnographic methods have been employed to study adolescents in their natural environments (Feldman et al. 1985; Akins and Beschner 1980; Bullington 1977). Trained ethnographers observe and interview people as they go about their daily routines in neighborhoods. From these studies it is possible to get an insider's view of drug use, the reasons and ways youngsters use drugs, and the consequences of use. In the mid-1970s reports were that inhalant abuse was "increasing," especially among young Southwest Hispanics and youngsters in Indian reservations. There were numerous media stories on "chronic inhalant abuse" based on statistics which showed that high percentages of Hispanic and American Indian youth had used inhalants at some point in their lives.

The media failed to report the distinction between *experimental* and *chronic* abuse, giving a false impression about the nature of the problem. Upon further investigation, using ethnographic methods, it was learned that most of these youth had used inhalant substances once, or at the most several times during their lifetime, and that only a small percentage were using inhalants regularly. Most preferred to use other substances like marijuana, which had become more readily available, was relatively cheap, and provided more pleasurable effects than inhalants. Alcohol use was considered to be the most serious substance abuse problem among young American Indians. The media, failing to report this distinction between *experimental* use and a *serious chronic* problem, caused unnecessary alarm. Unfortunately, few ethnographic studies of adolescent drug abusers have been conducted.

Much of the information about adolescent drug users comes from studies of clients in treatment programs. These studies shed light on adolescent drug abusers and their drug use patterns; but the adolescents who enter drug treatment (voluntary or involuntarily) are not representative of other adolescents who use drugs. Also, attempts to identify the most problematic drugs (that is, the "primary" drug of abuse) are difficult because the youngsters tend to be multiple drug users, shifting from one drug to another depending upon what is available (Farley et al. 1979).

Despite the limitations of the various survey approaches, much has been learned about the causes and the factors that predict adolescent drug abuse. It has been learned that no single factor explains adolescent drug use, and that this complex problem has multiple causes. For this reason, people who really want to understand the probem must resist the tendency to look for *the* cause, or *the* underlying problem, or *the* solution. The tendency for people to look for simple answers is understandable. It is only natural to want to cut through the complexities, seek clear answers and solutions, and find something concrete and understandable that can be addressed immediately.

In the real world, the challenge is not so simple. To understand alolescent drug abuse, one must understand adolescence as a time of experimentation and defiance. One also must understand the powerful influence of peer pressure during these formative years and the damaging effects of living in a family in which children are either improperly supervised, rejected, or abused. Many parents are poor role models who themselves use alcohol and/or drugs excessively.

The Availability and Cost of Drugs

Most drugs commonly used by adolescents are inexpensive and easily obtained. Good-quality marijuana can be purchased in most communities for $5 to $10 a gram. Posing as a high school student, a New Mexican reporter found out how easy it was for adolescents to acquire drugs:

> Reefer prices and quality are debated openly and often. During an Independent Living class a stocky, short-haired senior called out for someone to chip in with him on a marijuana purchase. While struggling with a worksheet . . . the instigator explained that he had all but $2 of the $8 asking price and promised to stash the drug at his home as a service to any financier.
>
> Marijuana sells for $1.50 to $2 a joint. The "lid," approximately an ounce of marijuana, is a passe quantity on the high school campus. Bowls—enough marijuana to fill a pipe bowl—are frequently used for measure. A slight freshman told me he sells "grams" of pot for $8. Large quantities costing $50 or more are readily obtainable.
>
> Speed isn't as popular as it used to be, but it's still readily available and inexpensive. Low-grade uppers run 10 for a dollar.
>
> The youths obtain booze through friendly of-age suppliers. A graduate is one regular source. Older brothers and sisters frequently can be counted on to provide liquor for underage siblings and friends.
>
> A slim, blond, 14-year-old girl goes off campus at lunchtime every day to smoke marijuana. "I smoke marijuana when I can get it," she said. "It makes me feel relaxed. I'm a really hyper person." (Linthicum 1983)

The Purity and Potency of Drugs

The effects of illicit drug use depend not only on the type of drug but also on the concentrations, purity, type of contaminant used to "cut" (increase the volume of) drugs, the method of ingestion, the characteristics of the user, and the environment in which drugs are used. The potency of marijuana differs from area to area and from day to day in various areas. Youngsters may purchase (sometimes to their disappointment) a low potency home-grown variety, or, at the other end of the spectrum, be lucky enough to secure sensimilla, a propagation of seedless female plants with relatively high levels of delta-9-tetrahydrocannabinol (THC), the mind-altering (psychoactive) chemical ingredient in marijuana. The average potency of THC in marijuana has increased notably since the late 1960s and early 1970s (Turner 1983). Potency can also be enhanced by use of drug paraphernalia like "bongs" (water pipes that concentrate marijuana smoke and cool it for deeper inhalation). Some drugs vary in potency because they are made in clandestine laboratories with little or no quality control standards (phencyclidine for example) or because they are diluted with other chemicals, some of which contribute to the drug's effects.

Adolescents cannot be certain of the potency of the drugs they purchase on the street. This uncertainty makes drug taking even more dangerous. For some drugs there is a fine line between a safe dose and an overdose, depending on the specific potency and amount ingested (see chapter 3, "Drugs and Their Effects on Adolescent Users" for information on specific drugs).

Methods teens use to "test" their purchases are far from scientific; mostly, they rely on prior experience, anecdotal evidence, and ill-placed confidence in the supplier. Thus, adolescents are likely targets for sellers of phony or low-quality (but sometimes highly potent and very dangerous) drugs. Their limited financial resources generally prevent them from buying in bulk (one way of obtaining better quality drugs).

Even sophisticated teens may fall for the sale of "look-alike" drugs, licit stimulants that are packaged to resemble prescription stimulants such as ephedrine, phenylpropanolamine, and caffeine. Used in excess (some users take many times the "normal" dose), look-alikes can also be very risky. For example, excessive doses of phenylpropanolamine, a decongestant used in look-alikes, can cause dangerous increases in blood pressure.

A drug's perceived potency also depends on the characteristics of the user. Two people may react differently to the same dose of a drug because of differences in their physiology, biochemistry, and personalities. The same person may respond differently to the same dose of a drug at different times because of the conditions under which the drug is used. The drug experience can also be influenced by the user's psychological state, or expectations, social pressures, or environment.

Types of Adolescent Drug Users

Adolescent drug users fall into three groups: experimenters, compulsive users, and floaters (users who float between the other two groups) (Jalali et al. 1981.) An important distinction between experimental and compulsive drug abusers is their reason for using drugs. Researchers have found that the reason (or reasons) individuals use drugs has a significant bearing on how they experience the drugs and on whether they remain experimenters or become chronic compulsive substance abusers (Jalali et al. 1981).

Experimenters are likely to be using drugs in response to peer pressure, boredom, simple curiosity, or the hope of having fun. Most experimenters do not have, and probably never will have, serious drug-related problems (Jalali et al. 1981; Hamburg et al. 1975). Experimenters (1) tend to use drugs infrequently and in small amounts; (2) generally limit experimentation to marijuana and alcohol; and (3) understand the difference between risk-taking and danger and between pleasure-seeking and reality avoidance. But experimenters are not protected from the dangers of drug abuse. Some will become compulsive users and the unlucky few will experience serious adverse reactions or accidents under the influence.

Of more concern are the compulsive users, individuals who are dependent on drugs and whose health and/or personal and social functioning are thereby threatened. For these teens drug abuse is not simply defined by the type of drug chosen but by the habitual or compulsive desire to use the drugs. Compulsive adolescent drug users devote considerable time and energy to getting high, talk incessantly (sometimes almost exclusively) about drugs, and become connoisseurs of street drugs. They generally have serious personal problems and take drugs to avoid problems and pain, or to cope with or relieve anxiety. Unable to handle pressure and responsibilities, most of these adolescents have a low self-image and poor relationships with their families.

Drug taking escalates during acute periods of stress and crisis and, ironically, often keeps these teens from seeking help for serious psychological problems. Far from providing the needed help, other than affording temporary relief from psychic pain and anxiety, the drugs tend to compound social and psychological problems. For example, some youngsters use drugs to relieve anxiety about school, yet attend school while high, assuring diminished school performance. This, in turn, increases family conflict, increases anxiety about school, and provides more incentive to use drugs.

No one knows for sure how many young people are compulsive users, but researchers estimate that 4 to 5 percent (depending on the geographic area) of U.S. youth between 15 and 19 use illicit drugs regularly (Beschner and Friedman 1985). Although the percentage is small, the numbers are large, encompassing more than a million teenagers in this country. This figure can be put in perspective by comparing it to a statistic that strikes fear in the public heart: during the peak of the heroin epidemic in the late 1960s, we were gravely concerned about the possibility that there may have been as many as 450,000 heroin addicts in this country.

Some adolescent drug users are classified as floaters because they move between the experimenter groups and compulsive user groups. Their needs and habits alter in response to changes in their environment and to their finding different means to resolve or cope with their problems. But they are always in danger of becoming compulsive users.

Compulsive Users Talk about Drugs

The author interviewed young compulsive drug users from different parts of the country to learn more about the drugs used. Five Maryland teens distinguished among various kinds of marijuana:

Jim:	It's like tasting good wine. You want the stickiest, the hairiest.
Ed:	Red, red seed husks.
Jane:	Indica.
Jim:	Got to look at it real close for the white crystals in the buds.
Tom:	The bad stuff is green, dark green, it smells bad, moldy like.
Jim:	Good weed has good sized buds. I look for a real sticky bud.
Ed:	I like the buds nice and tight and not too many seeds.
Mark:	I also go by smell and taste.
Jane:	It sort of smells like pine trees. You can tell if its potent by that.
Jim:	Anybody that's into smoking marijuana can tell the good stuff from the bad.

A Florida teen described how he uses quaaludes and PCP:

The ludes are good. There's a lot of interest in bootleg ludes and ludes with valium. At first that bothered me a little, because I saw people getting sick on them. Got to be very careful of ludes that are cut with strychnine. A good friend of mine ended up in the hospital after using them.

You can tell how good ludes are when you look at them . . . how hard they are . . . how smooth they are. The ludes I get are hard to break in half . . . you need a hammer. The good ones have the kind of tacky taste. You can bite through the bad ones; you can bite them in half with your teeth. The letters aren't all lined up on the bad ones, and they aren't stamped on the pill clearly. You can pretty much look at them and tell if they are good or bad.

As far as PCP is concerned, I used to do that all the time. I really enjoyed it, especially if it was a good batch. Once in a while I would have bad trips on PCP. I would get some bad stuff, and I would kind of lose it. Bad PCP trips would scare me to death. I was picking, sweating, and just sick for hours on end. After a while I learned how to determine the good from the bad. I'd see how it smelled and I'd burn it to see how it burned, to make sure I was getting good PCP. Sometimes it depends on what they cut it with. Good PCP has got a kind of smokey smell to it. I would burn it. If it had strychnine or something like that in it, it would stink when you burn it.

A young New Yorker talked about marijuana:

As far as what types of marijuana are around, Columbian, sensimilla, different quality stuff. Good Columbian, $45 an ounce, commercial Columbian about $30 an ounce. Commercial Columbian is everywhere. Gold is a little harder to get. Commerical Columbian is like a light brown, maybe kind of smells kind of sweet; gold Columbian has got more of a gold color to it, and it smells really good, sort of like chocolate. Whenever you inhale it, it just expands your lungs, inside your lungs; you can hardly hold it in. And the red bud is kind of sensimilla; it's just red and greenish brown, a lot of buds in it, real hard in it, real strong scent to it, real strong taste to it. That's the red bud; high real quick. It's about as strong as the gold Columbian, same price as the gold Columbian, the red bud is.

Sensimilla there is a lot of different kinds. Californian, Hawaiian sensi. Hawaiian marijuana is unbelievable; they got red buds with gold running through it. Green, purple, gold. Purple with a little bit of green running through it. Like the best pot there is. From Hawaii and California is about the best there is. That run around $170 to $210 an ounce. But it is hard to get. That kind of sensi is around $2,500 to $3,000 a pound. You can get it for $150 an ounce, and turn around and sell it for $180 to $210 an ounce. Hang on to it when everybody else is selling it for $180 an ounce; then sell it later for $210 an ounce.

Pretty easy for kids to spot heavy marijuana users. Changes in attitudes, drowsy, eat a lot, eyes are always red, a lot of times they have a lot of dollar bills from selling joints. Looking for something to drink. Losing respect for themselves in the way they dress, hair may not be combed, may not brush their teeth, shoes not tied, shirts not tucked in. Once they get past being into marijuana they usually do other drugs . . . then their outlook really changes, and they usually stop caring about anything. They are moving around a lot if they are on cocaine or speed. Can't sit still, talking too fast to understand.

Youngsters in suburban Pennsylvania talked about drugs:

Bob:	Less guys are using marijuana.
Larry:	It's mostly used in the sixth through eighth grades.
Betty:	In junior high school you just smoke pot. You start out smoking pot.
Frank:	The first time I didn't get high.
Bill:	The first three times I didn't get high.
Frank:	When you use pot, you feel like paranoid. Like I'll be walking into a class late, and I'll open the door, and I feel like everyone is staring at me.
Mike:	It's available; that's for sure. Everybody's still using it, but it's getting more expensive.
Joan:	Marijuana is boring.

Larry:	Marijuana burnt me out. You smoke more and more and you don't get high as easy. You smoke five or six joints to get high instead of just one when I first started getting high, when I got real high. It gets to the point where you're feeling dead when you get high.
Frank:	Yeah, it gets to the point where you get blah.
Mike:	There's all kinds of marijuana. Thai sticks are a lot of fun. Columbian is also good when you can get it.
Bill:	And, of course, there's hash.
Larry:	I get hash at _____. I got a half ounce last week. It's pretty good.
Ron:	Hash is hard to find. During the winter you get a lot of blond hash. During the summer you can get some good Columbian, sensi and black hash.
Bill:	You slice it down the middle, and it's like green inside. Sometimes you get hash with white streaks in it.
Frank:	Most of the marijuana you get is commercial weed.
Larry:	It's mostly home grown. We call it ditch weed.
Larry:	It looks good, but they just sell it to make money.
Ron:	Has anyone used mushrooms?
Bill:	I used mushrooms.
Frank:	I love the taste. I chew them.
John:	I always liked speed the best. I used to take a lot of speed.
Mike:	Speed never made me tired.
Bob:	Ludes make you feel like you're drunk.
Betty:	A lot of my friends use coke. I never bought it myself. Cocaine gives you a real high. Pot is boring.
Joan:	I prefer alcohol. There's always some alcohol at my house. I never get a hangover.
Larry:	I like acid, man. I don't get sick of it. It's always like reading a different book.
Mary:	When I first got here [moved into the community], I found something new. It's called "lovely." They say it's marijuana sprayed with embalming fluids.
Joan:	It's PCP. Lovely first became popular around here a few years ago.
Mike:	I call it green.
Bill:	They also call it the Bomb. It's where they take pot and spray some PCP on it and dry it in the sun.
Larry:	It gets you wasted. It's got a nasty flavor.

Mary:	It's the ultimate high. I never heard of it before I came here. When I came here, it was everywhere. When I met people here, the first thing they asked me is do I get high off lovely.
Larry:	When I use acid, I feel great, at the top of the world. But when I'm high on it, I don't know what I'm doing. Me and my friend bought some cigarettes in the 7-Eleven. When we walked out, we didn't know whether we paid for them. I started laughing and couldn't stop.
Mike:	I used to use a lot of acid, but last year when I took my exams I couldn't even see the paper. Yeh, the teacher came up to me and started talking. Her face was right here and I started laughing in her face. So I had to go down to the guidance room.

Youngsters from a small rural community in Ohio talked about drugs with equal savvy:

Lloyd:	There's all kinds of dope available—marijuana, acid, coke, uppers, downers, everything, just about.
Bob:	Alcohol's used more than anything else.
Carol:	With alcohol, you're talking about everybody in school. Everybody drinks.
Susan:	For me, it's mostly alcohol.
Charles:	There's more people that drink. There's a lot of people that drink. People that get high, get high every day.
Hank:	My mom was talking about it when she was in school. Used to be mainly drinking and then they got into pot before she graduated. It may be history repeating itself, just a cycle; it goes to almost strictly alcohol, then to pot, then to whatever else becomes available and back to alcohol. Good pot is pretty hard to find now.
Lloyd:	I use pot the most. When I would get high all the time, I would stay high all day. For a while, I would drink every day, then just two or three times a day. When I was taking acid, I would like to spread it out. If you tripped, like a few days in a row, you would just be so wired out afterwards. So I got to using acid once a month, once every two months.
Charles:	I started on speed and then on pot. For about six months, it was real heavy with pot. Then I drank more.

Wayne:	Pot is getting a lot stronger now. 'Cause, when I first started getting high, four or five years ago, I used to smoke a bag of pot in one day. Now, a gram, just a little gram of pot can last you two days. It's so good, that some people are just starting to get high. If you smoke some of that sensimilla, you can get freaked out on it.
Ruddy:	I use whatever is available. Sometimes there's a lot, and sometimes you can't find much of anything.
Warner:	Yeh, it's starting to get a little more scarce.
Lloyd:	I think it's just getting harder for some of us to get it because we're not around the people as much.
Bob:	I don't think it's more available.
Hank:	Its availablity has gone way down.
Wayne:	I get different highs from different pot. I've been getting really hyperactive. When I was using it a few years ago, I was more calm and laid back.

From these interviews of adolescent compulsive drug users, one can see that they are very knowledgeable about the drugs available in their communities. Whether from Maryland, Pennsylvania, Florida, New York, or Ohio, the youngsters have learned to distinguish the good drugs from the bad and find the quality they are looking for. Drugs have become an important element in their lifestyles.

Discovering a Child's Drug Problem

Adolescent drug abuse is insidious; it progresses slowly and, in most cases, destructive behavior and harmful effects are seen only after a youngster has had a serious drug habit for some time. With some substances, like alcohol, the physical damage may be irreversible. Short episodes of isolation and rebellion are usual during adolescence even without drug use. They may for a time mask the dramatic behavioral changes that usually accompany excessive drug use. Parents should be aware of these signs which, especially in combination, could indicate drug use:

Mood swings, irritability, depression

Slow, slurred speech

Diminished alertness

Weight loss or gain

Deterioration in school performance

Deterioration in relationships or radical change of friends

Parents may also discover that their children have a drug problem through more direct means:

The child may be picked up by the police or arrested, and the parents directed to seek treatment or turn the child over to a juvenile detention facility.

The child may suddenly have plenty of money (a clue he or she may be dealing) or may be caught stealing to obtain money for drugs.

The child may have been involved in a drug-related accident or have had an adverse physiological reaction (such as an overdose).

The child may have attempted suicide.

Drugs or drug paraphernalia may have been discovered by the parents or by a school official.

Thus, by the time parents discover the problem, it is likely to be serious. Like their adult alcoholic counterparts, teens confronted with their drug abuse almost always resort to denial, regardless of how long or how frequently they have been using drugs. Some parents believe their children, at least for a time, wanting to believe that there is not a problem. Some overreact and thus risk worsening the problem they are hoping to correct. Eventually, most parents begin to face the truth but find their children's refusal to do so hard to understand. Family conflict is likely to follow.

The Parents' Predicament

Parents who accept implicitly the stereotypical media portrayal of the pathological, spaced-out, assaultive, incorrigible adolescent drug user may fail to recognize early drug problems in their more "normal" child. Conversely, some parents may overreact to drug experimentation, classifying their children with heroin addicts roaming the streets in search of a fix. Both of these extreme reactions are inappropriate, and neither reaction will prevent or minimize drug abuse by their children.

Upon finding that their children are using drugs, most parents feel hurt, betrayed, or guilty. Many parents ask, "Why us?" or, after internalizing the problem, "Where have we failed?" Some feel helpless because they have a limited understanding of drug abuse and do not know where to turn or what to do. Others feel frustrated because, after learning about the problem and reaching for help, they find there is no simple "right" approach. Each family's problem is unique in some ways.

Faced with the reality that their youngster is using drugs, parents must gain control over their emotions, resist the urge to act precipitously, and try to look at the situation rationally and objectively. These are difficult but essential first steps. Initially, parents should try to gather as much information about their child's situation as possible. Hopefully, the child will cooperate in providing some of this information. Before jumping to conclusions, parents should find out what substances are being used, and how and why they are used.

It will be most difficult for parents to face the possibility that they are somehow involved in their child's drug problem. Indeed, in many cases the family itself may even be at the root of the drug problem. Some adolescents might use drugs to gain attention in a family that otherwise ignores them. Family therapists who specialize in treating substance abusing young people have found that the families of their patients are often in conflict, or are disengaged, or lack open communication, mutual respect, reasonable organization, and close, loving relationships. The parents and children often are alienated, and the parents may be poor models or may be overcontrolling. The drug use itself is of deep concern but cannot be treated outside the context of these other factors.

Families in which the parents regularly use alcohol face a special dilemma in arguing against their children's use of drugs. Research shows that children of parents who drink regularly are more likely to use drugs than children of parents who drink infrequently. Similarly, children whose parents use psychoactive drugs are more vulnerable to drug abuse. Alcohol, especially when abused, can be as dangerous as the drugs commonly used by adolescents. Furthermore, many parents use drugs such as tranquilizers to relieve stress—behavior similar to that they wish to discourage in their children.

What to Do

Parents who decide (or are required by the school or the court) to seek professional treatment for their children have several options. A clergyman or private physician may be able to provide some guidance for the family in finding an appropriate resource, since it is likely that professional help will be needed from someone who is trained to treat adolescent substance abusers. Initially, the family should seek the advice of someone who has an understanding of the overall problem and who can provide information about the various treatment options that are available. Good diagnosis and a careful evaluation of the youngster are the key to selecting an appropriate approach and should be done before treatment is initiated. The diagnosis and subsequent treatment plan should take into consideration the possibility that the youngster may have a learning disability (Meier 1971). In addition, substance abusers are more likely than nonabusers to be depressed, and to have other emotional and psychological problems, or to have serious physical problems. These problems, in addition to family history and the youngster's social functioning, must be considered in developing a treatment plan.

If youngsters are not motivated to seek treatment and are outside the control of their parents, there are few treatment options. In extreme cases, they can be legally committed to a hospital (inpatient) facility which provides diagnostic services, detoxification treatment, and psychological counseling, if such a facility exists in the community. Unfortunately, these services are scarce, and in some states it is difficult to work out the involuntary commitment procedure.

In recognition of the growing need for detoxification and emergency treatment for overdoses, private hospital (inpatient) treatment programs have been started in many communities across the country. But these programs are very expensive, costing as much as $10,000 per patient per month, and therefore available only to families with comprehensive health insurance. Some state and local governments support public inpatient treatment programs which are less expensive, but the capacity of these programs is usually limited.

Most hospital programs offer only short-term care, essentially to treat crisis situations and to diagnose medical and psychological problems. If long-term treatment is needed, the hospital will usually try to refer adolescents to less expensive outpatient, daycare, or residential (nonhospital) programs.

Nationally, there is only a small number of residential treatment programs designed especially for adolescent substance abusers. Patients usually stay in residential treatment for six months to one year. Compared to inpatient programs, residential programs are far less costly, averaging between $9,000 and $10,000 per year. Residential programs generally provide individual and group therapy, educational classes, parent participation, confrontational meetings, recreational activities, and shared responsibility for managing the facility; they generally lack the medical, psychological, and diagnostic services offered by hospital programs.

Residential programs may not be appropriate for teens who are in treatment against their will. Most do not have closed locked wards to prevent youngsters from running away. Many are located in remote areas to discourage escape attempts, but these locations make it difficult for parents to be involved in regular family sessions. For a number of reasons, residential programs tend to have high dropout rates (about 80 percent leave in the first few months) but those who do stay in these programs are likely to show improvement; and progress is roughly proportionate to the length of time in treatment (De Leon et al. 1984).

Daycare treatment programs offer many of the same services as residential programs, but without overnight accommodations. Some school systems support alternative education programs or daycare programs for substance abusing high school students. The drug treatment programs operate during school hours, serving adolescents until they are drug free and able to return to regular school classrooms. Unfortunately, only about fifty such programs have been established in the United States.

Almost all communities have outpatient drug treatment and counseling programs or community mental health centers supported by state, county, or city governments. These programs, which treat more than 80 percent of the adolescent substance abusers admitted to treatment, generally provide drug counseling services to adults and adolescents in addition to treating a broad range of psychological and behavioral problems. Outpatient clinics have very few controls and relatively little structure. Thus patients must be highly motivated to benefit from the counseling provided and make a personal commitment to attend regularly and participate actively. As in other treatment settings, family participation may be needed for treatment to be effective, and unfortunately few adolescent outpatient programs have family therapy specialists.

After hospital or residential treatment, many youngsters find it difficult to retain their newly learned lifestyle once they return to the former peer group, family, or school situation they had before treatment. A significant percentage revert to alcohol and marijuana use (Sells and Simpson 1979; Hubbard et al. 1983). Even those who develop understanding and coping skills find it hard to deal with their old environments and will likely require support and direction. This may come, in part, from the family, if family therapy of some sort has been provided; or it may come from aftercare programs that have the capability of treating youngsters as they adjust to the community. Outpatient programs can be instrumental in providing aftercare of teens discharged from inpatient and residential programs. This will, in turn, help adolescents in adjusting to their home and community lives.

Aftercare is based on the recognition that the treatment process should not end abruptly at discharge from a daycare, inpatient, or residential program. Aftercare programs usually have professional counselors or other support persons available when problems arise, anxieties build, and peer pressure or temptation to use drugs increases. Some aftercare programs make use of peer groups to provide support during the reentry process. These groups, consisting of other teens going through recovery, are organized and led by both professional and peer counselors. Teens often feel more comfortable talking openly to peers about their families, friends, and other relationships and also may be more receptive to feedback from their peers.

Parent participation is also very important during the aftercare process. In some cases the parents themselves will need help in developing and maintaining an appropriate and positive parent-child relationship. In short, almost all parents of adolescent substance abusers, even those who are well adjusted, will need help coping as their children readjust to family, friends, and school. The love and understanding of the parents certainly will be tested. They must be prepared to respond with their time and patience, setting appropriate limits and giving ongoing support.

References

Akins, C. and Beschner, G. 1980. *Ethnography: A research tool for policymakers in the drug and alcohol fields.* Rockville, Maryland: National Institute on Drug Abuse, DHHS Publication No. (ADM) 80–946.

Beschner, G. and Friedman, A. 1985. Treatment of adolescent drug abusers. *International Journal of the Addictions,* 20(6&7):971–993.

Borton, T. 1983. Pressure to try drugs, alcohol starts in early grades. *Weekly Reader,* April 25. Middletown, Connecticut: Xerox Educational Publications.

Bullington, B. 1977. *Heroin Use in the Barrio.* Lexington Books. Lexington, Massachusetts.

De Leon, G. 1984. The therapeutic communtiy: A study of effectiveness. Rockville, Maryland: National Institute on Drug Abuse, *Treatment Research Monograph Series,* DHHS Publication No. (ADM) 84–1286.

Farley, E.; Santo, Y.; and Speck, D. 1979. Multiple drug abuse patterns of youths in treatment. In eds. Beschner, G. and Friedman, A. *Youth Drug Abuse: Problems, Issues and Treatment.* Lexington, Massachusetts: Lexington Books.

Feldman, H.; Mandel, J.; and Fields, A. 1985. In the neighborhood: A strategy for delivering early intervention services to young drug users in their natural environments. In Friedman, A. and Beschner, G., eds., *Treatment Services for Adolescent Substance Abusers.* Rockville, Maryland: National Institute on Drug Abuse, DHHS Pub. No. (ADM) 85–1342.

Hamburg, B.; Kramer, M.; and Janke, W. 1975. A hierarchy of drug use in adolescence: Behavioral and attitudinal correlates of substantial drug use. *American Journal of Psychiatry* 26: 108–112.

Hubbard, R.; Cavanaugh, E.; Graddock, S.; and Rachal, J. 1985. Characteristics, behaviors and outcomes for youth in the TOPS. In Friedman, A. and Beschner, G., eds., *Treatment Services for Adolescent Substance Abusers.*

Rockville, Maryland: National Institute on Drug Abuse, DHHS Pub. No. (ADM) 85–1342.

Jalali, B.; Jalali, M.; Crocette, G.; and Turners, F. 1981. Adolescents and drug use: Toward a more comprehensive approach. *American Journal of Orthopsychiatry* 51(1).

Johnston, L.; O'Malley, P.; and Bachman, J. 1984. *Highlights from Drugs and American High School Students, 1975–1983.* Rockville, Maryland: National Institute on Drug Abuse, DHHS Publication No. (ADM) 84–1317.

Linthicum, L. March 10, 1983. Albuquerque Tribune, New Mexico.

Meier, J. 1971. Prevalence and characteristics of learning disabilities found in second grade children. *Journal of Learning Disabilities* 4(1): 1–16.

Sells, S. and Simpson, D. 1979. Evaluation of treatment outcomes for youths in the drug abuse reporting program (DARP): a followup study. In Beschner, G. and Friedman, A. eds., *Youth Drug Abuse: Problems, Issues and Treatment.* Lexington, Massachusetts: Lexington Books.

Turner, C. 1983. Cannabis: The plant, its drugs, and their effects. *Aviation, Space and Environmental Medicine,* 54(4): 363–369.

2
The Social History of Teenage Drug Use

Jerry Mandel
Harvey W. Feldman

There was a time, only thirty years ago, when we—the parents, teachers, clergymen, social workers, psychologists, and most of the adults who were responsible for the healthy upbringing of our nation's youth—did not concern ourselves with the problems associated with drug use. The reason was simple enough: young people, with few exceptions, did not take drugs and limited their consumption of intoxicating substances primarily to alcohol.

There were, of course, heroin addicts. But the number was so small that the 65,000 the former Bureau of Narcotics claimed existed in the middle 1950s were isolated in a few inner-city neighborhoods, with over half living in New York City and the remainder in slums and barrios of other major cities such as Chicago and Los Angeles (Anslinger 1951, 1959). Except among the street gangs of New York, heroin had not been reported to have filtered down to the adolescent age group.

There were also marijuana smokers. They, too, were limited in numbers and reportedly restricted to jazz musicians, artists, writers, migrant farm workers in the Southwest, or sporting life archetypes in the inner-city ghettos.

There were fewer cocaine addicts, so few in fact that estimates thirty years ago were not calculated. Even then the cost of cocaine was prohibitive for young people; but a major reason for its lack of popularity with adolescents throughout the country was limited knowledge. Information about the purchase of cocaine, routes of administration, and its effects and dangers hardly ever entered the world of youth.

In the 1950s and early 1960s narcotics had not yet piqued the interest of young people. And the language that usually accompanies such new activities had not yet emerged. Terms like "bad trip," "rip off," "bummer," "far out," and dozens more that moved from subcultural use to general acceptance and then into obsolescence had not been coined.

In the field of drugs and narcotics, innocence was an outgrowth of ignorance. What young people did not know, they could not put into words or actions.

Adults in the straight world were similarly ignorant. They had no reason to know that marijuana was rolled into "joints" and inhaled deeply in order to attain a feeling that slowed time, dried the mouth, and brought on unexplained laughter and hunger. It was commonly believed that heroin addiction resulted inevitably in a "living death," the details of which were physical and psychological decay too horrifying to contemplate. They shuddered at any injection, much less a hypodermic needle pumping an opiate directly into the bloodstream. Somewhere deep in the American unconscious was the belief that cocaine produced an immediate psychosis that left the user incapable of recovery. Most people were satisfied with this lack of information and were willing to be guided by myths and stereotypes that they had no reason to question.

Looking back over the last three decades, we may well ask, "What happened? Why did so many young people turn to drugs?" In order to understand this phenomenon, we should look at the history of drug policy and at adolescent drug use in the United States.

Early Hysteria about Youth and Drugs

Most drug histories begin with the passage of the Harrison Act of 1914, which essentially outlawed heroin and mandated the medical and pharmaceutical professions to control all other opiates and cocaine. At the time, there were probably as many opiate addicts per capita in the United States as at any other point in our history. Just prior to the passing of the Harrison Act, drugs and narcotics were sold openly in pharmacies throughout the country. Troy Duster's historical coverage of drug policy, *The Legislation of Morality* (1970), for example, begins with the statement, "There was a time when anyone could go to his corner druggist and buy grams of morphine or heroin for just a few pennies." That time was before the implementation of the Harrison Act.

In the numerous listings during this period of the kinds of people who comprised the nation's addicts, youth were markedly absent. Mentions of youth involved in drug use, in fact, did not regularly occur until after World War I when the implementation of the act began to have its effects.

In 1919, when the federal enforcers of the Harrison Act issued a binding opinion that almost all addicts could be "cured" in three weeks and that any physician providing opiates to an addict would be considered a criminal "pusher," addicts found themselves without legitimate access to narcotics. To avert an anticipated flood of sick and desperate addicts, forty local governments throughout the country sponsored and/or sanctioned the opening of drug treatment clinics to supply addicts with legal narcotics. In many of these clinics, maintenance doses of morphine or heroin were dispensed.

Of the ten or so clinics for which there are public records available to scholars, New York City's clinic was unique in several respects. Clearly, it was the most widely reported in the mass media. From the reports, it was hastily assembled with little more than a day or two given to planning (Hubbard, March 1920; *New York Times,* April 10 & 11, 1919). In order to staff the clinic, for example, a last-minute call for volunteer society women resulted in staffing interviewers who were not only untrained in the area of drugs but equally unfamiliar with the lower classes (*New York Times,* April 13, 1919).

Of all the clinics, the one in New York had the largest number of clients. And finally, *it was the only clinic in which young men showed up in vast numbers* (Hubbard, February 1920). This appearance of young people at the clinic in order to receive the free heroin and morphine that were used as maintenance doses for addicts was the first mention of widespread youth involvement in narcotics to appear in any public record.

In order to appreciate how misguided the ensuing concern for young people was it is important to understand who the typical early 1900s addicts were. The most common description of them was that they were adults, mostly professional people, intellectuals and artists, and housewives whose extensive dependence on narcotics made them docile, appreciative, but—without access to legal narcotics—desperately sick.

The New York clinic opened on Worth Street on the Lower East Side, right in the heart of the bursting immigrant Jewish and Italian populations. Quick to recognize the easily exploitable potential of the new clinics, young streetwise youths (not unlike the Bowery Boys or the Dead End Kids of 1940s film fame) seized the opportunity of lining up for free heroin, conned the matrons who interviewed them, and then sold their supply to addicts, many of whom were suffering from withdrawal symptoms while standing in line (Hubbard, February 1920; Graham-Mullhall, 1921). Dealing drugs went on in the park adjacent to the clinic, and sales were made directly to people standing in line. This behavior was considered so despicable by the legitimate clinic staff, and it was so unlike what they had expected, that authorities were convinced a new class of addicts had surfaced: young people who lied, cheated, and ignored the newly implemented Harrison Act (Hubbard, February 1920; Prentice 1921).

Despite the publicity that appeared in the *New York Times,* this repugnant and rarely seen behavior which linked youth with narcotics use and sale was *not* reported in any other drug clinic throughout the country. Further, we are not aware of any mention of addiction as a social problem among Jews or Italians during this period in any historical description of those immigrant populations in New York City. What occurred had little to do with addiction and much to do with the entrepreneurial opportunism of a poor population in a situation where the clinic gave out free heroin (and in its earliest days, cocaine) already inflated in price on the black market as a result of the Harrison Act.

In the middle and late 1920s, attention was again focused on youthful drug use, this time by a colorful Spanish-American War hero and former congressman named Richmond Pearson Hobson. Hobson had been a leading prohibitionist, and his speeches against alcohol were given wide circulation and publicity (Sinclair 1962) in newspapers and magazines. In the 1920s, Hobson dominated the drug references in the Congressional Record. Having been instrumental in helping to pass the Volstead Act, he became disenchanted by 1923 with Prohibition and turned his attention to heroin addiction. With a focus on "saving" youth, he claimed that teenage addiction was rampant and cited Harlem in New York City and Denver as centers of drug traffic and use among adolescents (*Literary Digest* 1924). In both locations, school officials and local leaders rejected his claims and denounced him as a publicity-seeking zealot. In neither city was there evidence of the kind of teenage drug use Hobson alleged. Nonetheless, his warning of demonic drug pushers seducing youth into addiction by such trickery as hiding heroin in snow cones got wide publicity through his brilliant use of the media (Lampman 1924).

Hobson founded several national organizations which carried his message throughout the United States. During the heyday of those organizations, hundreds of school systems set aside a week in February as "Narcotics Week" in which lectures and brochures prepared mostly by Hobson's organization were the content of the education. It was through Hobson's efforts that the myth of the "dope fiend" came into virtually unquestioned acceptance.

Possibly Hobson's major achievement in focusing on the connection between youth and drugs did not occur until a few months after he died with the passage of the Marijuana Tax Act of 1937. A few years prior, the Federal Bureau of Narcotics had reported that the extent of marijuana use and its allegedly lethal effects had been erroneously and substantially magnified. The Bureau's Anslinger, however, reversed his position on marijuana to conform to Hobson's image of the heroin "dope fiend" and transferred it to marijuana (Anslinger 1937). According to Anslinger, marijuana caused insanity, murder, rape, and (in something of a contradiction) impotence. All of these claims were made in Anslinger's book *The Traffic in Narcotics* (1953); and he asserted that youths were particularly vulnerable to the seductive ways of the marijuana pusher. His article entitled "Marijuana: Assassin of Youth" (1937) described gory murders which he attributed to the smoking of marijuana; and his most memorable image was of rosy-cheeked, innocent girls, lured to inner-city neighborhoods by a misguided sense of excitement, waking up after smoking marijuana for the first time with the realization that they had been debauched by lower-class males.

Apart from the stories that appeared in the mass media, most of which could be attributed either to Anslinger and the Bureau of Narcotics or Hobson and his various organizations, there was slight evidence that marijuana use had made significant inroads in the youth market. In the early part of the 1940s, Mayor Fiorello LaGuardia commissioned a group under the chairmanship of George B. Wallace to study the connection between marijuana use and the youth of New York City (1944). The researchers responsible for collecting the social data were, in fact, New York City policemen. Among the conclusions of the La-Guardia Committee were the following:

> Marijuana is used extensively in the borough of Manhattan, but the problem is not as acute as it is reported to be in other sections of the United States;

> The majority of marijuana smokers are Negroes and Latin Americans;

> The use of marijuana does not lead to morphine or heroin or cocaine addiction, and no effort is made to create a market for these narcotics by stimulating the practice of marijuana smoking;

> Marijuana is not a determining factor in the commission of major crimes;

> Marijuana smoking is not widespread among school children;

> Juvenile delinquency is not associated with the practice of smoking marijuana; and

> The publicity concerning the catastrophic effects of smoking marijuana in New York City is unfounded.

Youth and Real Drug Use

By the end of the 1940s, youth and drug use once again became national news; and, once again, it was Commissioner Anslinger who was the prime newsmaker. It was at this time that Anslinger stated that there were 65,000 addicts in the United States with about half of them living in New York City. And for once the alarm about drugs and youth had a basis in fact, as would be corroborated by such independent sources as *The Autobiography of Malcolm X* (1964), Claude Brown's *Manchild in the Promised Land* (1965), and Piri Thomas's *Down These Mean Streets* (1967). By the middle 1950s, heroin use had gained a foothold with inner-city white youth in New York. The use of heroin, however, was restricted almost exclusively to the former fighting street gangs that drew so much publicity during that era; and New York officials responded to the rise in heroin use among teenagers by opening a special adolescent facility at Riverside Hospital on North Brothers Island. Aside from the evidence that heroin use was identified in specific low-income communities in two or three of the largest U.S. cities, there were no reports that it had spread beyond the borders of slum communities (Anslinger 1951, 1959).

Between the end of the 1940s and the beginning of the 1960s, concern for heroin addiction among adolescents was a dominant theme among drug experts. From personal reports of the time such as Larner and Tefferteller's *The Addict in the Street* (1964) and Fiddle's *Portraits from a Shooting Gallery* (1967), both of which contained transcribed tape-recorded interviews, life for the young addict largely followed the stereotype Hobson had created some thirty years previously. Heroin users injected their drugs with hypodermic needles directly into the vein, developed expensive habits, stole in order to purchase their drugs, and generally lived an unsavory life outside the law.

What was also evident from these reports and from the authors' professional experience was that the life of the heroin addict was inextricably bound up with the criminal justice system. In many court situations, civil liberties were ignored as addicts depended on public defenders who, along with judges, physicians, and other professionals during that period of history, were less than sympathetic toward the addict's situation. Police, who understood that addicts were often rejected in their communities and within their own families, frequently ignored proper search and seizure procedures, or simply employed brutal methods either in arrests or in forms of street justice. Much of the corruption that evolved from the relationship between police and the despised addict of the 1950s and early 1960s has been documented in the *Knapp Commission Report on Police Corruption* (1972). It described police extortion, bribe-taking, illegal wiretaps, stealing money and narcotics, perjuring themselves, and even riding shotgun for selected narcotics dealers. These arrangements are mentioned here not because they were widespread throughout the United States but because they represented the general orientation in that period of history toward drug use and addiction. They permitted police and others in the criminal justice system to treat heroin addicts with little respect and to ignore due process of law. The ways in which addicts were deprived of their rights has been analyzed well by Lindesmith in *The Addict and the Law* (1965). The importance of this social and political orientation toward addicts and other types of drug users became significant for the total country because it was the existing framework for responding to the upsurge in youths' drug taking in what we call the Great American Drug Revolution of the 1960s.

Antecedents to the Great American Drug Revolution

Literary historians might note that the predecessors of the hippies were the avant-garde beats of the 1950s. In both Jack Kerouac's *On the Road* and in some of Allen Ginsberg's poems, there are romantic and positive references to drugs, mainly marijuana. The Beat writers may have had some influence in bringing attention to the harsh laws that regulated marijuana (possession in those days in many states called for as much as twenty years in prison) but their influence on the behavior of young people was apparently minimal and had little impact on broad societal patterns of behavior.

In 1962, President Kennedy convened a White House conference whose title introduced the term "drug abuse" into the American lexicon. This new interest in narcotics by a young and vigorous president followed a renewal of concern for other social problems that had been ignored. Kennedy's support for the Mobilization for Youth project on the Lower East Side of New York and the Haryou Act program in Harlem initiated a new and exciting venture into the social problems of juvenile delinquency and poverty, both of which had been ignored since the start of the Second World War.

At the White House Conference on Drug Abuse, over 400 drug experts from treatment agencies, hospitals, research centers, the courts, and the police attended. The two days of meetings at the State Department concluded with two major results: (1) it was generally agreed that the drug field was characterized by misinformation and inadequate information; and (2) the legal instrument of civil commitment was a new strategy that would emphasize medical treatment for addicts but still keep them very much attached to the criminal justice system. The Federal Bureau of Narcotics was scathingly criticized for its overstatement of the addiction problem. Isadore Chein, the social scientist who directed the major study of youthful narcotic use in the 1950s, which resulted in the book *The Road to H* (1964), noted that by confusing users with addicts, the government's narcotics police vastly exaggerated the number of addicts. Chein stated,

> We need desperately to have someone who knows how to count. . . . They [the Federal Bureau of Narcotics] do not know the difference between counting names on a list and counting addicts. The Commissioner would have been better advised to have said: "The number of addicts in the United States cannot be very much more than 46,798 and, in reality, it is doubtlessly very, very much less" (*Proceedings: White House Conference on Narcotic and Drug Abuse* 1962).

The Modern U.S. Non-Addictive Drug Situation: 1964–1984

The first rumblings of the new youthful drug use explosion occurred in 1963 and 1964 on both coasts of the United States. In Cambridge, Professors Leary and Alpert at Harvard University had begun their experiments with LSD. Many of their students and friends were claiming to have undergone profound religious and other mystical experiences through the use of LSD and marijuana. In the San Francisco Bay area, marijuana was fast becoming a popular drug among students at the University of California at Berkeley as well as other schools throughout the area. Similar pockets of marijuana and LSD advocates arose simultaneously in New York City. The pro-drug advocates who developed a toehold in these three cities were not distinguished by their numbers but by their influence among other youths in nearby cities and in other colleges. Illegal drug use grew quickly among the youth population. It was not the number of young people who began to "turn on" in ever-increasing proportion in the mid-1960s that was of such great importance, for we suspect that the sheer percentage of young persons who have taken an illegal drug in any given month over the past decade far exceeds the number in the mid-1960s. Rather, it was the social context and the meaning attached to drugs by the users themselves and those who were aghast at such use that made the period so special in the United States. Until the development of this new group of young middle-class drug users, the groups most closely identified with drugs were in the inner-city; and the most common societal response to their use was to classify them as criminals and to bring harsh sanctions against them.

What was distinctive about drug use in the middle and late 1960s? First, the reports of the actual sensations of the experience—the highs— were unique, at least to the initial wave of middle-class Anglo users. Users claimed that drugs enhanced sensuality, slowed time, enabled new solutions to old problems; for many users, drugs were reported to improve looking at art and listening to music. The experiences were often startling and even dazzling. For example, LSD users reported a flood of sensations and the breakdown of perceptions into raw elements (colors or sound particles, electrical currents, and the like) causing many to feel closer to a pure, natural order of life than they had before the drug experience. For many users, these internal explorations became religious experiences. Drugs were frequently used for introspection and for socializing, especially in natural and friendly surroundings. For the intellectual drug users, the new "consciousness-expanding" drugs, as they called marijuana and the psychedelics, were not addictive, escapist, tranquillizing experiences that deadened the senses. Unlike alcohol, which was viewed as facilitating aggression and sloppiness and which caused damage to one's liver, brain, and other organs, these new drugs were used for their enhancement of artistic and intellectual experiences.

For the first time in modern history, there were pro-drug advocates, who, despite the illegality of some of the drugs, were enthusiastic proponents of the experiences they induced. Even when opiates were legal, or when Prohibition was being repealed, no one urged the use of drugs or alcohol because they were good for the mind and the soul.

Another distinctive feature of this new drug use was the culture that emerged and supported it. In 1966 and 1967, youths from across the country flocked to communities such as San Francisco's Haight-Ashbury district, to Berkeley, to Boston, and to the developing East Village of New York City to become part of the burgeoning "counterculture." By the end of 1967 and the famous "Summer of Love," Haight-Ashbury was reeling from the onslaught of drifting, rootless youths who had pulled away from conventional families to seek unknown adventures. Countercultures began to spring up in cities across the country.

These communities usually shared several attributes, which were unique in U.S. cities. A substantial number of participants were young people on their own for the first time. Communal living among people who had previously been strangers became popular. The dress was costume-like, creative, colorful, and not (yet) styled for fashion shows. There emerged a field of art that ranged from street musicians to posters and murals. Writers who were identified completely with a sense of the social movement and a flair for a new idiom, which often included forbidden curse words, wrote for underground papers and new publishers. Dance halls catering to new "acid-rock" musicians and their followers offered exotic light shows and dances. Radical political events became a regular part of the community's activities and alternative forms of education such as the "free" university cropped up.

With regard to drugs and their consciousness-expanding capabilities, young people seemed deeply involved in experimentation and extensive dissection of the experience. They were absorbed in conversation about various drugs, prices, fluctuations in quality and character of one supply over another, in those local and national figures in the entertainment and political world who were associated with drugs, and the lyrics of popular music which might refer to drugs, ad nauseum. This concern for drugs permeated much of the press and television in both reporting and fictional accounts. Those young people who were preoccupied with drugs found support in knowing that the rest of the nation, hip or straight, was fascinated with the drama of new explorations into what was once forbidden behavior.

How was it that drugs and dress and music and art came to take on such importance that a veritable children's crusade engulfed the Haight-Ashbury district and other neighborhoods in cities throughout the country? At the time, most adults had images of drugs from the 1950s or earlier, when the subject was connected to only a small and outcast portion of the population. Many people believed that marijuana was a step to heroin addiction, that all drug uses outside of medical prescription was a sign of weakness and that users quickly became slaves to the drug. They believed that users were lured to drug experimentation by older, evil pushers who exploited their naiveté. What was viewed during that era as a "generation gap" was in significant part an *information gap* between young people who had learned some hard facts about drugs through their own experimentation and the friends and adults who accepted as truths the myths of public agencies. The divergence of opinions drove a wedge between the new drug users and the large portion of society, mostly adults, who honestly believed that a generation of young people was caught up in an inappropriate and immoral pursuit of pleasure and was blindly destroying itself.

Many drug users, on the other hand, thought of themselves as special. The new drug use erupted after a decade of political conservatism and what some writers viewed as cultural drabness in such best sellers as *The Organization Man* (1956), *The Man in the Gray Flannel Suit* (1955), and the other-directed people of *The Lonely Crowd* (1950). For many young people, breaking free of the constraining, formal adult world was exhilarating; and breaking the law by using illicit drugs made the step toward unconventionality even more exciting. From the start of this new wave of drug use, it was unclear how much of the excitement which surrounded drug use and the quickly formed counterculture was due to drugs themselves and how much to other major changes in society at large. Even without drugs as an issue, the 1960s would have been a decade of extraordinary change in the United States. The decade began with the presidency of the vigorous and handsome John F. Kennedy. Ushering in the decade was the civil rights movement with its sit-ins, freedom riders, and mass demonstrations that often ended in violence and arrests. Within two years of becoming president, Kennedy authorized the ill-fated Bay of Pigs invasion of Cuba and the commitment of military units to Vietnam. In 1963, the country was stunned by Kennedy's assassination; and by the following year, Lyndon Johnson had launched a series of legislative proposals that started the War on Poverty and gave the promise of a Great Society. By mid-decade, both civil rights and the Vietnam War were tumultuous issues which roused the passion of a dissenting youth population and contributed to the gap between the adult world that rallied patriotically to its government in a time of crisis and a new generation of youths who actively opposed what they saw as an unjust war. Political demonstrations became commonplace in some cities and were prominently reported in the mass media. In some cities, growing antagonisms between minority groups, particularly the black ghetto population, and local governments erupted in street violence that left city blocks charred by anger and arson.

How much of the alienation and antagonism between generations was related to drug use? To what extent was the rejection of previously unquestioned laws and assumptions about government and authority tied to drug-using activites? Twenty years have not given sufficient perspective to sort out those influences. Everything seemed to combine, at least for a while, in a coalition of youth (and some adults) around the issues of protest so that even young people from conservative communities such as the white working class took up the style, if not the content, of the counterculture. Even many youths who were not politically radical shared a common bond with those who were. Both groups selected drug use as an exciting activity and ran the risks of violating the law and antagonizing conventional society whether the aim was to protest the U.S. presence in Vietnam, to refuse military service, to participate in civil rights demonstrations, or to smoke marijuana.

Until the late 1960s, certainly until the presidential election in 1968, the counterculture's growth knew few limits. In response to the protests against the war, President Johnson announced that he would not seek reelection, and it appeared that the critics of mainstream politics had a powerful influence on the direction of U.S. history.

Why, then, did it end and end swiftly? First, there were many motives besides the idealized hippie version for being involved in the counterculture and with illegal drugs. Some youths came to the counterculture and brought with them the same entrepreneurial motives for profit at any cost that others had denounced in economic capitalism. Some of them sold adulterated drugs that resulted in serious adverse reactions; some simply ripped off users through shady dealing. And some youths, uninterested in religion or politics or transcendental experiences, simply wanted to take drugs and used the countercultural experience as a back-drop to cushion severe personal, psychological, and family problems. Almost from the beginning, there were divisions within the countercul-ture based on political and apolitical drug taking.

Perhaps most important, there was constant police harrassment that often resulted in arrest and the ensuing consequences of involvement in the criminal justice system. For many young people from middle-class backgrounds who selected poverty and an open, hippie lifestyle, the in-trusion of police and criminal proceedings were a calamity. Not only did an arrest affect one's life chances and require large sums of money for bail and attorneys, but it also often signified the collapse of the innocent trust which permeated the counterculture in its beginning years. The world of undercover agents, informants, and agents provocateurs and their intrusions into the everyday world of young people were a brutal counterpoint to the desire to live open, trusting lives with loving friends.

Finally, there was essentially no economy in these counterculture communities. Many young people merely dropped out of the straight world, and with a few marketable skills, they had a hard time making ends meet. If they could not make a living at the simple crafts they attempted, there was always the opportunity for dealing drugs. Even here, the occupational hazards from police and the brutality of rip-off artists and other heavy hitters from the street made dealing drugs harsh and dangerous.

Within a few years after forming, practically every urban counter-culture community in the country experienced a marked decline. Where once there had been hope, the streets reflected despair; and even on Haight Street in San Francisco, where the Summer of Love of 1967 ush-ered in an era of flower children, by 1970 the streets were empty except for pockets of burned-out speed freaks and heroin addicts. Stores were boarded up, and an ominous distrust was pervasive.

Many young people had trouble handling drugs. As new drugs en-tered the youth market, their potency was often unknown and their ef-fects frequently unfamiliar and frightening. Drugs were often of unreliable quality and adulterated with contents that were physically harmful. Other young people, hell-bent on rebellion for its own sake, simply took too many drugs, too often, and became burn-outs with brains so fried that their drug fantasies became their realities; and friends, neighbors, and even sympathetic health authorities were sometimes at a loss to help them. There were overdoses, admissions to emergency rooms, and bad trips that required aid from free clinics. And occasionally someone died at a young age as a direct result of drug consumption.

The coup de grace for the counterculture was probably not drug related; but the message received by the participants also affected drug users. By 1968, the outside world showed a nasty face. The Vietnam War had been escalating steadily, and the U.S. commitment had stabilized at over 500,000 men. In the spring of that year, both Martin Luther King and Robert Kennedy were assassinated. The enemy in Vietnam launched the Tet offensive. And in the summer of 1968, outside the Democratic National Convention in Chicago, the nation watched as police clubbed thousands of young demonstrators who had mobilized to protest. The conservative trend of the country continued with the election of Richard Nixon. Although the landmark Woodstock Festival, with over a half million young rock fans gathering for a weekend, was considered a roaring success in peace and love (despite open drug use without serious consequences), six months later at Altamont Festival in Northern California the atmosphere was different. Again youngsters took drugs openly, but this time there were numerous adverse reactions and fights. One spectator was stabbed to death in front of the concert stage.

In Berkeley, California, one of the symbolic centers of the counterculture, street people had claimed a plot of land which the university planned to use for campus expansion. Eventually, university officials called in the police. The confrontation between police and street people (augmented by thousands of students and local residents) resulted in battles with tear gas cannisters hurled back and forth and the eventual killing of an onlooker by a police bullet. Across the Bay at San Francisco State College, demonstrations turned violent with police riding horseback into crowds. In May, 1970, when U.S. troops invaded Cambodia, a large protest by students at Kent State University was met by the National Guard, who fired on fleeing students and killed several of them. At Jackson State College in Mississippi, students protesting discrimination in their community were also fired upon by police, and several nonviolent students were killed.

The message sent out to the counterculture, or what remained of it, was loud and clear: the larger culture was no longer willing to accept demonstrations and would use strong and forceful measures to control the actions of the protesters. During this period, budgets for law enforcement and drug treatment programs climbed steadily.

The message received by the counterculture could be illustrated by the drug arrest statistics which were reported in the Uniform Crime Reports (UCR) compiled by the Federal Bureau of Investigation (FBI). In 1963, there were under 30,000 drug arrests reported nationally, an arrest rate of 29 per 100,000 people. Through the rest of the decade, such arrests rose steadily, reaching 233,000 in 1969, a rate of 162 per 100,000 people. The proportion of drug arrestees who where teenagers under 18 increased almost four-fold from 1963 to 1969, going from 6 percent to 25 percent of those arrested for drugs. Similarly, the proportion of drug arrestees aged 18–20 rose two and a half times from 1963 to 1969. The growth in youthful drug use, which at first was most apparent in big cities, soon began occurring in the suburbs and late in the 1960s started showing up in rural areas. However, as the 1960s ended, the arrest rate for drugs was twice as high in the cities as it was in the suburbs and three times as high in the suburbs as it was in the rural areas.

The UCR data also show an especially marked increase in arrests among whites. Even though the number of blacks being arrested on drug charges was also increasing from 1964 to the end of the decade, the proportion of black drug arrestees under the age of 18, declined by half (from 26 percent to 13 percent) between 1966 and 1968, while the proportion for persons 18 years of age and over declined by a third (from 38 percent to 25 percent).

The Anglo counterculture was the most unexpected major drug development in the latter half of the 1960s and clearly the most widely covered in the media. Those groups that dominated all discussions of drug use prior to the mid-1960s—blacks, Puerto Ricans, and Mexican-Americans—had very different experiences. Judging from the arrest data, drug use among these youth populations also rose dramatically. Among these minorities, the new psychedelics such as LSD never achieved great popularity. But there were several ways in which lower-class youths adopted drug patterns of the counterculture and vice versa.

In several low-income minority communities, there was a marked decline in the use of heroin among young people. In some ways, this development may have reflected the hope provided by the civil rights movement for blacks from the early 1960s until the assassination of Martin Luther King, and paralleled a similar phenomenon among Mexican-Americans from 1968 to 1972 when the Chicano movement swept over many communities in the Southwest. By the end of the 1960s, the hope offered by the civil rights movement was also felt in mainstream institutions such as colleges and universities, which enrolled a higher rate of minority students than ever before and began to design special ethnic courses for them. The counterculture's preferences in drugs and drug lifestyles apparently influenced inner-city minority youth, who moved away from heavily addicting substances toward more controlled use.

By 1973, the Haight-Ashbury Free Medical Clinic researchers began to identify a new kind of drug consumer who managed to avoid addiction. Rather than the typical heroin addicts, the *polydrug user* emerged. Polydrug use was characterized by "psychological" addiction to an altered state rather than by a physical dependence on an addicting substance. As soon as ghetto and barrio youth started adopting a drug use pattern which was non-addictive, the significance of heroin lessened dramatically. The cultural cross-over occurred both ways: Anglo youth, starting in the late 1960s, often experimented with heroin, most notably in Vietnam but also in urban U.S. communities (Feldman 1963); and the differences between the new Caucasian and the old ghetto/barrio drug patterns lessened.

The Federal War on Drugs: The 1970s

The decade was only a few months old when President Richard Nixon announced a "War on Drugs." This was not the first time a political leader in the United States had announced such a war, but it was the first time that a War on Drugs was backed by huge increases in funds and a marked shift in government programs. In 1969, for example, the federal anti-drug budget was slightly under $40 million. By 1973, when the War on Drugs had hit full stride, $750 million in federal money was allocated, with approximately half going to law enforcement and half to treatment programs, most of which catered to heroin addicts. Throughout the United States, city and state governments vastly increased the funds they allocated to drug police and treatment programs. All of these increases were, of course, in addition to the millions of dollars being spent by courts, jails, and prisons to process and use the rapidly increasing number of people caught up in the new efforts to bring drug users into line.

The War on Drugs was hardly an instant success. Even with the demise of the counterculture, the number of drug users appeared to continue rising, especially in parts of the country such as the suburbs and the rural areas which previously had relatively few incidents of drug use. Perhaps the most important change during this period was the way the number of drug arrests soared as a result of the infusion of funds and resources. From 1969 to 1974, drug arrests rose from 233,000 to 642,000. The rate of arrests per 100,000 people reached 393 in large cities in 1970 and hovered at that level for several years, while a similar pattern took place in suburban and rural communities where it peaked in the mid-1970s. The proportion of young people among those arrested— both persons under 18 years of age and those 18–20—remained about the same as it had been at the end of the 1960s. Its slight decline in the last half of the 1970s reflected in part the decline in the number of youths in the populaton at large.

With the end of the counterculture, drugs became almost equal to alcohol popularity among young people. Drugs, in a sense, had become almost normalized. Instead of being championed by aggressive communities of users and charismatic and intellectual leaders, drug use became institutionalized in a quiet, somewhat acceptable fashion. Drug use con-

tinued without the blatant display of the 1960s, and without the deliberate attempts to proselytize. It had worked its way into the socialization
patterns of growing up in the United States.

As soon as drug use became common among "typical" adolescents,
so, too, did the presence of the police. Even though the War on Drugs
produced a network of drug treatment programs throughout the United
States, the route into those treatment programs often (maybe usually)
began with a drug-related arrest. Under these circumstances, the police
became the single most important case-finder so that a kind of symbiotic
relationship evolved between the treatment community and the criminal
justice system with drug users as the basic product which kept the industry vital.

Throughout the 1970s, arrests for drug charges averaged 575,000
per year. In each year of the 1970s, between 49 percent and 57 percent
of those arrested were under the age of 21. In 1972 when the arrest data
started differentiating arrests by the type of drug, it became apparent
that the vast majority of drug arrests were for marijuana. The pattern
has continued to the present time even though in the 1970s states began
to reduce the penalties for possession of small amounts and this change
significantly reduced the number of felony drug arrests from those states
that reported to the UCR system. The UCR does not indicate the type
of drug for which one is arrested by age; but from what we know from
other sources, the hard drug arrests are primarily of adults. The proportion, then, of teenage drug arrests which involve marijuana is higher than
the 62–72 percent figures listed in the UCRs throughout the 1970s.

In large cities, for black males aged 16 through early 20s, the likelihood of being arrested for drugs in any year of the 1970s, was over
one in fifty. In any five year span, the likelihood of arrest on a drug
charge for this group was about one in ten. Increasing the risk of arrest
served to change the character of drug dealing. The price of illegal drugs
soared as did the profit margin for those whose risk was now greater.
The ranks of "friendly" dealers, acting as middlemen for little or no
profit as described by street ethnographers in the late 1960s, diminished
dramatically (Mandel 1967; Carey 1968; Goode 1970; Blum 1972; Cavan 1972). In their place were young businessmen and women whose
interest was career opportunity and profit (Fields 1984).

For several years until the mid-1970s, both the number of arrests
and the percentage of all prisoners convicted of drug charges steadily
increased; but since then there has been a decline in numbers even though
the total number of all prisoners has increased. The continued high rate
of arrests for all types of offenses in conjunction with the decline in

arrests for drug charges suggests that the criminal justice system has become more lenient in its treatment of arrestees who are only drug users or low-level drug dealers, especially if the drug is marijuana.

One of the more visible consequences of the Nixon administration's War on Drugs was the proliferation of treatment programs. For the first few years that this national drug treatment system was operative—roughly from 1971 to 1977—it served a disproportionately large number of persons classified primarily as having opiate problems. During those years, a similarly disproportionately large number of clients in those programs were young adult black and Latino males. In the late 1970s, however, the backgrounds of clients throughout the country started shifting away from those who had strictly a heroin problem. Part of the reason for this shift was that responsibility for these programs moved away from federal control to state and local levels. As a result, treatment facilities started catering to victims of a variety of drugs rather than what was presumed to be the most damaging drug. During this period, methadone maintenance lost much of its lure for many (although not all) heroin addicts.

The major reason for the shift was a change in the drug-using practices of young people. By the middle 1970s, drug use as a rite of passage for adolescents had been in existence for approximately fifteen years. Collectively young people had been bombarded with drug information from a variety of sources and had developed a working knowledge of the dangers and the effects both from well-intentioned educators and from personal observations of older, more experienced peers. During that time, knowledge had been passed on, distilled and refined, so that the level of information available to young people was most often both accurate and detailed. In short, young people became highly sophisticated about drug use and its pitfalls. Of all the pitfalls associated with drug use, one of the least desirable was physical addiction. The result was that young people began to manage their drug use in such ways that inadvertent dependence became relatively rare. With regard to treatment programs, older addicts continued to show up on the treatment rolls; but their ranks were not significantly replaced by younger heroin addicts. Heroin overdoses, for example, which had been a good indicator of heroin use, started plunging in the mid-1970s. Young people simply moved away from heroin or experimented with it in ways that avoided physical dependence.

What caused the decline in heroin use among adolescents while interest in other drugs continued to remain high is not completely clear. Part of the answer is connected to the way methadone patients were viewed in their respective communitites (Hunt et al. 1985). During the

1960s and the early 1970s, the heroin addict seemed to enjoy a special position in the street hierarchy of prestige. Several ethnographic studies (Sutter 1969, 1972; Preble 1969; Feldman 1973) described heroin users as street leaders who commanded the respect of the neighborhood young people. When viewed from a street perspective—not only in slum neighborhoods but also in middle-class suburbs where young people had a respect for daring and a desire for action—heroin users took on a kind of role model status in which their lives were filled with excitement and challenge. They were seemingly in command of their lives and dominated a world that was packed with violence and competition. Once heroin users were moved into methadone maintenance programs, their lives changed dramatically and took on a much slower pace and a more dependent style. Instead of being constructed around the pursuit of heroin and the money with which to buy it, their days, centering upon a daily visit to the clinic, became far less eventful. Preble and Miller describe the change in the heroin addict's lifestyle and his decline within the peer system in an article called "Wine, Welfare, and Methadone" (1977). Rather than changing heroin addicts into conforming citizens, the greater impact of methadone maintenance was to reduce their importance as street leaders by allowing them to develop methadone addictions, which many addicts reported to be far more debilitating than the heroin addictions they had surrendered (Hunt et al. 1985). With their removal from the action on the streets, they could no longer be worthy of emulation, and heroin as a drug of fascination lost its appeal. Other drugs, however, did not.

The 1980s: Too Early To Tell

So far the 1980s mark yet another generation of youthful drug users, although the national trend is, of course, modified by vast differences between different social and ethnic groups (including the different histories of drug use in distinctly different communities). Based on several national data systems as well as recent ethnographic studies, the trends seem unmistakable; they are also supported by most of the arrest data presented on the Uniform Crime Reports. For the first time in recent history, the overall pattern of youthful drug use is in the direction of *decreased* use of illegal drugs.

The last published survey of high school seniors provides data for each of the last nine years from 1975 to 1983 (Johnston et al. 1984). For marijuana, the most widely used illegal drug, the numbers rose from 1975 to 1978, but since reaching its peak in 1978, use has dropped considerably. Of high school seniors in 1978, 37 percent had smoked marijuana during the thirty days prior to the survey, and 11 percent claimed to have smoked it daily during that month (Johnston et al. 1984). By 1984, the comparable figures were twenty-five percent and five percent respectively. For four classes of drugs—sedatives, tranquillizers, inhalants, and hallucinogens—drug use has clearly decreased since 1975. Only for cocaine and stimulants were the figures for "use in the last twelve months" higher in the 1980s than in previous years.

One clear trend shown in the drug treatment data has been the aging of the nation's heroin addicts. For several years now, youths have been less inclined to use heroin, and some recent ethnographic studies have found that when they do experiment with heroin, they do so with a conscious effort to avoid those practices which might lead to physical dependence.

Probably the most provocative official statistics about youthful drug use in the early 1980s are the Uniform Crime Report national arrest figures. These statistics show that teenage drug arrests have decreased every year since 1973, and that the decrease was never so steep as in the 1980s. Comparing the annual average of drug arrests in 1973–74 with that of 1982–83, the proportion of arrests for those under 18 years of age declined from 26 percent to 13 percent; and for those ages 18–20, the proportion dropped from 30 percent to 20 percent (Federal Bureau of Investigation 1973–83).

The Uniform Crime Report figures show two *opposite* trends occurring among young Anglos compared to young blacks and Hispanics in urban areas. Drug arrests for young Anglos, whether they are located in the city, the suburbs, or rural areas, are plummeting; in 1983, arrests were less than half of what they were in 1978. Drug arrests of urban black and Hispanic youth, on the other hand, have remained stable during those years. However, in each of the years since 1980 the rate for older blacks and Hispanics has steadily and significantly increased. There were 65 percent more drug arrests of urban blacks ages 18 and over in 1983 than there were in 1978 (Federal Bureau of Investigation 1978–83).

While it is encouraging to know that the drug arrests of white youth are on a downward spiral, our pleasure is tempered by the fact that arrest of urban blacks and Hispanics have soared so far in this decade. If the arrests statistics do, in fact, accurately reflect drug use patterns, then the United States has returned to a two-track system of drug use, and one can safely state that the interim period of the 1960s was something of an aberration in which criminal and chemical problems were "integrated" and shared by all races and ethnic groups much like alcohol during Prohibition. It appears likely, however, that the pattern may also reflect differing law enforcement between the races. One tentative explanation may be that in the 1980s law enforcement efforts may be an attempt to combine a War on Poverty with a War on Drugs.

Summary: Historical Guideposts for Providing Drug Services for Youth

The constantly changing and ever-varied patterns of youthful drug use provide some guidelines for those who hope to have an impact on adolescent drug problems. First, one can never assume that a unitary "drug problem" exists or that drug use patterns and situations—either over time or among different groups—remain constant. Inner-city black youths have a distinct pattern of drug use, which changes over time and varies among different inner-city ghettos. Latino youths also have unique drug use histories; and the general patterns of Mexican-American drug use in the Southwest and Far West differ considerably from the patterns among Puerto Ricans in New York City or other East Coast cities. Even with black and Latino youths, there are vast differences between drug use preferences, styles, and attendant problems in different regions of the country and in different cities in the same region.

Second, even if drug use for a given group of people were steady over the last few decades, the same consequences of drug use might be considered a problem at one moment, but an advantage at another. Marijuana use in the middle and late 1960s, for example, was considered to be advantageous by many young people because it generated new experiences and perspectives which led to disdain for traditional approaches and facilitated "dropping out" of the bureaucratic establishment. The same consequences today would be looked upon negatively by all but a handful of young people.

Third, the extent of drug use, and particularly the manner in which youthful users of illegal drugs approach these substances, may be postulated to be a reflection of the status of youth at a given period of history. When the prejudice experienced by racial and ethnic minorities was vast and virtually unquestioned in the public arena, there was hardly any experimentation with illegal drugs by most white youth, while at the same time there was substantial use of addicting drugs in some inner-city minority communities. In the latter half of the 1960s, when youth spearheaded what in a less stable society might have been a radical revolution, the use of drugs by young people from the most powerful classes in the United States soared, even to the extent that large countercultures emerged in many of our major cities; and for many youths, drug taking took on some transcendental meaning. Then, with the emergence of a generation concerned with individual self-advancement, whose formative experiences with the political system left them cynical instead of politically active, the use of non-addicting drugs became prevalent throughout the country. Today, drug use is less likely to be a central and dominant experience in the lives of the great majority of youths even though drug taking has become somewhat institutionalized. In the 1980s, at a time when Anglo youths for the first time in memory are more conservative than their elders, the indicators of illegal drug use among youth are down.

Fourth, even with the decline in arrests of young people in recent years, the number of persons under 21 years of age arrested for drugs in the 1980s, so far, averages about 250,000 per year. This level of arrests testifies to the continuing role of law enforcement in the lives of young people who, despite the constant protests of many responsible adults, continue to make drug use a part of their adolescent socialization rituals.

Fifth, the trends in drug use seem to defy prediction. Who, in 1962, could have predicted the upsurge in illegal drug taking among middle-class Caucasian youth during the last half of the 1960s? Who, in the midst of the counterculture's boom, would have predicted its sudden demise and the growing self-centeredness and eventual conservatism of young people?

— An important implication of this chapter is that the drug problems of specific youths are part of the general life problems of these youngsters. However much an expert might know about the general conseqences of a particular drug, it will be extremely difficult to advise or counsel a youth unless one knows the cultural background and life circumstances of that person. One cannot rely on uniform stereotype forms of treatment. In addition, treatment of Anglo youths having a problem with marijuana or PCP may not be applicable to black or Latino youths experiencing difficulties in their use of the same drugs.

Finally, the very illegality of many drugs favored by teenagers places adult advisors in a difficult situation. If the advisor, on the one hand, takes a strict prohibitionist view that is in keeping with current public policy, he or she will be in concert with the law; but in many cases, youths will tend to shut out any advice coming from someone who is antagonistic to their chosen lifestyle. Some youths are simply not interested in achieving total drug abstinence or in cutting out *all* illegal substances from their lives. If the advisor, on the other hand, opts for "reasonable" drug use, this position pits him or her against the prevailing laws and drug policies of the community, even though this option might be the preferred treatment strategy for some youths. Either the advisor takes an authoritarian position that is unrealistically prohibitive, or else the advice offered aids and abets illegal activity. Given the current laws regarding drugs and the fact that public opinion, since the repeal of

Prohibition, has always supported toughening drug laws, the dilemma is here to stay. For better or worse, anyone offering advice or counsel to youths is going to do so in far less than ideal circumstances.

None of the previous discussion should be taken to indicate that young people do not experience many drug-related problems, that concerned and reasonable adults have little to offer youths who experience such problems. On the contrary, we believe teenagers will and do welcome intelligent advice and direction from experienced and qualified adults. The major problem lies in tailoring the advice and help to the needs of different groups of young users. That in itself is a formidable task, but one that is both necessary and worth doing.

References

Anslinger, H.J. (with R. Cooper). 1937. Marijuana: Assassin of youth. *American Magazine,* July.

Anslinger, H.J. 1951. The facts about our teenage drug addicts. *Reader's Digest,* October.

Anslinger, H.J. 1953. *The Traffic in Narcotics.* New York: Funk and Wagnalls.

Anslinger, H.J. 1959. Current narcotic situation in the United States. *F.B.I. Law Enforcement Bulletin,* June.

Blum, R.H. 1972. *The Dream Sellers.* San Francisco: Jossey-Bass.

Brown, C. 1965. *Manchild in the Promised Land.* New York, New York: New American Library.

Carey, J.T. 1972. *The College Drug Scene.* Englewood Cliffs, N.J.: Prentice-Hall.

Cavan, S. 1972. *Hippies of the Haight.* St. Louis: New Critics Press.

Chein, I.; D.L. Gerard; R.S. Lee; and E. Rosenfield. 1974 *The Road to H: Narcotics, Delinquency, and Public Policy.* New York: Basic Books.

Duster, T. 1970. *The Legislation of Morality: Law, Drugs, and Moral Judgment.* New York: The Free Press.

Federal Bureau of Investigation. 1969–1983. *Uniform Crime Reports: Crime in the United States.* U.S. Department of Justice, Washington, D.C.: U.S. Government Printing Office.

Feldman, H.W. 1973. Street status and the drug user. *Transaction/Society,* Vol. 10, No. 4.

Fiddle, S. 1967. *Portraits from a Shooting Gallery: Life Styles from the Drug Addict World.* New York: Harper and Row.

Fields, A.B. 1984. 'Slinging weed': The social organization of street corner marijuana sales. *Urban Life,* Vol. 13, Nos. 2 & 3.

Goode, E. 1970. *The Marijuana Smokers.* New York: Basic Books.

Graham-Mulhall, Sarah. 1921. Experiences in narcotic drug control in the State of New York. *New York Medical Journal,* Vol. 113.

Hubbard, S.D. February 1920. The New York City narcotic clinic. *Monthly Bulletin of the Department of Health, New York City,* Vol. 10.

Hubbard, S.D. March 1920. Municipal narcotic dispensaries. *Public Health Reports* (U.S. Public Health Services), Vol. 35.

Hunt, D.; D. Lipton; D. Goldsmith; D. Strug; and B. Spunt. 1985. It takes your heart: The image of methadone among street addicts and its effect on recruitment into methadone treatment. *International Journal of the Addictions,* Volume 2. Spring.

Johnson, L.; P. O'Malley; and J. Bachman. 1984. *Highlights from Drugs and American High School Students, 1975–1983.* Rockville, Maryland.: U.S. Institute on Drug Abuse.

Kerouac, J. 1956. *On the Road.* New York: Viking Press.

Knapp, W. 1972. *The Knapp Commission Report on Police Corruption.* New York: George Braziller.

LaGuardia Committee on Marihuana. 1944. *The Marihuana Problem in the City of New York.*

Lampman, R.H. 1924. Heroin heroes—an interview with Richmond Pearson Hobson, *Saturday Evening Post,* September 20

Larner, J. and R. Tefferteller. 1964. *The Addict in the Streets.* New York: Grove Press.

Lindesmith, A.R. 1965. *The Addict and the Law.* Bloomington: Indiana University Press.

Literary Digest. 1924. Saving youth from heroin and crime. Vol. 81.

Malcolm X (with A. Haley). 1964. *The Autobiography of Malcolm X.* New York: Grove Press.

Mandel, J. 1967. Myths and realities of marijuana pushing. In J.L. Simmons (ed.) *Marijuana, Myths and Realities.* North Hollywood, California: Brandon House

New York Times. April 10, 1919. Fear outbreak by men needing drugs.

New York Times. April 11, 1919. Treat drug victims at municipal clinic.

New York Times. April 13, 1919. Drug victims keep city clinic jammed.

Preble, E. and J. Casey. 1969. Taking care of business—The heroin user's life on the street. *International Journal of the Addictions,* Vol. 4, March.

Preble, E. and T. Miller 1977. Methadone, wine and welfare. In R. Weppner (ed.) *Street Ethnography.* Beverly Hills: Sage Publications.

Proceedings: White House Conference on Narcotic and Drug Abuse. 1962. Washington, D.C.: U.S. Government Printing Office.

Prentice, A. 1921. The problem of the narcotic addict. *Journal of the American Medical Association,* Vol. 76, June 4.

Reisman, D.; R. Denny; and N. Glazer. 1950. *The Lonely Crowd.* New Haven: Yale University Press.

Sinclair, A. 1962. *Prohibition: The Era of Excess.* Boston, Massachusetts: Little, Brown and Company.

Sutter, A. 1969. Worlds of drug use on the street scene. In D. Cressey and D.A. Ward (eds.) *Delinquency, Crime, and Social Process.* New York: Harper and Row.

Sutter, A. 1972. Playing a cold game: Phases of a ghetto career. *Urban Life*, Vol. 1.

Thomas, P. 1967. *Down These Mean Streets*. New York: Alfred Knopf.

Wilson, S. 1955. *The Man in the Gray Flannel Suit*. New York: Simon and Schuster.

Whyte, W.H. 1956. *The Organization Man*. New York: Simon and Schuster.

3

Drugs and Their Effects on Adolescent Users

S. Kenneth Schonberg, M.D.
Sidney H. Schnoll, M.D., Ph.D.

Although drug use by adolescents was an unusual phenomenon prior to the 1960s, the past two decades have witnessed an explosion in both the extent and variety of chemicals abused by some teenagers. In the late 1960s and early 1970s, the abuse of such drugs as heroin, barbiturates, and amphetamines was responsible for extensive illness and mortality among youth. Those who treated teenagers needed to absorb a new body of knowledge concerning the physical and behavioral consequences of these agents. In some urban centers, drug-related illness, stemming primarily from the use of opiates and barbiturates, accounted for nearly 10 percent of hospital admissions. As both the lifestyle of these drug users and the illegality of their activities made it unlikely that they would seek medical care, only a small fraction of the most serious conditions were brought to the attention of a physician. Significant illness and dysfunction often went undetected, unaddressed, and unrecorded.

The availability of many other drugs, changes in the law, in enforcement practices, and in education, and the expansion of treatment may have all played a role in the decline in adolescent heroin and barbiturate use. The specific contribution of any one factor to this decline remains speculative. At present the abuse of opiates and barbiturates remains at a lower but rather constant level. Similarly, reports of illness due to these drugs are far fewer than a decade ago. However, a knowledge of the consequences of such drug use remains important. Vigilance is required for the understanding of disturbed behavior and other symptoms, when these occur in an adolescent, lest the role of drug use as the possible cause of the dysfunction be overlooked and an opportunity missed for meaningful intervention and treatment.

In addition to opiates, barbiturates, and amphetamines, a variety of other chemicals have become available in the adolescent drug culture.

Included are cannabis; the hallucinogens such as LSD, mescaline, and most recently phencyclidine (PCP or angel dust); the inhalants (volatile hydrocarbons) including those found in glue, cleaning fluid, and aerosols; and cocaine. There have been changes in drug popularity but each of these substances remains a rather constant part of the experience of many adolescents. Among the hallucinogens both lysergic acid diethylamide (LSD) and phencyclidine (PCP) enjoyed brief periods of extensive use with concomitant negative consequences. They now have become less dramatic but nonetheless persistent parts of the drug scene and some 15 percent of older adolescents will report some lifetime experience with hallucinogens. Inhalants were a drug of choice of some younger adolescent groups in the 1960s and 1970s though such use is now encountered with far less frequency. The data on cocaine use indicate a doubling of the rate of use in the past decade and current usage by 4.8 percent of high school seniors in 1983 (Johnston et al. 1984). The consequences of this abuse are now more frequently coming to medical attention.

Overlooked in the turmoil which accompanied the epidemic of drug abuse was the widespread use of alcohol by all segments of our population including adolescents. Learning to drink has been and remains a rite of passage for the vast majority of American youth. Nearly 95 percent of high school seniors in the United States have had some experience with alcohol and between 25 and 35 percent drink to the point of intoxication each month. The short and long term consequences to those teenagers who drink to excess and establish a persistent pattern of alcoholism represent a national health concern. Of equal importance is the impact of intoxication upon young people who will not become alcoholics. Accidents while driving under the influence of alcohol are the leading cause of death among adolescents and young adults and the prevention of such accidents is currently the subject of intense legislative and educational activity.

The effects of alcohol alone should raise serious concern, but an additional concern is the interaction of alcohol with other drugs of abuse. Alcohol often increases the level of intoxication occurring with other drugs by interfering with metabolism. This can increase the consequences associated with drug use. In today's climate of drug use, multiple drug use is the norm rather than the exception, making knowledge of alcohol-drug and between-drug interactions extremely important.

In less than a quarter of a century marijuana use has changed from a rare phenomenon to what many believe is a permanent and certainly pervasive experience of adolescents. Currently, over half of all high school seniors have had some experience with marijuana with nearly 25 percent smoking this drug at least once per month. The behavioral and physiological consequences of marijuana use have been the subject of extensive investigation. Beyond concern with an "amotivational syndrome" (loss of purpose and drive) or other aftereffects of intoxication, which marijuana shares with alcohol, there are concerns regarding a host of other behavioral and physical effects, many of which have not been fully clarified.

In effect, neither the ability to understand the developmental process of adolescence nor the ability to render care to teenagers can be achieved without a knowledge of drugs, their use, abuse, and consequences.

How Drugs Work

To understand drugs and their effects it is helpful to know some basic principles about the way drugs are taken into the body and how they act upon the body. For any drug to have an effect, several important things must happen. First the drug must be taken into the body. This is called absorption. Second, the drug must get to the parts of the body where it will exert its effects. This is called distribution or transportation. Third, the drug must combine with a specific part of the body, usually called a receptor, to exert its action.

To stop a drug's effect on the body, additional steps must take place. The first is usually the transformation of the drug into a form which can be easily removed from the body. This process is called metabolism. After the drug is metabolized, it is removed from the body. This removal of the drug is called excretion.

These five steps, absorption, distribution, action, metabolism, and excretion, occur for almost all drugs but not necessarily in the same order.

Absorption. There are many different ways drugs can enter the body. The most common route is oral: drugs are swallowed and absorbed through the intestinal walls. A drug that is swallowed usually does not have an effect until it passes through the intestinal wall into the body. This passage occurs very quickly for some drugs, like alcohol, and very slowly or not at all for other drugs. Marijuana is very slowly and erratically absorbed from the intestine.

Some drugs can be smoked or inhaled. Once inhaled, the drug crosses the membranes of the lungs into the bloodstream. Marijuana, inhalants such as toluene, found in glue and nitrous oxide, and nicotine are absorbed through this process.

Some drugs like heroin are injected by needle into the body. This method frequently leads to the development of infections when sterile techniques are not used.

Drugs can also be absorbed through the mucus membranes of the nose. This is called snorting and is the most common way to take cocaine.

Distribution. Once a drug enters the body, it is distributed by the blood to all parts of the body, not just the part where the drug has its expected effect. This means that the drug can act on other areas of the body. This is called a side effect of the drug. All drugs have side effects. Morphine exerts its primary action in the central nervous system, where it relieves pain, but it is also distributed to the bowel, where it causes constipation, a side effect of morphine. A side effect can be an adverse effect, but at times an effect originally considered a side effect can be useful, for example the constipation effect of opiates is effective in stopping diarrhea.

Drugs can also be distributed to parts of the body where they are stored without exerting a specific effect. Often a drug can be stored for a long period of time, slowly being released from the storage site, resulting in a prolonged period of action for the drug. The long duration of action of PCP (phencyclindine) is a result of storage in cells.

Action. A drug's action usually occurs when the drug combines with a specific part of a cell called a receptor. Once the drug combines with the receptor, a series of events takes place which result in the drug's effect. These events are not clearly understood at this time.

The receptors where drugs combine are not there just for drugs to react with them but also serve some function when the drug is not present in the body. Therefore, the drug serves to alter some function the cell is already able to perform. When a medication is taken as prescribed, these alterations in function may be extremely beneficial, such as making a failing heart beat better. In the case of abused drugs, however, these alterations can result in hallucinations, alterations in memory, or other effects which may not be expected.

Metabolism. Metabolism is the way the body alters a drug so its action is stopped and it can be eliminated from the body. Some drugs are metabolized very quickly and some very slowly. Some drugs are not active in the form absorbed into the body and must be metabolized to an active form before they can exert their effect. Heroin is metabolized to morphine, which is then active.

The process of metabolism is very complicated. In some cases, an active drug is metabolized to another active drug or metabolite before it is metabolized to a form that can be excreted. As more is learned about the metabolism of various drugs, we can begin to understand why some drugs have effects that last for a short period of time and others last for a long period of time.

Excretion. Excretion is the way the body eliminates a drug. This usually occurs after the drug is metabolized to a form that can be excreted. Most excretion takes place in the kidney, and the drug is eliminated in the urine. Therefore, urine testing is often an effective way to determine whether someone has taken a particular drug.

Reasons for, and Consequences of, Drug Use

Adolescents use drugs for many reasons, not all of which relate to the anticipated or known psychoactive effects of the substance. As with all other human behavior, motivations are complex and not always consciously understood by the individual. Motivations for adolescent drug use include expressing opposition to adult authority; identifying with a peer group; attempting to exhibit a desired personal attribute such as being "cool" or "macho;" marking emergence from childhood and dependence into a more mature and adult status; and coping with problems or painful experiences in one's life. However, regardless of motivation, drugs of abuse affect the user's thinking and perception. Although the effects, or consequences, are different for different types of drugs, there is much overlap of effects across drugs. A single drug most often has multiple effects and at times these effects are contradictory. Such effects vary from individual to individual and even within the same individual at different times and in different settings.

Many drugs are capable of producing a high—euphoria or elation. The most familiar high is the euphoria produced by alcohol (in some ways similar to that reported for marijuana). Other substances, in particular amphetamines, cocaine, and the opiates may produce a more intense euphoria which contributes to repetitive use, habituation, and addiction. In contrast, the inhalants, such as those found in glue, cleaning fluid, and aerosols, produce a short-lived high. Feelings of euphoria can also occur after taking barbiturates or hallucinogens. The hallucinogens, such as LSD and PCP, may also produce hallucinations, confusion, and loss of inhibition. Although most non-users would regard such effects as frightening and unpleasant, some users report feelings of elation and "mind-expansion." As close as one can come to describing a universal experience of drug abusers, regardless of the drug, is to say that many teenagers use them because drugs make them feel better, not worse.

The opiates, tranquilizers, barbiturates, and to some degree alcohol and marijuana, can help alleviate anxiety. All adolescents suffer from anxieties and pressures as they attempt to cope with profound physical and psychological changes. Lack of parental support, guidance, and understanding may weaken the adolescent's ability to cope and weaken ego strength at a time when ego strength is important. A logical argument can be made that for many adolescents, the repetitive use of drugs represents self-medication for anxiety, tension, and/or depression. In other words, adolescents may gravitate toward a substance which, they feel, relieves anxiety or in some other way enhances their ability to meet the demands of day-to-day life, such as improving their performance. These youngsters often believe that they function better, rather than worse, while self-treating with a drug of abuse. Unfortunately, this is often a misperception arising from lowered anxiety and decreased awareness of poor performance. Amphetamines are frequently used to counteract feelings of fatigue, in the quest for psychic energy, or in alleviating the depression encountered among abusers.

Once the adolescent begins to use drugs for producing good feelings at a time of stress he or she is in trouble (MacDonald 1981). Most drugs lead to psychological and emotional dependence. The concept of using a drug to achieve normal function, rather than a state of euphoria or mind expansion, is even more applicable to those who become drug abusers—compulsive, uncontrollable, or irrational users. When the abuser tries to stop drug use, a withdrawal or abstinence syndrome can develop. Feeling ill, physically and/or mentally, is a part of all abstinence syndromes and results in a strong desire to continue drug use in order to feel well. The intensity of withdrawal symptoms, the anxiety which accompanies abstinence, and the craving for more drugs place addicts in a separate class from non-addicts seeking better performance through drugs. Addicts will only feel well after drug use and have often lost the ability, at least to some degree, to achieve the euphoria which initially accompanied their drug use. Continued use to "get straight" is seen with all drugs of abuse including opiates, barbiturates, alcohol, amphetamines, cocaine, and tranquilizers.

Physical and Mental Consequences

Regardless of the motivations for using a particular drug or the psychoactive benefits perceived to be derived from that drug, the physical and behavioral consequences of drug abuse remain. These consequences are secondary not only to the pharmacological actions and side effects of the drug but also to the methods by which it is self-administered and the lifestyle of the drug abuser.

Alcohol

Alcohol and marijuana are the drugs most frequently abused by adolescents in the United States. Although very different substances pharmacologically, with different physiological consequences, they share two characteristics: both are widely used by adolescents as recreational drugs, and both have a major health impact upon teenagers.

Some 93 percent of the adolescents in the United States report having used alcohol at least once prior to graduation from high school, and for nearly a third of those that use began before high school. Daily drinking among high school seniors was at about the same level in 1983 (5.5 percent) as it was in 1975 (5.7 percent). However, the rate of occasional binge drinking rose from 37 percent in 1975 to 41 percent in 1979 (Johnston et al. 1984).

Alcoholism seems to run in families. Therefore, if one or more parents or close relatives is an alcoholic, there is a greater chance that the children may become alcoholics. Anyone who has a history of alcoholism in the family should be very cautious about the use of any drug which has a potential for abuse.

Physical damage due to alcohol abuse during adolescence is rare, with the exception of injury from accidents, and is mainly confined to instances where large amounts are consumed at a single sitting. Acute inflammation of the stomach (gastritis) with possible hemorrhage and inflammation of the pancreas may both result from an alcoholic overdose. Bleeding, severe vomiting, and changes in the composition of blood and other body fluids may mandate hospitalization for such an episode. Overdose reactions with pneumonia due to breathing foreign substances (for example vomit into the lung), cessation of breathing, and coma do occur, but are rare. Such overdose reactions are likely to occur in a teenager who is a novice at drinking and has no concept of his or her tolerance for alcohol.

The consequences of chronic alcoholism encountered in adults, such as chronic liver disease, inflammation of various nerves, and impaired memory for new events, are generally not seen in adolescents. Generally, adolescents have not used alcohol long enough to sustain serious physiological damage. Similarly, alcohol addiction with a specific withdrawal syndrome is quite uncommon during the teen years. The major withdrawal syndrome from alcohol marked by delirium tremens is rarely, if ever, observed in adolescents. A less severe withdrawal syndrome, characterized by tremors, excessive perspiring, agitation, disorientation, and occasional brief self-limited seizures has been observed in teenagers who had been drinking heavily over a period of weeks. Hospitalization may be required for such adolescents so they can be put under observation when discontinuing alcohol use. Even if the withdrawal symptoms do not develop, hospitalization can be used in these cases as an opportunity to begin an intervention designed to interrupt continued alcohol use and the physical risks associated with adult alcoholism.

Marijuana

The effects of marijuana depend on many factors—the type of plant, how it is cultivated, the potency of the preparation, the amount consumed, the person using it, and the environment in which it is used. Even different moods can influence the way a drug will effect an individual. While psychological effects can be so subtle that an inexperienced user is unable to detect them, the immediate physiological effects can be pronounced. There is usually an increase in pulse rate and a fall in blood pressure, the eyes become reddened, and there is a decreased ability to coordinate physical movements. The drug causes a distortion of perception of time and distance resulting in impaired thought processes. Highly susceptible youngsters who use high doses can experience perceptual changes, body distortions, and hallucinations. For the neophyte the effects can be frightening and result in panic or even temporary psychotic reactions. In view of these negative effects, why do youngsters continue to use marijuana? Some emotional effects can be quite appealing, especially to adolescents. A marijuana high is generally described as a dreamy and enjoyable feeling, somewhat like being mildly drunk on alcohol (Berger 1982).

In the last twenty-five years, marijuana among adolescents has gone from a rarely used substance to a popular intoxicant, deeply entrenched in adolescent experience. Currently some 55 percent of high school seniors have tried marijuana at least once, with nearly 6 percent using it on a daily basis. Over 20 percent report having had a first experience prior to entrance into high school.

As a result of its widespread use, its potential dangers, and the continuing public debate and controversy, marijuana has been the subject of extensive investigation. Marijuana is neither a benign drug nor among the more dangerous substances abused by teenagers. Research on the consequences of marijuana use is extensive, and definite effects upon brain, cardiovascular, pulmonary, endocrine, and psychological function have been demonstrated.

Of great concern has been the potential effect of marijuana upon brain function. The most common acute effect is temporary euphoria and intoxication, the desired result for most adolescents. However, anxiety, panic, confusion, hallucinations, and prolonged loss of contact with reality lasting several days have been reported in some cases. Permanent psychosis has not been clearly demonstrated to result from marijuana use. Marijuana causes acute changes in both the waking and sleeping electrical activitiy of the brain. However, these changes do not persist after use is discontinued and there is no evidence of changes in brain cell structure or an increase in the potential for seizures.

Negative effects on short-term memory and the ability to learn are of particular concern for the adolescent who smokes marijuana during the school day. To date, no evidence exists that the recreational use of marijuana during the weekend will impair learning during the subsequent school week. However, the prolonged use of marijuana, daily over months, may be associated with a more permanent deleterious effect upon behavior, called "the amotivational syndrome," characterized by lethargy and a loss of goal-directed behavior (Cohen 1980).

Initially, or when used occasionally, marijuana can cause bronchodilation for a short period of time, while chronic use has been associated with mild and reversible obstruction of the smaller branches of the bronchial tree. It is therefore not unexpected that a few asthmatic adolescents report relief of symptoms with marijuana smoking even though most do not tolerate the drug. As with tobacco, chronic use causes irritation and an increase in respiratory tract infection. Although results are as yet inconclusive it appears that heavy marijuana use can cause lung cancer. Effects on the heart and blood vessels include mild and transient rapid heartbeat and alterations in blood pressure which are of no significance during adolescence except in the teenager who already has heart problems.

In both males and females, marijuana lowers the secretion of sex hormones. In young men there is also a decrease in both sperm number and motility and some indication that the drug may lower blood levels of the male sex hormone testosterone. These effects are temporary and disappear when marijuana use is interrupted, and have not been demonstrated to have a deleterious effect upon male fertility. Similar effects upon menstrual patterns and ovulation have been reported in females, but these studies remain unconfirmed and have not yet demonstrated an impact upon fertility. Studies of large numbers of deliveries have failed to conclusively demonstrate that marijuana can harm the development of the fetus. These investigations have been hampered by the frequency with which mothers who use marijuana also use other drugs. Of particular concern to the teenager is the question of what effect, if any, will the hormonal changes shown to be present with marijuana use have upon the complex sexual and physical changes which characterize adolescence.

The effects of marijuana and alcohol upon motor function are of major and immediate importance. In addition to causing euphoria and a relative lack of concern for self-preservation, marijuana impairs motor coordination, reaction time, time sense, the ability to follow a moving object, and other sensory and perceptual functions. All of these skills and functions are necessary to safely operate machinery, including automobiles. Accidents, particularly automotive accidents, are the leading cause of death among adolescents in the United States. The relationship between alcohol and automotive fatalities has been clearly established in recent years—many fatalities involve an intoxicated adolescent driver. The relationship between collisions and marijuana has been more difficult to establish. The lack of a breath test or an easily performed blood analysis has been an obstacle to such documentation. However, both the effects of marijuana upon motor function and the automotive data which are available strongly suggest such a relationship. Thus marijuana emerges as a possible second leading cause, after alcohol, of injury and death among adolescents.

One of the primary concerns about marijuana use is that starting such illicit drug use will some day lead the young user to the use of more addicting drugs, particularly heroin. There is, however, nothing in the pharmacology of marijuana which leads to a physical need for more dangerous drugs. It is possible however that the deleterious effects of marijuana could cause complications and problems in the lives of adolescents and thus make them more prone to use more addicting drugs in later years.

Sedatives, Barbiturates, and Tranquilizers

Some of the drugs included in this group are Seconal, Tuinal, Nembutal, Phenobarbitol, Quaaludes, Glutethimide, Doriden, and Valium. Like alcohol, sedatives are depressants, and can cause symptoms of intoxication: drowsiness, agitation, intellectual confusion and impairment, emotional, slurred speech, and poor body coordination. These drugs can lead to both psychological and physical dependence. Withdrawal from these drugs can be more dangerous than heroin withdrawal. Although the number of adolescents who report having abused either barbiturates or glutethimide (a sleep inducer) has remained rather constant over the past fifteen years, the frequency with which these teenagers come to medical attention has noticeably declined. The medical consequences of sedative abuse can include overdose, addiction, and secondary complications which occur with the intravenous injection of drugs meant for oral use. For example, injected particles may end up as granular deposits in the lungs, liver, and other organs. The risk of death resulting from overdose is greater when alcohol has been taken in combnation with sedatives and barbiturates.

Sedative overdose is characterized by difficulties in walking and speaking, constant uncontrolled eye movements, lethargy, and coma.

Respiratory depression may be severe and may require mechanical assistance.

Unlike the opiate withdrawal syndrome, which generally does not result in a major physiological risk, withdrawal from sedatives may cause low blood pressure, convulsions, delirium, and death. Symptoms usually appear within thirty-six hours after the last dose and begin with restlessness, anxiety, and a sudden drop in blood pressure upon standing up (postural hypotension). When postural hypotension develops there may be a rapid progression to convulsions. Any teenager who has been using high doses of barbiturates for a month or longer should be considered at risk for developing a withdrawal syndrome and treated accordingly.

Amphetamines

Amphetamines are a large group of synthetic nervous system stimulants that are used to stave off lethargy and as "diet drugs" and antidepressants. After World War II, amphetamines became very popular street drugs in the United States. At the same time, they were used widely as prescription drugs. Amphetamines were used for a variety of purposes—to lose weight, to stay awake, to increase energy, and to get high. During the sixties, methylamphetamine, known as "speed," became popular for injecting and snorting. Those who injected the drug were called "speed freaks." Amphetamines, as well as non-prescription amphetamine-like substances, continue to be used and abused by adolescents either for weight loss or to enable them to remain awake.

Of the classes of drugs which are used illicitly by high school seniors, stimulants are the second most prevalent after marijuana. More than one-third (35.4 percent) reported having used stimulants at one time or another and 12.4 percent reported using stimulants in the last thirty days (Johnston et al. 1984).

The acute physical effects of amphetamines are dilated pupils, rapid heart beat, and the raising of the systolic (upper) blood pressure. In addition, chronic abuse leads to weight loss and persistent feelings of anxiety. The adolescent who has been abusing amphetamines on a continuing basis appears quite similar to patients with hyperthyroidism and an initial mistake in diagnosis can be made if the teenager conceals the habit and the physician is unsuspecting and less than thorough.

Although amphetamines are most often ingested they are at times abused via the intravenous route. Intravenous abuse of amphetamines carries the risk of infection and the accumulation of tiny contaminant particles in the body organs. In addition there have been rare reports of strokes, inflammation of blood vessels, and deaths secondary to either fever or disturbances of heart rhythm.

Both amphetamine overdose and withdrawal are marked by an hallucinatory state with paranoid (feelings of persecution), aggressive, and other behavior which may be indistinguishable from an acute functional psychosis. With abstinence there is usually a short period of lethargy, sometimes followed by the onset of the hallucinatory state.

Inhalants

The sniffing of certain substances (volatile hydrocarbons) contained in airplane glue, gasoline, cleaning fluid, and aerosols has generally been confined to younger children (11 to 15 years of age). Among this population inhalant abuse has slowly declined (an annual prevalence of 4 percent in 1983 according to the national high school survey) as drugs such as marijuana have become available. The effects of inhaling substances like gasoline can be similar to those of drinking alcohol. Symptoms include lack of coordination, restlessness, excitement, confusion, disorientation, difficulty in walking (ataxia), delirium, and coma. Repeated use results in giddiness, dizziness, and hallucinations. If inhalants are used continuously for long periods of time, damage to the brain, liver, kidneys, and nerves can develop. At times a young person will spray an inhalant into a plastic bag placed over the head, in an effort to increase the concentration of the inhaled substance, and fatalities from suffocation may result if intoxication leads to loss of consciousness. In addition, a syndrome of "sudden sniffing death" has been described consisting of inhalant abuse followed in rapid order by exercise or stress and then death. Irregular heartbeat stemming from the sensitization of the heart by these chemical vapors has been implicated as the cause of this syndrome.

Cocaine

Cocaine, a stimulant and euphoriant, is generally inhaled by adolescents. Sniffed or snorted, it enters the bloodstream through blood vessels close to the inner surface of the nose. Over the past decade the number of adolescents who report using cocaine has risen slowly but consistently. In 1983, over 16 percent of high school seniors had used cocaine at least once in their lives with almost a third of these teenagers reporting use within the past month (Johnston et al. 1984). With this widespread use, complications from cocaine are increasingly being brought to medical attention.

Cocaine acts primarily as a stimulant, somewhat like amphetamines, and produces an intense, short-lived euphoria for a few moments and stimulation for a period from two to three hours. It is the intensity of the euphoria that provides this drug with its popularity despite its expense. Excessive amounts may produce paranoid reactions, hallucinations, depression, and violent behavior. These effects are generally transient and often disappear before medical attention can be obtained. Other side effects of cocaine use include rapid heartbeat, high blood pressure, and rapid breathing.

Cocaine constricts the blood vessels, and thus the repetitive sniffing (snorting) of the drug may lead to irritation and ulceration of the mucus membranes of the nose. The injection of cocaine by the intravenous route is not a common practice. When it is used it carries the same risks of hepatitis, infection, and introduction of particles into the blood as has been noted for opiates and sedatives.

Cocaine may also be smoked. Although no figures exist, such "free-base" smoking amongst teenagers is presumed rare, in part because it is very expensive. Generally, the cocaine is dissolved in water, a strong alkali is added, and the basic cocaine is extracted with a solvent. The basic cocaine is more volatile than the cocaine hydrochloride salt (its original chemical form) and well suited for smoking. There are also some reports of coca paste smoking, particularly in the Miami area. Coca paste is a mixture of coca leaf, kerosene, and sulfuric acid, primarly produced for chemists who manufacture cocaine with it. However, coca paste also may be smoked. While full of noxious chemicals, coca paste provides a potent and inexpensive stimulant high.

Smoking cocaine brings on all its acute effects more rapidly. Chronic heavy smoking may lead to severe weight loss, insomnia, and psychosis. Evidence exists that pulmonary dysfunction, both acute and chronic, can result from smoking cocaine.

Overdose reactions, more common with intravenous abuse, are marked by tremors, delirium, and convulsions. Fatalities do occur after either acute respiratory failure or circulatory collapse. There is increasing evidence that an abstinence syndrome occurs in chronic high-dose users characterized by insomnia, depression, agitation, nausea, and headaches. As noted above, the expense of the drug places some limits upon the extent of use by teenagers and it is rare for any of the side effects of cocaine in teenagers to be brought to medical attention.

Hallucinogens

Over the past quarter century a variety of drugs capable of producing hallucinations have waxed and waned in popularity among adolescents. Included within this list are lysergic acid diethylamide (LSD), peyote (mescaline), 2, 5-dimethoxy-4-methyl amphetamine (MDA), and most recently phencyclidine (PCP or angel dust). All of these drugs are capable of producing chemically induced hallucinations and they therefore share the risk of accident and injury during an altered state of consciousness. A state of extreme anxiety is possible for any of these drugs and in years past such bad trips were encountered frequently in emergency rooms. The treatment for such episodes includes removal of the patient to a quiet environment with few external stimuli (most emergency rooms are inappropriate settings), and constant reassurance ("talking down"). The use of sedative medication should be avoided if possible as any further compromise in the level of consciousness may lead to more violent or bizarre behavior. Bad trips are self-limiting, usually lasting no longer than a few hours to a day. Except for injuries which may occur during a hallucinatory state this category of drugs has little potential for physical harm. An exception to this is phencyclidine (PCP).

PCP appears in multiple forms, as a powder, a capsule, and a tablet, and may be ingested, snorted, or smoked, the last being the usual method of use. PCP causes euphoria, loss of inhibition, agitation, confusion, stupor, paranoia, catatonia, and hallucinations. Toxic reactions include psychosis (mimicking schizophrenia), convulsions, coma, and death. Violent and bizarre reactions are not uncommon. Such reactions may last for days or weeks, in contrast to other hallucinogens with a much briefer toxic state. Fortunately, the number of adolescents entering emergency rooms with overdose reactions has declined rapidly in the past few years. Although over 6 percent of high school seniors still report some lifetime use of PCP, the number who have used it during the past year has declined from 7 percent in 1979 (when it was at its peak) to 3 percent in 1983.

Heroin

According to the most recent (1983) National High School Survey only 6 percent of the senior high school students reported ever using heroin and few of these students reported taking it in the past month (Johnston et al. 1984). In fact, between 1975 and 1979, the prevalence of heroin use among seniors dropped steadily and then remained constant during the ensuing years. Today, it is very rare for adolescents to mainline (inject directly into a vein) heroin and become addicted to the drug. Those who use it are most likely to snort or sniff it.

Why isn't heroin more popular among adolescents? There are several reasons. Today, adolescents have a choice of many different drugs—drugs that cost less and are more easily controlled. They have been educated about drugs: on the street, by way of the media, and through education programs. Heroin is physically addicting. Heroin use is dangerous and adolescents know it. It is risky to buy, possess, and use heroin. Heroin is not so easy to come by and quality and potency vary from day to day. Excessive doses can lead to coma and eventually death, usually from respiratory failure.

Given the fact that heroin is not currently popular among adolescents, why should we cover it in this book? Although the percentages appear small many adolescents are still exposed to heroin in this country and some do eventually become addicts. We also know that patterns of drug use change and drugs regain their popularity. When we go back into the history of narcotics use it is surprising to find that most users of the drug in the early nineteenth century were women (Austin 1978). It was sometimes prescribed by doctors for relief of menstrual pain.

We have learned a lot about street heroin in recent years. It is usually sold in the form of white powder, mixed or cut with at least one dilutent, usually lactose or some other sugar.

Many problems can result when the drug is injected. Injecting heroin under the skin (skin popping) can result in infections and abscesses, damage to the fat layer under the skin at the injection site, or skin ulcerations. This is more likely if the heroin has been cut with an irritant. A clear physical sign of narcotics use is scars or tracks on the skin along the course of veins. Some users attempt to sterilize the needle tip prior to an injection by passing it through a flame. As a result carbon and other material is deposited on the needle and subsequently under the skin adding to the disfigurement of the tracks. It is also possible that insoluble particles will be injected accidentally along with heroin. Those who attempt purification by pouring through wads of cotton to filter the drug may end up with cotton fibers in their circulatory system.

Abscesses under the skin are potential sites for the growth of the organism causing tetanus (a disease characterized by violent spasms, stiffness, and prolonged muscle contraction.) However, tetanus, which has been reported in adult addicts, has not been seen in teenagers. This is probably due to residual protection against tetanus from childhood immunizations. The administration of tetanus antitoxin should be routinely considered for every adolescent heroin addict.

Acute bacterial (Staphylococcus aureus, for example) inflammation of the membrane lining the cavity where the heart is contained (endocarditis) is among the more serious complications of intravenous drug abuse. This diagnosis should be considered in every teenage addict with a fever of unknown origin.

Viral hepatitis is among the most frequently encountered infections among teenage heroin addicts. The existence of hepatitis in this population will escape detection if liver function tests are not routinely performed. It has been our experience that nearly 40 percent of teenage heroin users will have laboratory evidence of liver dysfunction. These abnormalities may persist indefinitely even after heroin use has been interrupted. Liver biopsies performed on more than 100 teenage heroin users having abnormal liver function test results revealed a diagnosis of chronic persistent hepatitis. The addict who experiences symptoms of acute hepatitis may not seek medical attention due to a reluctance to expose the habit to medical scrutiny.

All opiates cause smooth muscle contractions in the bowel, which frequently results in constipation. The occurrence of ulcer disease, appendicitis, hepatitis, or inflammation of the fallopian tubes carries special risks for adolescent addicts. Abdominal pain, which is the warning sign of these conditions, may be misinterpreted by the adolescent as a sign of withdrawal and therefore treated with increasing doses of narcotics. Since the narcotics effectively mask the pain, these teenagers may not seek medical attention until after very serious complications have occurred.

A third of female adolescent heroin users stop ovulating and lose their menstrual cycles. The younger the girl the more likely that this will happen to her. Normal menstrual periods with ovulation may not return for many months after cessation of opiate use. However, sex counseling or contraceptive counseling is mandatory for these girls as they have often come to believe that they are infertile when realistically they are at risk of unwanted pregnancy during the rehabilitative process. The as yet unknown long-term implications of hormonal changes in the developing adolescent due to opiate use are a further cause for concern.

Weeks of daily opiate use are required to produce withdrawal symptoms. Most teenagers who use opiates intermittently do not have withdrawal symptoms when they are hospitalized or when other circumstances separate them from the drug. For adolescents who are physically addicted, symptoms of abstinence will first appear twelve to thirty-six hours after the last dose, with the later onset being associated with the use of methadone rather than heroin. Symptoms of withdrawal include dilated pupils, tearing, yawning, gooseflesh, muscle cramps, diarrhea, rapid heartbeat, and high blood pressure. It is extremely uncommon for the adolescent in withdrawal to have serious physiological problems. Treatment for withdrawal can be on an outpatient or an inpatient basis with the latter preferred in most circumstances. A variety of treatment regimens have been used including simple reassurance and support without the use of other drugs. When necessary, methadone can be used in the treatment of withdrawal symptoms in teenagers, reducing or eliminating most symptoms of abstinence with the exception of diarrhea and occasionally insomnia. Abstinence is attained by gradually and systematically reducing the daily dosage of the drug used. Difficulty with insomnia may be expected for days or weeks after abstinence has been achieved and an effort must be made to avoid self-therapy with barbiturates for sleeplessness. Most teenagers can complete the withdrawal process with few physiological or behavioral problems.

Commonly encountered a decade ago, opiate overdose reactions among adolescents have become quite rare. The overdose reaction is characterized by lethargy, respiratory depression, coma, fluid in the lungs, and occasionally death.

Multiple Drug Abuse

Over the years it has become evident that large numbers of persons labeled as single-substance abusers are in fact abusers of more than one substance (Whitehead 1974; Judd and Gerstein 1981). One of the most dangerous and least understood adolescent drug use patterns is multiple drug or "polydrug" abuse. Adolescent substance abusers tend to be multiple-substance abusers, using different drugs sequentially and/or concurrently. Research studies show that adolescents entering drug treatment programs have, on the average, used more than five different substances. Studies have shown that over 95 percent of pot smokers drink alcohol and vice versa and the effects on behavior are probably synergistic (Macdonald 1981).

All drugs have multiple actions. Individuals have multiple responses to a single drug. What happens when individuals take different drugs at or about the same time? The dangers are compounded. The hazards of combined abuse include overdose, coma, and death (Kaufman 1982). The margin of safety decreases and the chances of adverse reactions increase significantly. Studies have demonstrated that the frequency of adverse reactions for any individual increases in proportion to the number of drugs taken. We also know that drugs, which alter the body chemistry, can interact unfavorably with certain foods. Two or more drugs may act similarly (synergism), may have opposing effects (antagonism), may when acting similarly have a summation effect (additive), or may have an effect that is greater than the sum of their doses (potentiation) (Greene 1980).

Many of the overdose cases seen in hospital emergency rooms are the result of drug combinations such as barbiturates and alcohol. Barbiturates alone are very dangerous substances and when combined with alcohol or other drugs they become many times more deadly (Berger 1982). Alcohol speeds up absorption into the bloodstream and adds to their depressant effects on certain essential physiological functions.

It is not surprising that young street users attempt to enhance the effects they are seeking by using different substances in combination. Judd and Gerstein (1981) studied individuals who commonly and frequently used alcohol, barbiturates, and hypnotics and minor tranquilizers. One of the major effects common to these three drug classes, which have a reciprocal pharmacological relationship and cross-tolerance to each other, is the depressant effect on specific nervous system functions.

Diazepam, a commonly used tranquilizer, can have serious effects when used with alcohol or other drugs. Alcohol increases the sedative effects of diazepam and diazepam increases the intoxicating effects of alcohol. Diazepam also increases the effects of other sedatives, antidepressants, and narcotic drugs.

An example of how this can result in serious problems was recently uncovered by a reporter in Washington, D.C. (Hochman 1985). On investigating why a number of high school students had been hospitalized for drug overdoses, he found that they had been affected by a combination of drugs. The students had used tranquilizers along with another prescription sedative which aggravated the effects of the tranquilizers.

A number of investigators have been studying the interactions of marijuana with other drugs. Secobarbital and smoked marijuana were found to have additive effects on psychomotor impairment and on subjects' responses and ratings of symptoms on a modified version of the Cornell Medical Index questionnaire (Dalton et al. 1975). Additive effects on heart rate and blood pressure were observed when amphetamines and marijuana were combined (Evans et al. 1974). Alcohol and cannabis were found to have synergistic effects in some users (MacAvoy and Marks 1975). Kepperman and Fine (1974) found that some young amphetamine abusers used small amounts of alcohol to counteract the effects of the amphetamines. In addition, alcohol was used as a sedative following an amphetamine binge.

Summary

The pharmacology of drugs—the absorption, distribution, metabolism, and excretion of chemical substances and their effects on the body—is not easy to comprehend. When attention is focused on the adolescent substance abuser the problem becomes even more complex.

The effects from using drugs vary from individual to individual. Not only does a person's physical make-up influence the effect a drug might have but many psychological and social factors influence the effects as well. Unlike teenagers in earlier decades, adolescents today tend to use a variety of substances. A single drug has multiple effects. When a youngster switches from one drug to another or uses drugs concomitantly, drug interactions are likely to occur, making the effects even less predictable.

In purchasing illicit drugs on the street, it is generally impossible for a youngster to know the actual quality or strength of the substances or the particular contaminants included. Even marijuana varies considerably in form and potency. Adolescents are never sure of the quality and potency of the drugs taken.

Despite these complexities, it is becoming increasingly important to understand the pharmacology of drugs used by adolescents and the potential consequences of use on the health of young people who are at the peak of their biological and psychological development. In this chapter we have reviewed the drugs that are commonly used by adolescents and the potential health consequences from using them. We hope this information will provide the reader with a better understanding of the drugs, how they work, the reasons for using them, and the consequences of such use.

References

Austin, G.A. 1978 *Perspectives on the History of Psychoactive Substance Use,* Rockville, Maryland: National Institute on Drug Abuse

Berger, G. 1982. *Addiction: Its Causes, Problems, and Treatments.* New York: Franklin Watts.

Cohen, S. 1980. Cannibis: Impact on motivation. *Drug Abuse and Alcoholism Newsletter,* 9(10): 1–3.

Dalton, W.S.; Martz, R.; Lemberger, L.; Rodda, B.E.; and Forney, R.B. 1975. Effects of marijuana combined with secobarbital. *Clinical Pharmacology and Therapeutics* 18(3): 298–304.

Evans, M.A.; Martz, R.; Lemberger, L; Rodda, B.E.; and Forney, R.B. 1974. Clinical effects of marijuana dextroamphetamine combination, *Pharmacologist* 16(2): 281.

Greene, B. 1980. Sequential use of drugs and alcohol: A reexamination of the stepping-stone hypothesis. *American Journal of Drug and Alcohol Abuse* 7(1): 83–99.

Hochman, A. 1985. Drug Mixture Blamed in Virginia Overdose Cases. *Washinton Post,* April 6, Page 9.

Johnston, L.; O'Malley, P.; and Backman, J. 1984. *Highlights from Drugs and American High School Students: 1975–1983.* Rockville, Maryland: National Institute on Drug Abuse, DHHS Pub. No. (ADM) 84–1317.

Judd, L. and Gerstein, D. 1981. The role and significance of alcohol and sedative use in the multisubstance abusers: An investigation of two patient samples. In *Drug and Alcohol Abuse: Implications for Treatment,* ed. Gardner, S. Rockville, Maryland: NIDA, DHHS Pub. No. (ADM) 82–958.

Kaufman, E. 1977. Polydrug abuse or multidrug misuse: It's here to stay. *British Journal of the Addictions,* 72(4):339–347.

Kepperman, A. and Fine, E. 1974. The combined abuse of alcohol and amphetamines. *American Journal of Psychiatry* 131(11): 1277–1280.

MacAvoy, M.G. and Marks, D.F. 1975. Divided attention performance of cannibis users annd non-users following cannabis and alcohol. *Psychophar-macologia* 44(2): 147–152.

Macdonald, D.I. 1981. *Remarks on relationship of moderate marijuana use and adolescent behavior.* Paper delivered at NIDA Conference on Marijuana Research, June 3. Rockville, Maryland: National Institute on Drug Abuse.

Whitehead, P. 1974. Multidrug use: Supplementary perspectives. *The International Journal of the Addictions* 9(2): 185–204.

4

Getting Busted for Drugs

James A. Inciardi

Most adolescents today have some awareness of illicit drugs and drug problems. Nearly everyone over the age of 10, even if they have never experimented with drugs, either knows someone who has talked about it with friends, or has heard about it from parents or teachers. They know, too, that drug use is against the law. Drug education messages and school health programs point to the physical and psychological problems that can result from the abuse of marijuana, alcohol, cocaine, and other drugs. However, information about the legal issues involved is seldom made available. As a result, most youths—especially those who do abuse drugs—pay little attention to the potential legal consequences, which can be very serious.

With respect to drugs, the law, and getting arrested (or getting "busted" as many adolescents refer to it), there are many questions that need to be addressed:

What are the current laws regarding illegal drug use?

How are these laws enforced in different localities?

What are the penalties for breaking these laws?

What is the potential for getting arrested?

If arrested, what is likely to happen? Is going to jail or reform school possible?

How are the laws and penalties applied to juveniles as opposed to adults?

Under the law, what constitutes a "juvenile"?

What happens in the juvenile court? Do juveniles need lawyers? Can they even have lawyers?

Do adolescents have any legal rights? What, if any, are they?

Can adolescents be processed through the adult criminal courts?

What goes on in the adult courts?

Where does someone turn for help? What alternatives are there?
What if someone cannot afford a lawyer?

One reason these questions are rarely dealt with by schools and drug
education programs is that there is a wide range of responses. The laws
vary from state to state. What may be legal in one location may be illegal
just over the state line. Police procedures for enforcing drug laws are
different, depending on law enforcement resources and community attitudes and pressures. Moreover, these legal procedures can change from
year to year, month to month, or even week to week. Court processing
for juveniles is different than for adults; even what constitutes a "juvenile" can vary from one state jurisdiction to another. Legal rights also
vary depending on the age of the offender. Sometimes these rights are
ignored. Finally, what ultimately happens can depend on the background
and conduct of the offender, the nature of the offense, and the resources
and services present in the locale where the arrest occurs. In this chapter,
these issues are discussed, and some specific examples provided.

The Laws, the Penalties, and the Probability of Arrest

All fifty states, as well as the federal government, have laws prohibiting
the possession, cultivation, sale, and sometimes even the use of certain
drugs. The best known prohibited drugs are marijuana, hashish, heroin,
LSD, PCP, and cocaine. There are also laws which apply to the lay use
of prescription drugs such as barbiturates, other sedatives such as quaaludes, and amphetamines ("speed"). The laws vary depending on the
drug. Moreover, as noted earlier, they can be quite different in each state.
The following are examples of the statutes governing marijuana:

> *In Alaska,* the possession or cultivation of any amount of marijuana
> in the privacy of your own home is legal.

> *In Delaware,* the possession of any amount of marijuana (whether
> for personal use or not, and even in the privacy of your own home)
> can result in up to two years in prison plus a $500 fine; the culti-
> vation of any amount can result in up to ten years in prison plus a
> $10,000 fine.

> *In New Jersey,* where all penalties can be applied to juveniles (but
> rarely are), possession of up to 25 grams of marijuana (less than one
> ounce) calls for imprisonment for up to six months plus a $500 fine;

the sale of such a small amount can result in as much as five years in prison and a $15,000 fine.

These examples demonstrate the tremendous range of penalties, which can vary according to the amount of marijuana involved and intent of simple possession as opposed to cultivation or sale. For large amounts of marijuana or for more dangerous drugs such as heroin, the penalties can be even more severe. Some states have mandatory penalties for certain drug offenses. Under Florida's drug-trafficking law, there is a mandatory minimum sentence of fifteen years with no parole. On January 20, 1983, 35-year-old Eugene (Mercury) Morris, the former All-Pro running back of the Miami Dolphins, received a twenty-year sentence under the Florida law for selling 456 grams of cocaine (just over a pound) to an undercover law enforcement agent. Unless an appeal to a higher court changes this sentence, Morris cannot get out of prison until 1998.

Even without such mandatory penalties, judges have the power to impose severe sentences, as in the case of *Hutto v. Davis,*[1] which reached the United States Supreme Court in 1982. In 1973, Virginia law enforcement officers raided Davis's home and seized 9 ounces of marijuana. Davis was convicted on two counts of "possession with intent to distribute" and sentenced to a term of forty years. On the grounds that the sentence was "cruel and unusual" and in violation of the Eighth Amendment of the Constitution of the United States, he initiated an appeal. Ultimately the Supreme Court ruled against Davis.

The point is that one should know the drug laws in his/her state. It is important to know not only what the various penalties are for the possession and sale of drugs, but also what other kinds of drug laws exist. Some states prohibit the possession of "drug paraphernalia," (any implements that can be used in the handling or consumption of an illegal drug). Moreover, in some places such as Ohio, one can be convicted of being a "drug abuser." Proof of possession or sale is not necessary, just use. The local library is a resource for information on state criminal codes and local drug laws.

What is the probability of arrest for drug charges? Official statutes offer a mixed picture. According to the FBI's *Uniform Crime Reports,* there were some 580,900 arrests for drug abuse violations in the United States in 1980. Over 400,000 of these arrests involved marijuana; about 12 percent of the persons arrested were under age 18, and almost a third were under age 21.[2]

Given the fact that many millions of people use marijuana and/or cocaine, and that many others use heroin, LSD, PCP, "speed," and "downers," these figures suggest that the chances of getting arrested are relatively low. However, enforcement policies, community pressures, and the status of the user can affect things. A black heroin user who lives in an urban ghetto has a higher chance of arrest. For a white middle-class marijuana user who smokes at a friend's house occasionally, the chances of arrest are almost nil. Using drugs regularly, using more than one kind of drug, or using drugs in public increases the probability of arrest. For those who violate the traffic laws with drugs in their possession, the chances of arrest increase even further. Involvement in drug sales escalates the possibility of arrest.

The probability of alcohol-related arrests is high, and jail terms are becoming more frequent. In 1980, there were 1.1 million arrests for drunkenness and 1.3 million arrests for driving under the influence of alcohol (or other drugs); about 80,000 of these persons were under age 18.[3] The penalties (if any) are minimal for drunkenness. On the other hand, there is currently a national crusade against drunk drivers. Also, drunk driving combined with a fatal auto accident can result in a homicide charge.

Whether any person arrested for a drug-related incident will be processed through the criminal court or the juvenile court, or processed at all, depends on a variety of crucial factors: the age of the defendant, the nature of the offense, any prior record, and the particular laws and policies of the jurisdiction. Furthermore, as in *Hutto v. Davis,* the courts are the last strongholds of feudalism, where, like medieval lords, judges have almost unlimited power to decide what happens to an offender.

The Juvenile Justice Process

Police officers who encounter juveniles involved in delinquent activities (including drug violations) have several alternatives available for handling the offense. First, there are *informal* options. The officer may simply release the youth with a reprimand. It is also possible that a trip to the police station may occur, where a "juvenile card" is filled out briefly describing the incident; and/or the parents may be called in for a discussion, after which the youth is released. These are informal adjustments which do not require a court appearance. A typical adjustment of this type might occur when a police officer is called to investigate a homeowner's complaint about a group of youths smoking marijuana behind his garage. Since the offense is not serious and the homeowner is likely to be satisfied if the youths leave and promise not to return, the officer would most likely take them to the police station and then release them. The incident would be terminated, if the juveniles did not give the officer a hard time and none of them was a serious drug user appearing to need some sort of treatment.

Second is the the *formal* option of taking the youth into official custody. In this case, a petition is filed with the juvenile court. The question then arises of "what constitutes a juvenile"? All fifty states have juvenile courts with varying jurisdiction over children under a specific age. In most states, this age is 17, but the range can be as low as 14 or 15. In Oklahoma, for example, youths over 14 may be tried as adults. Moreover, youths over 16 are automatically certified as adults in that state if they have committed a serious felony offense. (Almost all drug crimes are felonies, and drug sales are considered "serious.")

The Petition and Intake Hearing

The juvenile adjudication (decision-making) process begins with the *petition* filed with the court by the police. Like an arrest warrant, this petition specifies the particular offense; the name, age, and residence of youth; the names and residences of his or her parents or guardians; and a description of the circumstances of the offense.

After the petition is filed, an *intake hearing* is held. This hearing is conducted by the court as a preliminary examination into the facts of the case. However, it is not presided over by a judge, nor does it occur in open court. Rather, the hearing officer is usually a referee with a background in social work or the behavioral sciences, an attorney, a probation officer, or someone else assigned to the juvenile court. The purposes of this hearing are to protect the interests of the child and to quickly dispose of those cases that do not require the time and expense of formal court adjudication.

The intake hearing can range from a brief examination of the facts to a lengthy investigation into the youth's family background, including interviews with parents, contacts with teachers and school officials, psychiatric or psychological testing, and even a medical examination. The depth of this investigation will vary by the nature of the offense, whether the child is a repeat offender, and the court's policy and workload. Most states, however, do require relevant witnesses to be present to testify.

Depending on the hearing officer's judgment of the sufficiency of the evidence, the need for court intervention, and, again, the policy and philosophy of the court, three things can happen:

1. the officer can dismiss the case, in which case the matter is over, no further court processing is required, and the youth can go home;

2. the officer can make an informal judgment, such as involving the youth in an informal probation or restitution program, or refer the case to some other agency, such as a drug treatment program; or

3. the officer can authorize an inquiry before the judge (the adjudication inquiry), which represents the next stage in the juvenile court process.

The Adjudication Inquiry

At the *adjudication inquiry,* which is generally closed to the public and the media, the judge determines whether the facts of the case and the offender's behavior warrant a formal hearing by the court. This inquiry is similar in purpose to the intake hearing. But the judge is ruling on the need for further processing. He can dismiss the case, order a formal adjudication hearing, or refer the juvenile elsewhere.

In recent years, the juvenile justice system in the United States has sought any number of alternatives for avoiding the official adjudication of youths. One method is *diverting* juveniles out of the court system and into community agencies for counseling and treatment. These "diversion programs" include the Youth Service Bureaus, school-related programs, police social service units, family therapy groups, and numerous other human services agencies which can provide a variety of programs and help for youth in trouble. There are special programs for young drug abusers. This diversion network emerged as a result of the juvenile court's functioning as a social agency to treat and care for young people rather than prosecute them.

If a juvenile court judge at an adjudication inquiry orders that the defendant attend therapy groups or some other treatment program, the youth has two options. The first is to follow the judge's orders. If the treatment sessions are attended and the youth gets into no more trouble during the course of treatment, the judge generally dismisses the case. If the youth abuses this order, an adjudication hearing is scheduled. The other option is for the defendant to request an adjudication hearing.

Adjudication and Disposition Hearings

An *adjudication hearing* is not a trial. It is legally classified as a civil rather than a criminal process. A judge presides over the hearing *on behalf of* the child to determine whether the child actually committed the alleged offense, and, if so, to use the misconduct described to determine whether the youth's parents are providing adequate care, supervision, and discipline. The judge relies on any clinical, social, or diagnostic reports on the child. Should the judge determine that no misconduct occurred, the case is dismissed. If youthful misconduct *is* apparent, a disposition hearing is ordered.

At *disposition hearings,* juvenile court judges have extremely broad discretion. They have the power to dismiss the case, give the juvenile a warning, impose a fine, order that restitution be paid, require that some community service be performed, refer the offender to a community agency or treatment facility, or mandate commitment to a juvenile institution.[4]

Gerald Gault and the Constitutional Rights of Juvenile Offenders

The juvenile court process, as mentioned earlier, is not a criminal proceeding. It is not a matter of *State v. Child;* there is no prosecutor who acts on behalf of the state to prove the guilt of the youth; there is no jury. Rather, it is a civil process designed, at least in theory, to aid and protect the child. But as such, is the youthful defendant in the juvenile court protected by the Bill of Rights? Does the juvenile have the same constitutional rights enjoyed by adult defendants in criminal trials? The answer is no, and until the case of *In re Gault*[5] only recently, juvenile courts seemed to accord few, if any, rights at all.

On June 8, 1964, Gerald Francis Gault and a friend, Ronald Lewis, were taken into custody by the sheriff of Gila county, Arizona. Gerald was then still subject to a six month's probation order as a result of having been in the company of another boy who had stolen a wallet from a woman's purse. Gault and Lewis's trip to the police station on June 8 was the result of a verbal complaint by Mrs. Cook, a neighbor of the boys, about a telephone call made to her in which lewd and indecent remarks were made.

At the time Gerald was picked up, his mother and father were both at work. No notice that he was being taken into custody was left at the home, and no other steps were taken to advise the Gaults that their son had, in effect, been arrested. Gerald was taken to a children's detention home. When his mother returned home that evening, she learned from the Lewis family that Gerald was in custody. Mrs. Gault went to the detention home and was told by deputy probation officer Flagg that her son was indeed there and that a hearing would take place at the juvenile court the following day.

Officer Flagg filed a petition with the court on the hearing day, but a copy was not served on Gault's parents. The petition was formal, but very brief. It made no reference to any factual basis for the court action, but merely recited that "said minor is under the age of 18 years, and is in need of the protection of this Honorable Court;" and that "said minor is a delinquent minor."

On June 9, Gerald, his mother, his older brother, and probation officers Flagg and Henderson appeared before the juvenile court judge.

Mrs. Cook, the complainant, was not there. No one was sworn in at the hearing; no transcript or recording of the proceedings was made; no record of the substance of the proceedings was maintained. From later testimony it appears that Judge McGhee had questioned Gerald about the phone call, but that there were differences of opinion as to how he answered. Judge McGhee and Officer Flagg stated that Gerald admitted making one of the obscene statements. Mrs. Gault recalled that her son had said he had only dialed Mrs. Cook's number and handed the telephone to his friend Ronald. At the conclusion of the hearing, the judge said he would "think about it." Gerald was not sent home, but returned to detention. Several days later, however, he was driven home, with no explanation as to why he had been held in custody for almost a week. Then at 5 P.M. on the day of Gerald's release, Mrs. Gault received the following note on a plain piece of paper, signed by Officer Flagg:

Mrs. Gault:

Judge McGhee has set Monday, June 15, 1964 at 11 A.M. as the date and time for further hearings on Gerald's delinquence.

Flagg

Present at the June 15 hearing were Gerald and his parents, Ronald Lewis and his father, Officers Henderson and Flagg, and Judge McGhee. Again, there was conflict about what Gerald actually had admitted to. Mrs. Cook again was not there; in fact, the judge denied Mrs. Gault's request that her son's accuser be present. The only contact the court ever had with Mrs. Cook was a telephone call by Flagg on June 9.

At the June 15 hearing a "referral report" was filed with the court; yet its contents were not disclosed to the Gaults. This report charged Gerald with "lewd phone calls." At the conclusion of the hearing, the judge committed Gerald Francis Gault as a juvenile delinquent to the State Industrial School till age 21. Since Gerald was only 15 years old, that meant a jail term of almost six years for a crime which, if committed by an adult, would have resulted in a fine of $50 or less. Furthermore, no appeal was permitted by Arizona law in juvenile cases.

Under a writ of *habeas corpus*, a petition that questions the legality of incarceration, the Gaults managed to initiate the appeal process. But both the local Superior Court and the Supreme Court of Arizona dismissed the writs filed by the Gaults. Gerald Gault remained in detention at the State Industrial School.

In 1967, three years after Gault's arrest, the United States Supreme court reviewed the case. The Supreme Court ruled against the Arizona courts, holding that Gerald Gault had been denied the following basic rights:

1. notice of charges;
2. right to counsel;
3. right to confrontation and cross-examination of witnesses;
4. privilege against self-incrimination;
5. right to a transcript of the proceedings; and
6. right to appellate review.

The result of the Supreme Court's decision was to extend these constitutional guarantees to every case in every juvenile court in the United States.

Thus, prior to the case of *In re Gault*, the juvenile court had almost unchecked power, and most constitutional rights were totally denied. As Supreme Court Justice Abe Fortas put it, "Under our Constitution, the condition of being a boy does not justify a kangaroo court." Subsequent to *Gault*, additional rights were applied to the juvenile process. The *Winship* [6] case, decided by the Supreme Court in 1970, required "proof beyond a reasonable doubt" for an adjudication of delinquency. The case of *Breed v. Jones*[7] in 1975 extended to juveniles the Fifth Amendment protection against double jeopardy. Still, however, juveniles have no right to bail while awaiting a hearing, nor do they have a right to a hearing before a jury.

Dispositions in Juvenile Drug Cases

The previous discussions have broadly described the general procedures of the juvenile court as they occur in most cases. To detail the distinctions between the numerous possible variations of this process would require many volumes. This, however, does not answer the questions of what would actually happpen and whether a jail term would be likely in the case of a juvenile arrested for a drug law violation.

As mentioned earlier, there are numerous alternatives open to the police, to the intake referee, and to the juvenile court judge. Moreover, these alternatives are shaped by community sentiment, the defendant's behavior and prior record, court policies and workload, and the resources and facilities available in the local area. Given this situation, what are the realities of the situation?

In most (if not all) urban areas, the courts are overwhelmed with serious juvenile crime. As such, they are neither willing nor able to process fully the drug experimenters, social/recreational users, and youths found in possession of the so-called soft drugs (marijuana, amphetamines, organic solvents, and inhalants. The majority of cases are settled informally at the intake hearing; the youth is dismissed to the custody and supervision of his or her parents.

Chronic users, those found in possession of harder drugs (such as heroin or barbiturates), and youths arrested for drug sales or possession of large amounts of drugs are a different matter. The case of the chronic user will most likely be referred for treatment in lieu of official adjudication since most urban areas have a variety of drug treatment programs. In other cases, if any adjudication of delinquency is made by the judge, probation is most likely, assuming that the defendant cooperates and is not a chronic offender. Arrests of adolescents for drug sales can be treated severely by commitment to a juvenile institution or processing through the adult court.

Less populated areas present a different picture. In smaller counties, where crime rates are lower than in the cities, police generally have closer ties to the community and police-citizen relationships are personal. In such settings, the novice drug offender is more likely to be handled informally or processed through a diversion unit based at the police station. Similarly, juvenile defendants with serious drug problems are placed in treatment, *if treatment services are indeed available.*

Conversely, the courts usually reflect community values, which are often quite conservative. The juvenile courts may operate solely as a functional deterrent for the sake of community protection. For the repeat offender or the serious drug seller, rehabilitative treatment is less likely.

In general, the majority of juvenile court systems across the country are attempting to make fair and practical decisions regarding which juveniles are released, processed through the court system, treated, or incarcerated. However, the lack of resources in some counties results in inadequate prehearing investigation and a restriction in the amount and type of services that can be made available, especially to the poor.

Finally, there is the issue of a criminal record. Does a referral to the juvenile court result in a criminal record? Does an adjudication of delinquency result in a criminal record? The answer to both questions is no. The juvenile court process is not a criminal proceeding. Rather, it is a civil action. Thus, any youth processed by the juvenile court has *not* been convicted of a crime.

Juveniles in the Adult Courts

In most states, the juvenile courts have some flexibility to waive jurisdiction over certain minors, thus sending them to the trial courts for criminal processing. Generally, the factors influencing this decision include the age of the youth, the type of crime committed, the defendant's prior record, and the juvenile court's prior experience with the child. Any or all of these factors can be crucial. Consider the Michigan law, for example, which is not unlike those in many other states:

> In any case where a child over the age of 15 years is accused of any act the nature of which constitutes a felony, the judge of probate of the county wherein the offense is alleged to have been committed may after investigation and examination, including notice to parents if address is known, and upon motion of the prosecuting attorney, waive jurisdiction; whereupon it shall be lawful to try such child in the court having general criminal jurisdiction of such offense.

Thus, the potential exists for a juvenile drug offender to be processed through the adult courts and perhaps be convicted and sent to prison. However, *in practice, juveniles are rarely turned over to the criminal courts.* The few exceptions involve instances of murder or rape, repeated armed robberies, or other violent crimes. A case in point was 15-year-old John Anthony Cruse, tried and convicted in an Alabama court and sentenced to life imprisonment: Cruse had shotgunned his foster mother to death. As such, juvenile drug law violations are not frequently seen in the adult courts. However, given public sentiment about drug use, a youth arrested repeatedly for drug sales or possession of large quantities of drugs with the intent to distribute could find himself being prosecuted in the state trial courts. Furthermore, in those states that designate persons 16 years of age or older as adults, the criminal courts become the entry point for the handling of virtually all offenses, even minor drug violations.

Criminal Penalties for Drug Law Violations

Given the numerous possible penalties for drug law violations that are listed in the criminal codes, judges have extremely wide discretion in most cases.

For a first offense of "simple" possession (which assumes a small amount and no intent to distribute), a fine or probation is likely. Subsequent convictions can also result in probation, but terms of imprisonment are possible. As with the juvenile court process, diversion alternatives are considered for chronic drug users. Many court systems will permit formal treatment in lieu of criminal processing. However, this alternative is not available in all courts. It is generally only the large urban areas where court diversion programs exist for individuals dependent on drugs.

Again, given the reality of criminal justice in the United States, a prison term for most drug violations is not likely. The penitentiaries of most states are so overcrowded that only the most serious offenders find their way into them. The courts will generally try other mechanisms, such as probation or diversion into treatment.

Most drug offenses are handled through the *plea bargaining* process. It is generally estimated that more than 90 percent of all criminal convictions result from negotiated pleas of guilty.

Plea bargaining takes place between the prosecutor and the defense counsel and/or the accused. It involves discussions about an agreement under which the defendant will enter a plea of guilty in exchange for some prosecutorial or judicial concession. These concessions are of four types:

1. the initial charges may be reduced to some lesser offense, thus insuring a reduction in the sentence imposed;

2. in instances of multiple criminal charges, the number of counts may be reduced;

3. a recommendation for leniency may be made by the prosecutor, thus reducing the potential sentence from one of incarceration to probation; and

4. in instances where the charges involve a negative label, such as child molesting, the complaint may be altered to a less repugnant one, such as assault.

The widespread use of negotiated pleas of guilty comes from the overcrowded caseloads in the criminal courts. Proponents of the plea bargaining process maintain that it is beneficial to both the accused and the state. *For the accused,* plea bargaining:

1. reduces the possibility of detention during the extensive pretrial and trial processing;

2. extends the potential for a reduced sentence; and

3. reduces the financial costs of legal representation.

For the state, plea bargaining:

1. reduces the overall financial costs of criminal prosecution;

2. improves the administrative efficiency of the courts by having few cases go to a full and time-consuming trial; and

3. enables the prosecution to devote more time and resources to cases of greater importance and seriousness.

Plea bargaining should never be engaged in without the advice of counsel and without a full understanding of its implications. However, for those drug offenders against whom the state has a strong case, it can mean the difference between going to jail and remaining in the community. In the case of *Hutto v. Davis* mentioned earlier in this chapter, Davis had been charged with possession of marijuana with intent to distribute. The jury found him guilty and he was sentenced to forty years. Had Davis negotiated his plea, offering to plead guilty to simple possession (without any intent to distribute), he might have received probation. Plea bargaining can also involve a reduction of charges on promises of a guilty plea and entry into treatment.

The Criminal Court Process

What can one expect to find in the criminal courts? How are cases processed? How many trips to court are involved? Does the drug violator have rights? What is likely to happen?

Before addressing these questions, it must be pointed out that criminal justice in this country is grounded in the philosophy of "due process of law" as guaranteed by the United States Constitution. Due process of law is a concept that is impossible to define precisely, but in contemporary U.S. law it asserts a fundamental principle of justice rather than a specific rule of law. It implies and comprehends the administration of laws which do not violate the very foundations of civil liberties; it requires in each case an evaluation based on a disinterested inquiry, on a balanced order of facts exactly and fairly stated, on the detached consideration of conflicting claims, and on a judgment mindful of reconciling the needs of continuity and change in a complex society. Or as statesman Daniel Webster once maintained, due process suggested "the law which hears before it condemns; which proceeds upon inquiry, and renders judgment only after trial."[8]

Arrest

The criminal justice process begins upon arrest. In most jurisdictions, an arrest warrant is required in misdemeanor cases, unless the crime has been observed by a police officer. Felony arrests can be made in the absence of a warrant if the officer has "reasonable certainty" (also referred to as "probable cause") that the person being arrested is indeed the offender. There are many rules which govern the police search of suspects and the seizure of evidence. If these rules are violated, the search and seizure is illegal, thus negating the worth of the evidence seized.

Booking

Booking is the administrative record of an arrest, whereby the accused's name, address, time and place of arrest, and the arrest charge are entered into the police log. Booking can also include fingerprinting and photographing of the suspect.

The booking phase represents the first point at which the defendant can drop out of the criminal justice process with no further criminal proceedings. Charges may be dropped if the suspect has been arrested for a minor misdemeanor, or if there was a procedural error by the police (such as lack of probable cause for arrest or illegal search and seizure) and this decision can be made by an assistant prosecutor or someone of high rank in the police system. Booking is also the first point at which some defendants can be released on bail.

Bail, taken from the French term *baillier* meaning to deliver or give, is the most common form of temporary release. It involves the posting of financial security by the accused (or someone on his or her behalf), *guaranteeing* an appearance at trial. Release on bail can occcur immediately after the accused has been booked under the following circumstances:

1. if the accused has been arrested pursuant to an arrest warrant, the warrant may specify the amount of bail required, and upon payment, the individual can be released;
2. in most misdemeanor arrests, bail schedules are available for determining immediate payment.

In all other circumstances, bail is set at a later stage of the criminal process.

Initial Appearance

Due process requirements mandate that within a "reasonable" (not extreme or arbitrary) time after arrest, the accused must be brought before a magistrate and given formal notice of the charge. Such notice occurs at the initial appearance. In addition, the accused is notified of his or her legal rights, and bail is determined for those who did not receive such temporary release during the booking phase. *Release on recogni-*

zance (ROR) can also occur as a substitute for bail, typically recommended by the magistrate when there is some indication that there is no substantial risk that the accused will fail to appear for trial. In this situation, rather than posting some financial security, the accused is released on his or her own personal *recognizance*, or obligation.

In extremely minor offenses, such as "drunk and disorderly" or other cases where a simple citation has been issued, summary trials and sentencing are conducted at this initial appearance, with no further court processing. Finally, the magistrate presiding at the initial appearance can determine that the evidence available is not sufficient to warrant further criminal processing and consequently dismiss the case.

Preliminary Hearing

Because of the complexity of criminal processing and the delays generated by overloaded court calendars, many jurisdictions have abolished the initial appearance and proceed directly to the preliminary hearing.

The major purpose of the preliminary hearing is to protect defendants from unwarranted prosecutions. Thus, the presiding magistrate seeks to:

1. determine whether a crime has been committed;

2. determine whether the evidence establishes probable cause to believe that the defendant committed it;

3. determine the existence of the probable cause for which a warrant was issued for the defendant's arrest;

4. inquire into the reasonableness of the arrest and search and the compliance of the executing officer with the requirements of the warrant; and

5. determine the appropriate bail or temporary release if not already addressed.

The preliminary hearing, like the initial appearance, is not universal. In some jurisdictions, the defense may waive this hearing in order to keep damaging testimony temporarily out of the official records in the hope that by the time the trial occurs witnesses have forgotten some things, become confused, or have disappeared. However, other defense attorneys will insist on the use of this hearing as a tactic for gaining insight into the strengths and weaknesses of the state's case.

Determination of Formal Charges

Whether the initial court processing does or does not include an initial appearance and/or preliminary hearing, the next step in the criminal justice process is the formalization of charges. One mechanism is the *indictment* by grand jury. The indictment is a formal charging document based on the grand jury's determination as to whether there is sufficient indication to warrant a trial. If a majority decision is reached, and a "true bill" is signed, the indictment would contain the following information:

1. the type and nature of the offense;
2. the specific statute alleged to have been violated;
3. the nature and elements of the offense charged;
4. the time and place of the occurrence of the crime;
5. the name and address of the accused, or, if not known, a description sufficient to identify the accused with reasonable certainty;
6. the signature of the foreman on the grand jury showing that it has been returned as a true bill; and
7. the names of all codefendants in the offense charged, as well as the number of criminal charges against them.

Since the grand jury does not weigh the evidence presented, its finding is by no means equivalent to a conviction; rather, it simply binds the accused over for trial. Should this tribunal return a "no bill," that is, should it fail to achieve the required majority vote and thus refuse the indictment, the accused would be released.

Grand juries are available in approximately half of the states and in the federal system, but in only a limited number of jurisdictions does this represent the exclusive mechanism for sending a defendant to trial. The most common method for bringing formal charges is the *information,* a charging document drafted by a prosecutor and tested before a magistrate. Typically, this testing occurs at the preliminary hearing. The prosecutor presents some, or all, of the evidence in open court (usually just enough to convince the judge that the defendant should be held over for trial). As indicated earlier, however, the preliminary hearing is sometimes waived, and in those circumstances the information is not tested before a magistrate.

Arraignment

After the formal determination of charges, through the indictment or information, the actual trial process begins. The first phase in this segment of the criminal justice process is the *arraignment,* at which the accused is taken before a judge, the formal charges are read, and the defendant is asked to enter a plea. There are four possible pleas in most jurisdictions:

1. *Not Guilty.* If the not guilty plea is entered, the defendant is notified of his or her rights, a determination is made of his or her competence to stand trial, council is appointed if indigency is apparent, and in some jurisdictions the defendant can elect to have a trial by judge or a trial by jury.

2. *Guilty.* If a plea of guilty is entered, the judge must determine whether the plea was made voluntarily and whether the defendant has an understanding of the full consequences of such a plea. If the judge is satisfied, the defendant is scheduled for sentencing; if not, the judge can refuse the guilty plea and enter "not guilty" into the record.

3. *Nolo Contendere.* This plea, not available in all jurisdictions, means "no contest" or "I do not wish to contest." It has the same implication as the guilty plea but is of considerable legal significance in that an admission of guilt is not present and cannot be introduced in later trials.

4. *Standing Mute.* Remaining mute results in an entry of a not guilty plea. It has its advantages in that the accused is not waiving the right to protest any irregularities which may have occurred in earlier phases of the criminal justice proceedings.

The Trial Process

The complete trial process can be long and complex. It may begin with a hearing on pretrial motions entered by the defense to *suppress* evidence, *relocate* the place of the trial, *discover* the nature of the state's evidence, or *postpone* the trial itself. Subsequent to the pretrial motions, if any, the jury is selected, and the trial proceeds as follows:

Opening statements by prosecution. The prosecutor outlines the state's case and how the state will introduce witnesses and physical evidence to prove the guilt of the accused.

Opening statement by defense. The defense, if it elects to do so, explains how it plans to introduce witnesses and evidence in its own behalf.

Presentation of state's case. The state calls its witnesses to establish the elements of the crime and introduces physical evidence; the prosecutor accomplishes this through *direct examination* of the witnesses, followed by their cross-examination by the defense.

Presentation of the defense's case. The defense may open with a *motion for dismissal* on the grounds that the state failed to prove the defendant guilty "beyond a reasonable doubt." If the judge concurs, the case is dismissed, and the accused is released. If the judge rejects the motion, the defense's case proceeds in the same manner as the state's presentation.

Prosecutor's rebuttal. The prosecutor may elect to present new witnesses and evidence, following the format of the state's original presentation.

Defense surrebuttal. The defense may again make a motion for the dismissal; if this motion is denied, the defense, too, can introduce new evidence and witnesses.

Closing statements. The prosecutor and the defense attorney make closing arguments which sum up their cases and the deductions that can be made from the evidence and testimony.

Charging the jury. In jury trials, the judge instructs the jury as to possible verdicts and charges them to retire to the jury room to consider the facts of the case, to deliberate on the testimony, and to return a just verdict.

Return of the verdict. Once the jury has reached a decision, they return to the courtroom with a verdict, which is read aloud by a member of the court. The jury may be *polled,* at the request of either the defense or the prosecution, whereby each member is asked individually whether the verdict announced is his or her individual verdict.

In the case of a trial by judge, those elements involving the jury are eliminated, and the judge makes the determination of innocence or guilt.

Post-trial motions can also occur if the defendant is found guilty. The defense is given the opportunity to seek a new trial or have the verdict of the jury *set aside* (revoked).

Sentencing

Subsequent to conviction or the entry of a guilty plea, the defendant is brought before the judge for imposition of the sentence. The sentencing process may begin with a pre-sentence investigation which represents a summary of the offender's family, social, employment, and criminal history, and serves as a guide for the presiding judge in determining the type of sentence to be imposed. Depending on the nature of the offense and the sentencing guidelines established by statute, a simple fine might be imposed or adjudication to probation in the community. Sentences involving imprisonment can vary widely, and can include:

1. the *definite,* or "flat" sentence, which involves a fixed period of time;
2. the *indeterminate* sentence, which has a fixed minimum and fixed maximum; and
3. the *indefinite* sentence, which has neither a fixed minimum nor a fixed maximum.

And finally, the terminal and most severe form of sentence is the death penalty.

Appeals and Release

Subsequent to conviction and sentencing, defendants found guilty may appeal their case to a higher court. Appeals are based on claims that due process was not followed or that the sentence imposed was cruel and unusual in violation of constitutional rights.

Release from imprisonment occurs after the time specified in the sentence has been served, or if the offender is released on *parole* (a conditional release after only a portion of the sentence has been served). Release from prison, or any type of sentence, can also occur through *pardon* ("forgiveness") for the crime committed, which serves to bar any further criminal justice processing. Other factors which can affect a sentence are the *reprieve,* which delays the execution of a sentence, and the *commutation,* which reduces a sentence to a less severe one.

The Rights of the Accused

A thorough discussion of the rights of the accused is impossible here, for any meaningful treatment of the subject would take many volumes. Those constitutional guarantees which apply to criminal defendants are mentioned in the Bill of Rights, but over the years they have been subject to varying interpretation. The Supreme Court of the United States serves as the ultimate interpreting body for the Constitution, and its decisions on behalf of the accused are binding on the lower courts. However, what has occurred over time has been a proliferation of cases which relate to individual incidents, thus making it difficult to make many general statements about defendants' rights in all situations. As a result, only the most basic rights are listed here. It is best that a defendant's attorney, who understands the precision of the law as well as the details of his or her client's case, address the finer issues of constitutional matters.

The following rights are considered basic to processing in the criminal courts:

1. *The Right to Counsel.* In all criminal cases, whether felony or misdemeanor, the accused has the right to have counsel present at interrogation, trial, and numerous other phases of the criminal justice process. If the accused cannot afford to hire an attorney, the court will provide one. This right, furthermore, applies to both criminal and juvenile court cases.

2. *The Right Against Self-Incrimination.* The Fifth Amendment holds that no person shall be compelled to be a witness against himself. This means that a defendant does not have to testify against himself in court or at any other stage of the criminal process. Thus, if an accused is forced to confess under threat of physical harm (in a police interrogation room, for example), that confession is invalid and cannot be used as evidence against him.

3. *The Right to be Free of Unreasonable Searches and Seizures.* The Fourth Amendment holds that persons have the right "to be secure in their persons, houses, papers, and effects, against unreasonable searches and seizures." Thus any evidence obtained illegally cannot be used against a defendant.

In addition to these, defendents have rights to a trial by jury and a speedy trial, as well as protections against double jeopardy (being tried more than once for the same crime) and cruel and unusual punishment.

For the juvenile and the adult, the right to counsel is the most significant by far. An attorney can be a defendant's ultimate protection and guarantee of fairness. Having an attorney present throughout criminal processing increases the chances of fair treatment and reduces the potential for conviction.

Conclusion

Something must be said at this point about what to do if a drug arrest occurs. The *first* thing to do, in all cases, is to get an attorney, preferably one who is familiar with drug cases (and the juvenile process if the defendant is a youngster). *Second,* never say anything to the police or the court without the advice of counsel. *Third,* find out what the diversion alternatives are in the community. A willingness to enter treatment or to receive counseling is something that many judges like to see. For more serious drug crimes (if the defendant is guilty, and the state has a strong case), discuss the possibilities of plea bargaining. *Fourth,* if innocent, never enter a plea of guilty.

Finally, although it has been emphasized that the police and the courts are willing to handle the majority of drug cases both quickly and inexpensively, there are exceptions. Moreover, although most criminal justice personnel across the nation are committed to just and fair treatment, there are exceptions. There are "the big-bellied sheriffs" for whom racism, cynicism, and brutality have become a way of life; there are prosecutors and state attorneys who, for political reasons, see convictions at any cost as the be-all and end-all; there are probation officers and public defenders who have reduced themselves to being civil service hacks, who hate themselves and their jobs, and for whom red tape and official procedure are more important than justice and humanity; and there are judges who believe that all drug users are "junkies," that all junkies lie, and that "once a junkie always a junkie."

Notes

1. *Hutto v. Davis,* 454 U.S. 370 (1982).
2. U.S. Department of Justice, Federal Bureau of Investigation, *Crime in the United States—1983* (Washington, D.C.: U.S. Government Printing Office, 1984), p. 179
3. Ibid.
4. For a more detailed discussion of the juvenile justice process, see H. Ted Rubin, *Juvenile Justice: Policy, Practice, and Law* (Santa Monica: Goodyear, 1979).
5. *In re Gault,* 387 U.S. 1 (1967).
6. *In re Winship,* 397 U.S. 358 (1970).
7. *Breed v. Jones,* 421 U.S. 519 (1975).
8. For a detailed examination of the concept of "due process of law" and a complete discussion of the criminal justice process, see James A. Inciardi, *Criminal Justice* (Orlando: Academic Press, 1984).

5
Weedslingers: Young Black Marijuana Dealers

Allen B. Fields

Introduction

In the past fifteen years, there has been a flood of literature concerning the use of drugs by young people. Studies have focused on the social and psychological characteristics as well as the age of users at the time of initial experimentation (Kandel 1982; Jessor et al. 1980); why youth use marijuana (Hendin et al. 1981–82; Segal et al. 1982); and the presumed negative consequences associated with continued and heavy use of marijuana (Petersen 1980). But there is little current information about young people who sell the drug. This chapter, in addressing that information gap, provides a historical perspective on marijuana dealing and describes the currrent routines and activities of young black males who sell marijuana and, increasingly, have become part of the drug traffic scene.

Studies conducted during the 1960s provide some understanding of the activities of street dealers during this decade. By examining marijuana sales from the perspective of those involved, Mandel (1967), Carey (1968), and Goode (1970), for example, were able to show that the popular image of the 1930s "dope pusher" was woefully incorrect. According to this image, one that predominated until the early 1960s, the marijuana dealer was an adult male, employed by a highly organized criminal apparatus, who tried to seduce youth into a life of drug dependency. He was said to give away marijuana under false pretenses for the purpose of getting youth "hooked" so that he could insure a steady clientele of high paying users. However, later studies showed that marijuana dealers were often youths who distributed small quantities of marijuana for minimal profits, for example "free smokes" for the seller, and often at cost or without payment to close friends. In some communities, there was little differentiation between the role of marijuana dealer and user. Goode (1970) states:

It is not simply that the user must purchase his drug supply from the seller to consume the drug, but the user and the seller are largely indistinguishable, there is no clear-cut boundary between them. Selling and using involve parallel activities. *The seller and user inhabit the same social universe.*

Several researchers have examined the motives of street dealers and the cultural context in which marijuana use and sales occur (Carey 1968; Mouledoux 1972; Reich 1970). In the 1960s and early 1970s, young people heavily involved in selling and using marijuana were designated as "the counterculture" (Davis 1967), "the alternative culture" (Roszak 1968), the "new bohemia" and "hippiedom" (Yoblonsky 1968; Wethues 1972; Cavan 1972). They were seen as having a unique set of values and motive for dealing. Membership in the counterculture meant a commitment to hedonism, spontaneity, expressivity, but above all to the value of anti-materialism (Carey 1968; Goode 1970). The dealer's motives grew out of counterculture group norms which renounced the profit motive. Dealers and customers generally had close personal relationships and it was common for a dealer to supply marijuana to friends as a favor (Mandel 1967, Carey 1968, Mouledoux 1972). Those suspected of being primarily interested in marijuana dealing for monetary reasons were subject to severe sanctions and were often ostracized by customer-friends (Mouledoux 1972).

Further investigation of the cultural context of hippiedom showed how youths made the transition from user to street dealer. Carey reported that street dealers seldom arrived at the decision to sell marijuana after careful and systematic thought. Rather, most youths began dealing drugs by drifting into it, primarily to keep ("hold") a sufficient quantity of marijuana around for frequent personal use. Once the decision to hold was made and acted upon, it was inevitable that friends would ask to buy small quantities and , in honoring their requests, the holder eventually became a part of the "give-and-take."

In the late 1960s, many dealers had ideological commitments and some were interested in promoting revolutionary changes (Goode 1970; Young 1971; Reich 1970; Mouledoux 1972). Mouledoux (1972) suggests that many street dealers saw their role as promoting social and personal change by helping to create new modes of perception among drug users. Maintaining a street dealership was not for the purpose of building a clientele of drug-dependent youth.

Carey (1968) argues that given the legal climate of the 1960s, the user's risk of arrest was greatest when he made purchases of marijuana. By purchasing an amount sufficient for his own personal use once a month instead of once a week, the user-dealer could reduce his risk of arrest. Moreover, holding served to reduce the inconvenience of having to seek out sources when the dealer wanted to replenish supplies, and the problem of having to bother friends, especially at odd hours of the night, when the desire to use was highest.

The careers of street dealers were generally short-term. First, the rewards of supplying friends eventually wore off, as the task of periodically giving them small quantities soon became too time-consuming. Second, for dealers who supplied more than three or four friends, it was inevitable that they would find friends-of-friends calling upon them for supplies and the risk of arrest increased accordingly. Third, a street dealer, particularly a novice, occasionally purchased inferior merchandise and since he sold primarily to friends, he was obliged to correctly identify the quality of his product, scale down his price accordingly, and at times absorb a monetary loss. In essence, street dealing no longer represented a convenience. As a result dealers either stopped selling at the street level or moved to middle-level dealing, where profits justified the risk and inconvenience.

Since these early studies, there have been few attempts to give us any new insight into marijuana dealing at the street level. Except for studies of Latino dealers (Alvidrez 1973; Flores 1981), the general trend has been for researchers to study white dealers (predominantly in university settings) and middle-level dealers (Liebe and Olson 1976).

There is little current information available on young marijuana dealers. However, the following questions will be examined in this chapter:

1. Who is most likely to become a street dealer?
2. At what age do young people begin to engage in street dealing, and what roles exist at this specific level in the marijuana distribution network?
3. What is the cultural context and the range of motives for dealing marijuana?
4. How do youths become street dealers and what factors help explain the maintenance of street dealerships?
5. What purposes are served by selling marijuana and how long do dealers continue selling the drug?

Data and Methodological Considerations

Data were collected during a three-year ethnographic study of drug-using patterns among youth in a predominantly low-income black communtiy of San Francisco. Three different research methods were used: (1) recorded observations of street-level marijuana sales; (2) informal discussions with youths involved in sales and purchases; and (3) tape-recorded interviews of dealers and buyers.

> *Observation:* The investigators located areas in the community where substantial numbers of youths gather on a regular basis and recorded observations of drug sales taking place in these areas. These data were easily collected since, unlike the cloak of secrecy that surrounded marijuana sales in the late 1960s, low-level marijuana sales are generally conducted in the open, in areas along the main transport routes that link the community to surrounding neighborhoods, and in full view of all who travel the route and/or pass through the areas.
>
> *Informal discussion:* Informal questions concerning marijuana sales were asked of young marijuana sellers who had been contacted. The following are examples of the questions asked during informal discussions with marijuana sellers: (1) How long have you been "slinging weed" (selling marijuana)? (2) How often do you sell marijuana? (3) How do you keep from getting busted by the police? (4) Who do you usually sell your weed to? Since these questions were asked during the course of normal discussions with young dealers they were answered with candor.
>
> *Formal Interview:* Fifteen high-status marijuana dealers were interviewed and five of these interviews were tape recorded. In order to verify the accounts of respondents, information was sought where possible from a respondent's friends or associates and from others who were equally knowledgeable about marijuana sales and use among youth.

The Marijuana Market

The current drug dealing scene is very different from the 1960s and early 1970s, when marijuana sales were conducted from apartments and houses, and the actual transactions between dealers and customers remained hidden. Today, marijuana dealers make no attempt to conceal their behavior. Indeed they hawk their wares obtrusively on the street and confront all passersby. Individuals passing through an area in which drugs are sold are likely to be confronted by dealers showing their wares in the same way others may peddle flowers at an intersection, although marijuana dealers are likely to be much more aggressive.

Areas in the community which lend themselves to sales of marijuana are favored by adolescent dealers for several reasons. First, each is located along a major transportation route that links the community to adjacent neighborhoods and metropolitan communities, and substantial numbers of potential customers pass through. Second, each has features which attract large numbers of youths (recreational facilities, amusement centers) guaranteeing a steady population of possible buyers. The dealer need not move about the community in search of potential customers. Third, the location provides the kind of visibiltiy that a dealer needs to successfully transact business. Regular clientele know where to find him and he is in a good location to attract new customers. In addition, he is less likely to be arrested by law enforcement personnel. "Flop," a 22-year-old dealer, explained how visibility reduces chances of arrest:

> If you hang in a house or apartment slinging, you can't see who's outside and the rollers [police] can sneak up and you gone. . . . You can see them long before they see you and all you got to do then is hide your weed.

Obviously, there are occasions where being visible in the marketplace works against the dealer. Undercover police occasionally infiltrate the community, gather evidence of selling activities, and arrest dealers. But most dealers feel because they are visible, law enforcement officials must show their hand before attempting an arrest.

In addition to marijuana sales, the marketplace functions as a multipurpose area for youth, such as a central source of information on past, current, and future events. Many of the items highly valued by youth— stereo sets, designer clothing, jewelry, automobile parts, and accesssories—are bought, traded, and bartered with few questions raised about how or where they were obtained. The only questions generally asked are about the quality of an item and what kind of mutually acceptable deal can be made for its purchase. Bartering among youth often takes place in a festive atmosphere. Large portable cassette players or car sterios are used to produce music. Entertainment is sometimes supplied by youths who dance to or attempt to reproduce the sounds of a favored group or singer. Refreshments consisting of beer, soft drinks, hamburgers, and marijuana are often served.

The operation of the marketplace is relatively standardized. Marijuana sales and purchases are most brisk during weekdays and between the hours of 9:00 A.M. and 5:30 P.M. Little dealing occurs on weekends because most youths leave the community to engage in other activities.

Little bartering of marijuana occurs in the marketplace since the quantity and price for different grades of marijuana are generally accepted and adhered to by both seller and buyer. Thai stick (Buddha), a type of marijuana grown in Thailand, which is considered the most potent of the cannabis family amongst respondents, sells for $10 a bag. The quantity in a $10 bag of Buddha is about 1 gram. Less potent grades of Columbian (gold) and sinsemilla (sensi), indica, and the least preferred home-grown (marijuana that is grown in or near the community) are also available. However, youths seldom use formal measures to evaluate the quantity of marijuana in a bag. As Roy, a 17-year-old frequent visitor pointed out:

> In a $5 bag, if it's right (correct amount), you can get about eight joints. If you get a skimpy bag, you get about five or six. Or like if you roll it as pinheads, you know, like tiny joints, you should get about fifteen joints. But most of the fellows don't be 'bout no pinheads. Roll fat, they roll them fat. Yeah, a tiny bit smaller than a regular size cigarette. If you can roll good, you supposed to get about seven or eight, if you get a good bag.

Situations do occur where, because of limited supplies in the marketplace, buyers will settle for "skimpy bags." As Kev, a 20-year-old customer, stated:

> People usually supposed to sell fat bags. But when there ain't no action on that [little marijuana in the area] they just have to take what's there or do without.

But these situations are rare and the buyer generally expects to receive the "right" amount for his money.

Like specialty shops of the conventional marketplace, dealers specialize in particular grades of marijuana. Young people know that Buddha, for example, is typically purchased in only one area. It is not impossible to buy Buddha in areas that specialize in the sales of gold or sensi, but there is little chance of "scoring" Buddha outside the area in which it is generally sold. The reasons for this differentiation are related to cost. Each area in the marketplace draws its regular customers from neighborhoods in close proximity which reflect differences in the social and economic status of the residents. Youths in low-income neighborhoods seldom want to pay the price for a $10 bag of Buddha since they can get twice as much for $10 if they buy such grades as Columbian. Weedslingers are well aware of this socioeconomic fact. For example, when R.R. was asked why he and the fellows who worked one particular area sold only gold and not Buddha, he stated:

> Buddha is too expensive and moves too slow. Gold moves fast and some-

times, if you get lucky, you sell five or six bags at one time. Most people who buy Buddha ain't gonna buy more than a bag at one time and there ain't that many people around here [the area in which he sells] that wants to buy. You could be on the corner all day and not make but 'bout 10 or 20 dollars for your troubles. Everyone who hangs there smokes gold, so you can sell that by just walking up and down the street. Most of my steady customers are into gold. If they want anything else, they just have to look for it elsewheres. Every once in awhile one of these niggas might get his hands on some Buddha but, you know, most of the time he will keep it for himself and sell the other kind (gold).

In summary, studies have shown the overwhelming majority of marijuana transactions take place in a few specific areas of the community. These areas comprise the marijuana marketplace and are favored by dealers because of their strategic locations, the large numbers of potential customers that they attract, and the visibility they afford dealers. Business in the market is conducted during specific hours of the day and the quantity and price of marijuana are relatively standard. Finally, each area comprising the marketplace seemed to specialize in a particular grade of marijuana, with prices for a bag ranging from $5 to $10.

The Market Behavior of Weedslingers

Youths in the area label the activities of persons who sell marijuana in the marketplace on a consistent basis as "slinging weed" or "weedslinging." The behavior of weedslingers resembles the behavior of the small-scale entrepreneur, especially in the way they organize the purchase, transportation, storage, and packaging of marijuana. They make bulk purchases of as much as a pound of marijuana from regular contacts, often outside the community, on a regular and consistent basis. The regularity with which they purchase from these outside contacts and the amount that they buy insures both the quality of marijuana and a margin of profit. While dealers who buy the drug in the community usually pay as much as $50 for an ounce of marijuana, Flop, one of the regular weedslingers, explained how its business arrangement gets established:

A pound costs me three hundred from the White boy. That is his nickname. That's what he like me to call him. And he is White, his nationality is White and he don't live around here. I don't buy in Ship City, not really. I know where to get it cheaper. You get it cheaper and you get better merchandise, quality stuff, outside the community. But you got to know how to organize it.

Weedslingers are also responsible for transporting and storing the drug in relatively safe places in their community. Although transportation is relatively routine, for those who live with parents, storage can pose problems. Dealers will commonly exhange small samples of marijuana for storage space in the apartments of others or acquire space in the homes of more receptive relatives and girlfriends.

Weedslingers seldom carry large quantities of the drug with them into the marketplace. Their preparation for sales in the marketplace consists of setting aside a quantity of the drug for personal use and packaging the remainder in $5 or $10 bags which they sell to a regular clientele of adolescent consumers or others who visit the marketplace.

Weedslingers tend to have regular business hours because the specific time that customers might purchase marijuana cannot be predicted. Chris, an 18-year-old weedslinger, provided an additional reason for the stabiltiy of weedslingers in the marketplace:

> You got to be here regular. You know, you got to be 'round whenever your customers show up. You never know when they gonna be looking for you for a buy. If you ain't 'round, they just gonna say fuck that nigga and buy from the competition. You be givin' up customers. You just be givin' way your steady customers. That ain't too cool for your business. You be givin' away customers and steady paper [money].

Weedslingers are aware of the consequences of failing to maintain stable hours. They know that there are competitors waiting.

Reducing Business Risks

Maintaining regular business hours in the highly visible marketplace increases the risk that accompanies the weedslinger's enterprise. Part of the risk is directly related to the severe criminal penalties that result from conviction for sales of the drug. The activities that occur in the marketplace are constantly monitored by law enforcement personnel. In fact, during one period of time during the study many of the activities occurring in the marketplace were recorded on video tape.

In additon to the risk from police, weedslingers are subject to local predators—disgruntled customers or older persons bent on robbing them. They also risk loss of profits resulting from thefts of merchandise. Perhaps the words of Bone, a 16-year-old dealer, best illustrates what is generally acknowledged by the dealing and adolescent community. In response to a question about the nature of life on the streets of Ship City, Bone stated:

You gotta be careful out here. If you ain't, niggas will rip you off. Them dope fiends [older males who are believed to be hooked on heroin] will take a nigga out [kill] to get money for dope. You got to watch it all the time. They steal, they rob, they do all that. They robbed blood [a term used to describe an associate], almost put him in the hospital. They took his money and weed.

Weedslingers have devised a number of techniques to reduce some of their risks, the most common of which are (1) participation in the informal communication system of the market; (2) relocating their enterprise; and (3) the use of deception.

The informal communication system of the marketplace is a type of early warning network. When police are active in one area, weedslingers either phone or carry this infomation to other areas of the marketplace. Such a system is believed to provide enough time for other dealers to take the necessary measures required to reduce their risk of arrest.

How does the communication network function? On one occasion the author observed the usual complement of dealers gathered in the central area of the marketplace. At 3:30 P.M., most community youths were passing through the area on their way from school, so business in the area was quite brisk. C.C., a 24-year-old dealer, was closing a marijuana transaction when a car screeched to a halt directly in front of a large gathering of young people. The driver, a young man in his late teens, yelled. "they are trying to set something up." Upon hearing this warning, dealers began to leave the area. Some ran to cars parked along the main thoroughfare, others ran up side streets, while others went in different directions. It took only a few seconds for the corner to become devoid of marijuana dealers. Only one dealer remained and he explained how the driver knew that the police were planning to raid the corner:

There are a number of ways that the fellows know. Most of the time the rollers [police] will hit one corner first. See, they don't usually have enough men to hit all the corners at the same time. Usually, they might hit the corner up the street and there are always people around when the bust go down. They don't get busted and they run ahead of the rollers to let the other fellows know about the bust so they can split. Other times, the fellows just know who the police are, even though they try to hide their shit by coming in unmarked cars. They know them. So, if the fellows see them, they know that a bust is about to go down and they tell the other fellows.

Among the measures weedslingers take in response to police activity in the marketplace is simply to move the enterprise to another area in the community. These areas are generally known by local adolescents but tend not to be under the same amount of police pressure as the marijuana marketplace. Police activity in the marketplace may momentarily disrupt transactions in one location, but it has little effect on sales in the entire community.

Weedslingers engage in secretive or deceptive behavior to reduce the chances of being convicted for sales in the marketplace. Past experience has taught them that it is not possible to avoid being stopped periodically and searched by police. This point was clearly made by "Little Ricky," one of the youngest dealers in the marketplace familiar with police activity:

> The cops sometimes stop and search you for nothin'. You can just be standing on the corner, not doin' anything, man, and if they feel like stopping and searching you, they will.

Weedslingers have learned, either from their own experiences or the experiences of others, what it means to be arrested for possession or sales. They know that to be caught with more than two grams of marijuana is to risk arrest and conviction for sales. For this reason, they store the bulk of marijuana that they bring to the market in places that they can watch, and that are within easy reach. Roy a 17-year-old dealer, explained the rationale for this market behavior.

> How I keep from getting busted for sales is, well, I just put mine in a bag and just sit it over by a garbage can. If somebody come, I look around and I'll just go get about two grams and just show them, see which they want. If they only want one, I'll take one back and put it back in the bag. You never keep that on you. You just go over and get a few grams so if they bust you, it's only for possession. You know, possession don't carry as much time as sales do. Get caught for sales, whew, that's big time.

Efforts to reduce the risk of arrest and conviction for sales of marijuana are also evident in the way weedslingers attract new customers. To inform potential customers of the product they have for sale, weedslingers use a variety of hand signals and body gestures. In a commonly used signal, the weedslinger extends one arm in front of his body, opens his hand to reveal five separate fingers, and shrugs his shoulders and tilts his head in a kind of questioning manner. This means "would you like to buy a five-dollar bag of marijuana?" Weedslingers are also able to signal the grades of marijuana available. Raising both arms above about their heads, forming a "T" with their hands and opening and closing one of their hands twice, dealers ask the potential buyer "Are you interested in buying a $10 bag of Thai stick?" There are variations on these basic signals and gestures, but all are designed to attract the attention of a prospective buyer without the type of bartering that would draw the attention of police.

Although police who regularly patrol the community are aware of the meaning of these signals and gestures, dealers believe that so long as they do not disrupt the flow of automobile traffic the signals are the easiest and safest way to attract new buyers. As one dealer stated, "They can't bust you for that [gesturing and signaling] even if they know what they be 'bout."

Finally, weedslingers must constantly guard against community informants who, in discovering the location of areas in which the bulk of their marijuana is stored, will trade information with police to avoid their own arrest for some illegal activity. To reduce the likelihood of this occurrence, the weedslinger will keep secret the location of these areas by separating the activities that occur in them—storing, cleaning, and packaging—from the sales that take place only in the marijuana marketplace.

Weedslingers must also take measures against the chance of being "ripped off" while in the marketplace. One of the more common ways they are ripped off is by a sneak thief who has discovered where they have hidden their marijuana. To protect against rip-offs, dealers are very secretive while in the marketplace and generally engage in deceptive patterns of behavior. When asked how he keeps people from stealing his market stash, Chris, a relatively new member of the dealing scene, explained:

> To keep the fellows from stealing it, you don't show where you put it. You don't let the fellows see where you go when you get your stash and come back with it. They just see you walk away and when you come back, you just have weed on you. See, you make 'em think that you be having it in your pocket. That's the way most of the fellows do it if they'd don't want to get ripped off.

Because of these measures dealers always appear to be on the move, unable to stay in one place in the marketplace for any length of time. When they are stationary for brief periods, they are constantly glancing about as if expecting to see someone who might mean disaster for them. For the most part, this is subterfuge to keep watch over their stash.

Another type of market rip-off occurs, although with far less frequency than thefts of marijuana stashes, during times in which dealers are letting prospective buyers examine the merchandise. A dealer often allows a prospective buyer who remains in his car to examine the merchandise but in doing so he runs the risk that the buyer will drive off without paying. An illustration of this type of "burn" was provided by "Bro," a 22-year-old weedslinger:

> It seldom happens, but you can be too trusting and get burnt. I was on the corner and these dudes drove up and wanted to buy some weed. They double parked in front of the hall and I gave 'em four bags of gold to inspect. We were about to close the deal but they was blocking traffic and when some old lady behind them started blowing her horn, they said that they would pull forward so she could get by. They pulled up but they kept going with my weed. Niggas burnt me for four bags.

Marketplace dealers who have been burned cannot say whether burns are planned or whether the thieves merely seized an opportunity. They do recognize, however, the effects that repeated burns can have on their corner's reputation. C.C. explained some of the more serious of these consequences as follows:

> You know, if a nigga rip you off out here, it's like he's ripping off the corner. And if these niggas out here ever get the idea that they can rip off the corner and get away with it, the fellows might as well forget about makin' money, won't nobody be able to work here. Everybody be thinking: niggas on that corner easy. So you be spending all your time watching out for them and don't have no time to take care of your thing. You got to control the corner, you can't go letting niggas rip you off. They got to know that your place of business ain't no place to be fucked with. You gotta be hard 'cause, if you ain't, niggas don't respect nothin' else. Business be getting all fucked up. Cause, rollers be lookin' for fellows that be packin.' You can't make no paper with them always around.

Controlling the areas in which marijuana transactions occur is the most common way that weedslingers discourage burns in the market-place. "Being hard" is the basic technique of control. Each of the areas must have a reputation of being frequented by dealers who are tough and willing to use force and violence where the need arises, to "let niggas know that your place of business ain't no place to be fucked with." Toughness and a reputation built upon the use of force and violence are believed by dealers to be the only things that a burn artist respects. Where such reputation does not exist or is lost, the ultimate result is to give up control of one's money-making enterprise.

Weedslingers are quick to show just how hard they are when the occasion presents itself. A case in point was illustrated by Flop in response to a question about how he had crumpled the front end of his car:

These dudes had come by the corner to buy some weed. Blood gave them a couple of bags to inspect, but instead of paying him, the niggas took off. Me and some of the fellas jumped in my car and took off after 'em. You can't let niggas take the corner. It gives other niggas the idea that they can do it. So, we was chasing the mother fuckers and was just about to catch them. But we couldn't get them to stop. The niggas knew they were in for a serious ass kicking, so they don't stop. So, I just rammed my car into the back of theirs and the dude lost control and ran into the side of this building. But by the time we could get out of the car, they were stepping [running] up the street, niggas was stepping, blood. We couldn't catch 'em. So, to let the niggas know that they don't be comin' up here ripping off the corner, Blood say: "Let's fuck up their car." We tore that car up. Bloods was banging on the mother fucker with irons, hammers, anything they could get hands on.

In sum, weedslingers are solely responsible for organizing and managing their sales of marijuana in the marketplace, including purchasing, transporting, storing, cleaning, and packaging the drug. Like the small businessman, weedslingers must also assume much of the risk that is associated with their enterprise, and to continue in business, they must find ways to reduce or eliminate these risks.

Who Becomes a Weedslinger

Not everyone who sells marijuana in the marketplace becomes a weedslinger (selling as a means of livelihood). Some youths sell small quantities of marijuana to close friends, but the seller's concern is not profit as much as not having to assume all the costs involved in supplying friends. Others, referred to as "runners" by community youth, sell marijuana on a periodic basis for "employers" (middle-level marijuana distributors who live in the community) and restrict their market sales to occasions in which some special event (party, spectator sports event, musical concert) requires them to raise small amounts of money. Once a sufficient amount is raised, runners stop dealing until some new event requires them to resume their market sales. Still other youths, "riders," work exclusively for one employer and sell marijuana on a regular and consistent basis. Riders are distinguished from weedslingers by virtue of their dependence on employers for the merchandise they sell in the marketplace and, thereby, their emloyee status. It is difficult to say just who in these categories of sellers will become weedslingers, but there are ways to identify those who have the greatest likelihood of becoming weedslingers.

To become a weedslinger, a youth must meet certain conditions that

current weedslingers view as fundamental to the success of their enterprise. At the very least, the youth must possess (1) individual autonomy;
(2) commitment to the work ethic; and (3) dealing techniques (which
include entrepreneurial knowledge and skills).

Autonomy

The amount of time that a youth can spend in the marketplace is of
fundamental importance to becoming a weedslinger. Unlike the white
street dealer of the 1960s, whose buyers consisted of a small circle of
close friends, the weedslinger needs to build a clientele of customers from
among persons whom he may know only vaguely or not at all. Since
most of these prospective clients are only in the marketplace sporadically,
a potential weedslinger must be able to spend time in the market culti-
vating and convincing them that he is reliable and has available a consistent source of quality marijuana. To have the time that is necessary
for this endeavor, the youth must have some individual autonomy, freedom from such responsibilities as having to attend school, work, and
similar obligations that limit the time he can spend in the marketplace.
It is also important that he be free of strict adult control and supervision
since either could limit the periods that he is available to the market and
the activities that he can engage in there.

Commitment to the Work Ethic

Success as a weedslinger requires commitment to an ethic that prescribes
a certain approach to selling marijuana in the marketplace. While the
"hang-loose" ethic of dealers described by Goode (1970) and Carey
(1968) legitimized a sloppy, easy-going, and laissez-faire approach to
marijuana sales, commitment to the weedslinger's ethic means that one
approaches sales as work. Ruben, one of the older and more established
weedslingers of the marketplace, explained this approach:

> Most of the older guys are on the corner everyday. They ain't out here
> to bullshit. They know that to make paper you gotta treat slinging like
> a job. That's the way they feel about it; it's a job, what they do for a
> livin'. I work from nine to five and, after that, I'm off until the next
> day. That's the only way to make paper out here, you gotta stay on
> your job.

Adherence to this ethic increases a youth's chances of becoming a
weedslinger in several ways. First, it reinforces a perception among potential customers that the youth is reliable, since it means that he will be

in the marketplace on a daily basis and during very specific hours of the day. Second, it informs employers that the youth is serious about selling marijuana, and thereby lays the foundation for establishing an exclusive business relationship with one employer. Third, such adherence helps inform both customers and employer that the youth is in the marketplace to make money, not "to bullshit," and thereby restricts the contacts he has with them. In turn, this type of relationshp reduces the amount of time that a potential weedslinger has to spend with a customer or employer, allowing him to increase his volume of sales and profits. Profits, after all, are a major resource that a youth must have to translate his job into a market enterprise.

Dealing Techniques

"Dealing techniques" are the complement of skills and knowledge that a youth must learn in order to work as a marijuana entrepreneur. Langer (1977) has suggested that the potential weedslinger must acquire entrepreneurial *knowledge* and *skills*.

Entrepreneurial Knowledge. Before a youth can establish an independent marijuana enterprise, he must first acquire rudimentary knowledge of the actions and tasks that make up the practical affairs of even the most sporadic seller of marijuana in the marketplace. Ray, one of the periodic sellers in the marketplace, described how he acquired this knowledge and what it entailed:

> You have to listen to them [knowledgeable youths] when you ask them how you start. They tell you who the people are that got good weed, what things you go to look out for, what you gotta do in order to, um, to keep selling weed. They teach you, you know, they teach you what kind of precautions to take and stuff like that. You gotta know, like who you selling weed to, if you see the police. . . . You gotta learn all that 'fore you can sell out here [in the marketplace].

Any youth who successfully sells marijuana in the marketplace must know how to reduce the risk associated with selling marijuana, "know what things you got to look out for. . . . what kinds of precautions to take . . ." in order to "keep selling." Without this knowledge, one's success as a periodic dealer, let alone a weedslinger, is severely limited by police and predators. Even more important is the fact that the potential weedslinger must know a "business contact" (middle-lever distributor) who will supply him with marijuana. This knowledge is generally acquired through sustained interactions with established dealers in the marketplace who have contact with, and who are willing to introduce youth to, middle-level distributors. The introductions generally take place after the regular dealer feels comfortable with guaranteeing the trustworthiness of the neophyte. Once the introduction is made, the neophyte must establish his own arrangements with the distributor.

Initially, the arrangement that a potential weedslinger makes with middle-level marijuana distributors is a runner-employer relationship. Employers are generally adult males who live in the community. They may at one time have been weedslingers who were a principal source of marijuana in the marketplace. Youths whom they hire (runners) receive $1.00 for each $5.00 bag of marijuana they sell, usually receiving between ten and fifteen bags on consignment. Thus, the industrious runner can earn no more than $15.00 per day.

The majority of youths who sell marijuana on a periodic basis are runners and seldom rise above this position. Potential weedslingers, though, eventually move from being runners to being riders. This occurs when they begin to work exclusively for one employer and when, as a result of their commitment to the weedslinger's work ethic, they are seen as a reliable source of profits by the employer. The employer, in attempting to keep a good employee, will then increase the runner's profits from $1.00 to $2.00 for each bag he sells. Once this occurs, the potential weedslinger will increase the number of bags he gets on consignment from fifteen to twenty-five bags. If business is brisk, the potential weedslinger may earn as much as $50.00 per day, assuming that the rider does not take out a small quantity of the drug for his personal use and that he has the skill necessary to sell some twenty-five bags of marijuana.

To rise from rider to weedslinger, a youth must know how to convert the money he makes while working for an employer to merchandise (marijuana) and then convert this merchandise into profits that can be reinvested in his independent business. Chris, a 19-year-old weedslinger, described one of the more common ways that capitalization occurs:

> You work for somebody 'til you get enough [money]. You have to get enough to buy, yeah, to buy a quarter ounce, $50. So, when you make that much, what you do is buy it [the quarter ounce], bag it up in little baggies. You just make it up and just go and sling it. Some of your friends, they be on the corner and everybody know what's going on there. So, when you get the money [from selling], you put a couple of dollars on the side and take the rest and go re-cop. You buy a couple of more [ounces of marijuana]. See, each time you cop, you get more action [get marijuana at a lower price and make more sales] and then you make more [money]. You get a little more paper, you get a little more weed and you build up like that.

Weedslingers work for an employer until they are able to raise the initial capital needed to begin their own enterprise. They then sever relationships with employers by purchasing enough merchandise, usually from contacts they have made with persons outside the community, to get started on their own. The profits realized from the sales of their own merchandise are, with the exception of the few dollars that they spend on personal items, reinvested. Over time, the continued capitalization of resources results in a reduction in the price that they have to pay for bulk purchases, a greater volume of sales in the marketplace and, thus, the eventual establishment of their own independent marijuana enterprise. There are, obviously, other ways that youths become weedslingers, but this method is the most common.

Entrepreneurial Skills. A potential weedslinger is aware of the "sociogenic" (Goode 1970) basis of a market enterprise, and realizes that being a successful weedslinger requires that he have certain interpersonal skills. He knows that success rests upon having the manipulative skills found, for example, in the successful car salesman. Each salesman must be able to manage the impressions that business contacts and customers have of him. During business hours, he must give others the impression that he is congenial, that he is confident of his abilities, and that he is knowledgeable about the dealing scene. He must appear to be fair, and his merchandise should give the appearance of being the highest quality available. To give others this impression, the potential weedslinger must, at the very least, have good conversational and communicative skills.

In negotiating confrontations with representatives of the legal system, youths must also be skilled in reducing impressions that they are contesting the authority of police. Weedslingers sense that to give police the impression that they are questioning police authority, especially when they are holding marijuana, would likely only end in their being searched and arrested. They understand that weedslingers must be able to confront these encounters without the expression of fear or anger and that they must be able to use persuasion and wit to talk their way out of a potentially serious situation. In problematic situations, such as confrontations with police and other youth, the potential weedslinger must project a demeanor of self-control. Blumer et al. (1967) describe this as consisting of:

A deliberate and self-conscious attempt to control oneself in all aspects of one's daily life. It means, generally, being unruffled in critical situations, keeping one's head, acting wisely, showing calm courage [and] being smart.

This demeanor is reflected in aloofness. Although he takes an active part, the potential weedslinger always appears removed from those interactions that have no direct bearing on business. He seldom engages in the type of expressiveness (loud and boisterious behavior) that could undermine his image of self-control or draw attention to his actions. Except for those interactions that are related to his enterprise, he maintains a relatively low profile and acts as though he is little concerned with or interested in other marketplace activities.

Summary

The young black marijuana seller in the 1980s differs in several basic ways from his white counterpart of the late 1960s. Part of this difference is a result of increased market price and legal changes which have affected street dealers of all ethnic groups. Other aspects involve cultural variations—motivations, job opportunities, and values.

Starting at the end of the 1960s, a nationwide police crackdown on marijuana sales, in combination with an expanding market for that drug, resulted in an increase in the cost of marijuana. Even though the profit margin for the marijuana seller might not have changed in terms of the percentage of investment, the dollar value of the profit at each level of dealing soared. Additionally, at least in California, legal changes have altered the risk factor for street-level marijuana dealers. In the mid-1970s, a new state law made it only a misdemeanor to be in possession of less than a ounce of marijuana. Hence, increases in the potential profits to be realized, reductions in the risk to dealers carrying less than an ounce, and changes in the law served to create a niche for the type of sales in which weedslingers are presently engaged.

Such market and legal factors only partially explain the black weedslinger's style of dealing. To some extent, cultural differences account for the different dealer styles. Weedslingers, for example, seldom drift into street dealing; they are far more systematic in selling marijuana than was the case with the street dealers studied in the 1960s. This tends to be true because the weedslinger's motive for entering street-level marijuana sales is principally to acquire money and has little to do with reducing the risk associated with personal use of the drug. Several writers (Carey 1968, Mandel 1967) noted that middle-class whites often cut back on the low-level sale of marijuana when it seemed to impinge on their alternative career plans. By contrast, the decision of young blacks to become weedslingers is made after careful thought has been given to alternative ways of raising money. On the one hand, the likelihood of a black youth finding good-paying legitimate work in the inner city is slim.

On the other hand, the decision to become a weedslinger is made after thought has been given to the legal consequences of engaging in more serious forms of illegal behavior such as burglaries, purse snatches, and muggings.

Part of the explanation for the differences in decision making and motivation between the weedslinger and the low-level Anglo dealer of an earlier era can be found in the value systems of the two cultures. Contrary to the hang-loose ethos of yesteryear's "love generation," inner-city black youth value behavior that demonstrates self-control. Unlike marijuana dealers of the 1960s, young black sellers are more businesslike. They are less likely to give marijuana to their peers as a friendly gesture. Supplying friends implies weakness and defines the individual as an easy touch, someone who can be used and readily manipulated. Finally, behavior that demonstrates successful achievement in competitive spheres of valued activities, such as marijuana selling, earns respect among inner-city black youth. Those who engage in sales of marijuana provide an important service for marijuana-using youth. More important, however, is the fact that young men who achieve the status of weedslinger are clearly viewed as successful entrepreneurs among their peers.

References

Alvidrez, S.R. 1973. "Drug Use Trends in California." In O. Ramano (ed.), *Voices*. Berkeley, California: Quinto Sol.

Blumer, H. and Sutter, A. 1967. *ADD Center Project Final Report: The World of Youthful Drug Use*. Berkeley, California: School of Criminology, University of California.

Cavan, S. 1972. Hippies of Haight. St. Louis: New Critics Press.

Carey, J.T. 1968. *The College Drug Scene*. Englewood Cliffs, New Jersey: Prentice-Hall.

Davis, F. 1967. Why all of us may be hippies someday. *Transaction* 5:10–18.

Flores, E.T. 1981. Dealing in marijuana: An exploratory study. *Hispanic Journal of Behavioral Sciences* 3: 199–211.

Goode, E. 1970. *The Marijuana Smokers*. New York: Basic Books.

Hendin, H.; Pollinger, A; and Ulman, R. 1981–82. The functions of marijuana abuse for adolesents. *American Journal of Drug and Alcohol Abuse* 8 (H): 441–456.

Jessor, R.; Chase, L.; and Donovan, J. 1980. Psychosocial correlates of marijuana use and problem drinking in a national sample of adolescents. *American Journal of Public Health* 70:604–613.

Kandel, D. 1982. Epidemiology and psychosocial perspectives in adolescent drug use. *Journal of the American Academy of Child Psychiatry* 21(4):328–347.

Langer, J. 1977. Drug entrepreneurs and dealing culture. *Social problems* 24: 377–386.

Lieb, J. and Olson, S. 1976. Prestige, paranoia and profit: on becoming a dealer of illicit drugs in a university community. *Journal of Drug Issues* 6: 356–367.

Mandel, J. 1967. "Myths and Realities of Marijuana Pushing." In J.L. Simmons (ed.), *Marijuana, Myths and Realities*. North Hollywood: Brandon House.

Mouledoux, J. 1972. Observations on drug traffic and reflections on its communal and ideological aspects. *Toxiconamies* 4(1): 81–97.

Petersen, R.C. 1980. Marijuana and Health. In *Marijuana Research Findings*. Research Monograph. 31. Rockville, Maryland: National Insitute on Drug Abuse.

Reich, C.A. 1970. *The Greening of America*. New York: Random House.

Roszak, T. 1969. *The Making of a Counterculture: Reflections on Technological Society and Its Youthful Opposition*. New York: Doubleday.

Segal, B.; Cromer, F.; Hobfoll, S.; and Wasserman, P. 1982. Patterns of reasons for drug use among detained and adjudicated juveniles. *The International Journal of the Addictions* 17(7): 1117–1130.

Westhues, K. 1972. Hippiedom 1970: Some tentative hypotheses. *Sociological Quarterly* 13(1):81–89.

Yablonsky, L. 1968. *The Hippie Trip*. New York: Pegasus.

Young, J. 1971. *The Drug Takers*. London: Paladan

6

Marijuana in the Lives of Adolescents

Barry Glassner
Cheryl Carpenter
Bruce Berg

Much has been written about the potential dangers of marijuana and the possibility that early marijuana use leads to more serious drug involvement. A considerable investment in marijuana research has been made in recent years and a great deal has been learned about the drug and its effects. For example, we know that marijuana is no ordinary drug. It is complex, containing hundreds of known chemicals. The principal active ingredient is D-tetrahydrocannabinol (THC), a lipid-soluble psychoactive ingredient stored in, and slowly released by, the body.

A primary concern about marijuana is the effects it may have on the brain and on behavior. There is evidence that marijuana leads to short-term memory loss, decreased attention span and perceptual changes that can affect school performance and driving ability (Macdonald 1984). Marijuana can also cause acute paranoia, which occurs most often in the naive user during early experimentation. A combination of hypotension and tachycardia is also possible with very potent forms of marijuana. The user becomes flushed, appears shaky, and may develop nausea and vomiting. Cases of allergic reactions to cannabis products have been reported and hypotensive episodes may be an allergic reaction (Schnoll 1979).

There is still much that is not known about the effects of frequent long-term marijuana use. For example, there are unanswered questions about the possible adverse effects of the drug on the body's immune response system, basic cell metabolism, and other areas of functioning (Dupont 1979; Peterson 1980). New methods of growing and producing marijuana have led to increased concentrations of THC and it has been acknowledged that risks to health and functioning rise with increased potency.

Despite all that has been learned about the potential effects, we know very little about the long-term consequences of marijuana for adolescents. Researchers have experienced difficulty isolating the effects of marijuana, since most regular adolescent marijuana users also take other drugs (Farley et al. 1979). In addition, many questions have been raised about the generalizability and interpretation of research findings, the validity of self-reports and the viability of the so-called stepping stone theory—that marijuana use leads to more serious drug abuse (Penning and Barnes 1982).

A recent nationwide survey shows that more than one out of every four youngsters (27 percent) admits using marijuana (Miller et al. 1983). In another national study, 57 percent of the high school seniors reported using marijuana. Of particular concern is the fact that 27 percent of the students had used it in the past month and 6 percent reported daily marijuana use (Johnston et al. 1983).

Much can be learned from surveys about the extent and patterns of use. However, to a large extent, much is still unknown. What do all of the statistics really mean? How can we better understand adolescent drug use?

It has been demonstrated that ethnographic research methods can be employed to obtain a more detailed inside view of drug users. The study method employed is usually participant observation in which a trained observer spends large segments of time observing and interviewing people as they go through their daily routines within the context of their home community (Feldman et al. 1979).

Using ethnographic techniques (field observation) and formal interviews, the authors studied young men and women in a city in New York state for eighteen months, to determine how drugs fit into their daily lives. The similarities and differences between frequent drug users and other adolescents, including family lives, attitudes about drugs, and friendship patterns, were examined. Particular attention was given to heavy drug users, young men and women who reported having used marijuana every day for at least several weeks at a time. These daily users were compared to a random sample (representative of "normal" youths) in the same communities.

In-depth interviews were conducted with 100 subjects 12 to 20 years of age. Forty were randomly selected from the community, another 40 were chosen from field observations which indicated they were routinely involved in drug use (and used marijuana daily), and 20 were youths serving sentences at local juvenile detention facilities, most of whom had also been seriously involved in drug use. The 100 subjects were interviewed confidentially by individuals they came to trust, and interviews usually lasted for five hours or more (over two or three sessions). The investigators tried to "get behind" the statistics and explore the significance of the drug experience for that particular population. The two groups of 40 each are compared below on their drug use patterns and on other characteristics.

Patterns of Drug Use

As expected, it was learned that many youths engage in occasional marijuana and cigarette smoking and drinking. Specifically, 73 percent of the random comparison sample say they drink alcohol, 38 percent use marijuana (76 percent of those high school age or older), and 63 percent smoke cigarettes. All of the daily marijuana users drink alcohol, and all but one smoke cigarettes.

Major differences emerge in the data on heavy marijuana smokers, or those who use drugs other than marijuana. None of the randomly selected youths smokes marijuana daily, and only 23 percent have ever used other drugs, compared to 95 percent of the daily marijuana users. In terms of often abused drugs, 8 percent of the random sample and 55 percent of the daily marijuana users have taken valium (without being prescribed to do so by a physician); 15 percent of the random sample and 68 percent of the daily marijuana users have taken amphetamines ("speed"); and 8 percent of the random sample and 70 percent of the daily marijuana users have tried cocaine.

The literature suggests a standard sequential pattern of the young drug use career (Kandel and Faust 1975; Kandel 1975). This study generally confirms this trend: Nearly all of the drug-using adolescents started with cigarettes and marijuana, with three-fourths beginning with cigarettes, then trying marijuana. After these substances, there is no clear pattern to the next drug used, and several are used within a short time of the first use of the harder drugs. The most common drug choices after marijuana are speed, LSD, and valium, though other drugs are also frequently reported. Typically, the first use of marijuana was during the ages of 12 through 14, with the next drug following within a year's time.

Family Life

In comparison to the random sample, the daily marijuana users far more often come from families which are notably unpredictable from the child's point of view. Usually, this is the result of adults who appear and disappear from the home, or from strife within the family. Most commonly, these youths reported difficulties which stemmed from complications related to their parents' divorces or desertions. An 18-year-old white female told the following story:

A. I think I grew up a little too fast. I was exposed to a lot of different things when I was younger.

Q. Like what?

A. Well, like my mother spent a lot of time bartending, and, there were times, where like, you know, she couldn't get a babysitter or something, I would have to go to work with her. And it wouldn't be like a daytime job, she would bring me anywhere at night. . . . I can remember a couple of afternoons, where I sat in the bar, drinking Cokes and watching all these drunken businessmen and things come in . . .

Q. Do you think your childhood was average?

A. Not really, not with my mother's divorce. I'd lived in 18 different places in 18 years, you know. My stepmother was the mother out of Cinderella, and she hates little kids, and at the time my father got married, I was 5 and she couldn't deal with me at all. We got into wild hassles as I got older. About the time I was 13, and more or less able to take care of myself, we got to be friends. My father and stepmother both came up for graduation, and all of the sudden, some problems are starting up again, between her and I, for some reason.

Like most others who discussed difficult times, this subject did not see herself as coping with troubles by using drugs. Indeed, she thinks her unusual experiences sometimes help her to cope:

A. I've experienced a lot of different things, and sometimes I think I know too much, for being 18. And other times, I think it's been really good for me, because it's going to help me handle anything that might, you know, jump in my way later on . . . I'm going to know a little bit about how to handle it if I've had some kind of experiences like that.

Or consider a 17-year-old white female, whose parents separated when she was five. Soon after, her mother met a musician and frequently travelled with him and took along the children. After that period, the family lived through "extreme poverty, and with no lights and no hot water, and no food, bugs, and lots of nasty things." Earlier than adolescence, she became "very independent."

A. I did not depend on my mother at all. After a certain point I couldn't talk to her, I didn't talk to anybody. I kept everything in and figured it all out myself. . . .

Q. Do you think your childhood was average?

A. No, by no means. . . . My mother was not married, and then she was separated for a long time, and she was young, and she had friends and she went out a lot . . . and we had a lot less money and very much less resources.

Q. How about your adolescence? Do you think your adolescence has been average so far?

A. Yeah . . . because it's maybe a little more intense than everybody else's, but not much more. I grew up a lot faster than everybody; I was always older.

Although their family lives are stressful and often disturbing, few of the daily marijuana users speak of their relationships with parents as generally negative. When asked about such issues, as a group, they gave responses as favorable as those of the random sample, differing primarily in the fact that one parent was more often missing. A typical response from a 14-year-old white male:

Q. How would you describe your relationship with your parents?

A. With my mom, pretty good. With my father, okay, and with my stepmother, there's no relationship.

A 13-year-old white male:

Q. What's your relationship to your parents like?

A. It's good. We understand each other.

Q. Are you closer to one of them than to the other?

A. Closer to my mother.

Q. How come?

A. She raised me and brought me up. My father would never be around.

Another difference between heavier drug users and the random sample, however, is the passion of those negative relationships that do exist between parent and child. Sentiments like the following from an 18-year-old white male were voiced:

Q. How would you describe your relationship with your parents?

A. Well, with my father, real good. With my mother, you know, I'd just rather not know her. She's just been, you know, a bitch for a long time.

Activities important to the youths varied between daily marijuana users and members of the random sample. Although roughly the same percentages report having had good times (even fondest memories) with their families, there are differences in the types of activities reported. When asked to recall the best times of their lives, for example, about one-third of each group mentioned activities with parents. The randomly sampled subjects tended to talk about specific and conventional activities (visiting grandparents, vacations). A 14-year-old white male:

A. Um, we always have a family vacation. And I've always loved taking family vacations. And no matter how far apart, my father works from 7:30 till 6, and then goes back out at night, and I barely ever see him and my mother's working, and my brother is at East State University, and the only person I really see is my sister. And just that two-week vacation brings us together and is really nice.

In contrast, the daily marijuana users recall whole periods of time. Typically, these are when they lived with one rather than the other divorced parent, and engaged in unconventional lifestyles. The 17-year-old white female previously quoted described the best times of her life as follows:

A. Our last year [living] in Canada. When I was 7. My mother had broken up with my father when I was 5, and she got a boyfriend, and when I was 6, her boyfriend, and she really fell in love with him, and it was really a good relationship, except for there was a lot of drugs, and he was a professional guitarist, and all her friends were really cool, really nice people, musical type people. And we'd go for rides, we'd go, she would, she was only 26 at the time, and she was still very young, and so we had more fun.

The nonconventionality they have experienced carries over into their own self-images—many place a high value on being different from "goody-goody" or "brainy" youths at their schools—and into the future. Asked what they will be doing ten years from now, the daily marijuana users frequently talked of having "a job where I will make a lot of money." When pushed by the interviewer to specify the sort of job, 40 percent of the daily marijuana smokers could not do so, and many of those who did respond offered careers such as rock musician or professional basketball player. A 14-year-old black male:

A. I'd say I'd have a nice job. What kind of job? Well, it wouldn't be a job, basketball star, you know. Like to get paid and play basketball for a team.

Even those with more conventional expectations often expressed these in glamorous terms. A 16-year-old white male:

A. I'll be rich, have a nice car, nice fine women in the car, and you got it from there. I don't know; I think I'll be doing pretty good.

Q. But what do you think you'll be doing?

A. I used to think I'd be doing something, now I may be doing something else.

Q. Like what? What's this something you think you might be doing?

A. I want to go into sales management. I thought about it, I might be getting a house this year, and get some houses and rent them out. You make good kinds of money that way.

These are strikingly unlike the conventional responses from randomly sampled youths. A 14-year-old white male:

A. I hope I'll be a teacher. That's what I want to be. I don't know what I'll be like, whether I'll be a teacher by then, but I should be out of college by then.

A 17-year-old black female:

A. Well, what I'm hoping to be like? Well, I want to be a good secretary. I'd like to be an executive secretary. And I want to have a nice place. I don't want to be married. We'll see, 'cause I don't want to get tied down. I don't know why, and I want to have a nice place, a nice car, and that's it. . . .

Similarities among Youths

Despite these differences, daily marijuana users appear to be more like than unlike other youths. Surprisingly, there was little variaton between daily marijuana users and random subjects on a variety of social variables. Consider a few examples:

Slightly more of the daily marijuana users have held jobs than have members of the random sample (25 percent and 18 percent, respectively). Of those who have held jobs, about the same percentages (40 percent and 35 percent, respectively) found the jobs rewarding and say that they expected the experiences would help them in work or careers as adults.

Members of both groups say they have a religious affiliation (83 percent in each group). In fact, more of the daily marijuana users report that their parents emphasized religion to them than did subjects in the random sample (80 percent and 70 percent).

About half of each group have been victims of assault (55 percent of the daily users and 45 percent of the random sample), usually being struck by other youths during arguments, and sometimes being attacked in the streets. Fewer daily marijuana users (20 percent) than randomly selected subjects (45 percent) have had their property stolen.

Beyond these general indicators—and the fact that daily marijuana users come from many socioeconomic and ethnic backgrounds—the study found similarities in attitudes, even about drug abuse. By definition, drugs are part of the daily lives of those subjects who are daily users, and not of those who never or seldom use drugs. Yet few of the daily users view drugs as a *necessary* part of their daily routine. They share with the random sample a desire to avoid "addiction" or "getting hooked" and do not define their present activities as dependency related. Members of both groups hold disdain for those persons (sometimes including their past selves) who need drugs or alcohol to "get through the day," or who "lose control of" or "can't handle" the drugs they use. One 15-year-old white male daily user sums up this overall disdain in his description of a youth nicknamed Larkin, who embodies what both daily users and random subjects refer to as "burnout":

A.   This Larkin, he's really weird, he's like a burnout. I don't like to hang around with him; I don't really hang around with him. I just, you know, get pot from him, get high from him once in a while.

Q.   Well, what do you mean burnout? Why do you call him that?

A.   He's just weird, he's eerie kind of. I'd, he gets high just about every day. And then he owes everybody money. He just owes everybody money, just from everything to do with pot.

Q.   Is it mainly pot, or does he do other things?

A.   He does, he does acid a lot. And—he's just weird.

The daily users as well as the random subjects make a clear distinction between burnouts and themselves. Keeping oneself in control seems to be a major distinguishing factor. Members of neither group show respect for persons who allow themselves to get out of control, nor do they enjoy being out of control themselves. Note the emphasis on maintaining control from a 16-year-old white female from the random sample:

Q.   So, let me see if I have this straight. You never let yourself get out of control.

A.   No.

Q.   And that's intentional on your part?

A.   Um hum.

Q.   Because you don't like the feeling?

A.   Yeah.

Q.   What types of people let themselves get out of control?

A.   Um . . . um . . . Maybe people that don't really care or they care but just um, just want to see how, how they, it can take them I guess.

Q.   What do you mean they don't care about what?

A.   Just things around them. You know, themselves.

Among daily users this theme emerged mainly in arguments for choosing to engage in daily use of one drug over another. Consider the following explanation for nonuse of PCP, given by a 17-year-old white male daily user:

A.   It was scary.

Q.   What was scary about it?

A.   The fact—you know, I just didn't like the fact of, you know, it taking over my body. I like to, I like to kind of be in control and stuff and I wasn't really.

Q.   How about when you get high on regular pot. Do you lose control then, too?

A.   Not usually, no. I'm kind of a, you know . . . just basically slow down.

Q.   So, it's not the same kind of problem, you're not, not-using pot because you're afraid of losing control?

A.   No.

Rules for Drug Use

The daily users and randomly sampled youths differ in their rules for addiction and loss of control. Subjects in the random group choose occasional use or totally refraining from drug use in order to avoid becoming a "druggie" or "burnout." Random subjects proceed with caution with all drugs so as not to get "messed up," "in trouble," or "lose control." Consider the foundation of cautionary rules in the following statements by a 15-year-old black male and a 14-year-old white female, both from the random sample:

Q.   Um, so you have some pretty specific reasons for not using drugs? Which are?

A.   I don't want to mess up my head. I want my friends, and I want my body. Cause I don't want to, I don't want to screw it up.

Q.   Do you think it's really wrong? I mean, obviously, it is against the law, as you said, for kids your age. But other than that, do you think it's bad stuff, too?

A.   I think if you know how to control, I mean, if you don't drink all the time. If you know how to control yourself like, uh, I know some people who drink every week. You know a lot of beer and stuff like that. I don't think that's good. Especially because we're underage.

Q.   Why?

A.   Because they don't have control over themselves to drink that much. You know that's how a lot of crime goes on. They don't know how to control themselves. They drink too much.

The foundation of the random sample's cautionary rules tends to be conventional knowledge about drugs. As in the above quotes, "it's illegal" and "it's dangerous" emerge as concerns. These concerns are rooted more often in indirect experience of marijuana, alcohol, and other drugs than in personal experience. Parents are sometimes the source of knowledge about drugs for members of the random sample. A 15-year-old black female:

Q.   You mentioned before that they've told you it was bad for you, mess up your mind and all. How can you believe them about that?

A.   They're my parents. I think it's my duty to believe what they say to me. Um, if they didn't say it, I don't think I'd believe anybody.

Another form of knowledge, based upon indirect experience, is from seeing others whom the randomly selected subjects don't want to be like or to be associated with. A 13-year-old white male:

Q.   You hang around with those guys at all?

A.   No, no.

Q.   You don't get along with them?

A.   No, not at all.

Q.   Why?

A.   'Cause they do, they're creeps. They drink all the time. They smoke all the time. They'll sit on the corner before and after school and smoke. I don't like them. They're not fun.

The daily users are also cautious about the dangers of what they consider addictive drugs and drugs that could "freak them out" or cause them to lose control. The criteria by which they decide a drug is addictive or might hurt them or make them lose control are also rooted in experiences provided by others, but in addition are based on the daily users' own drug experiences. Note the cautionary rules denoted by a 16-year-old white male and a 15-year-old white female:

Q.   You said you wouldn't try angel dust.

A.   No, not that, I heard too much shit about that stuff.

Q.   Like what?

A.   It makes you crazy and kill yourself.

Q.   O.K., why did you tell him you didn't want to get high with PCP?

A.   Oh, that stuff will kill ya.

Q.   Why do you think it'll kill you?

A.   Cause what I hear, that stuff is pretty potent; you can freak out on that stuff. I don't get into freakin' out.

Although rules such as "that stuff will kill ya" become the explanations for avoiding drugs, such rules are not static. "That stuff will kill ya" is applied by the daily users to anything from airplane glue to LSD. Drugs deemed safe for daily use are viewed as irrelevant to cautionary rules. It is necessary, therefore, to provide ad hoc rules for drugs used daily. These ad hoc rules are part of the subjects' legitimization of their daily use of a particular substance.

In most cases, marijuana is made an exception to the cautionary rules. Two major justifications emerged among daily users.

1. It is normal to smoke pot; everyone smokes. This theme is elaborated by a 16-year-old white male:

A.   I figure, put it this way, here especially at Oxford High, any school, if you're 16, and you haven't partied yet, there's something wrong. 'Cause this is the kind of life that people are living right now, smoking pot.

Q.   Tell me about that, what makes you think that?

A.   It is, man, if you just talk to other people, and you get high with a lot of people, man, you just find out that, there's not, there's maybe one out of twenty people that don't get high.

Q.   Um hum.

A.   And there's those fucking brains and even those brains be getting high later.

2. Pot is mild compared to truly addicting drugs; even if you're hooked on it, it doesn't hurt you. A 14-year-old white female:

Q.   So, what's the difference between getting hooked on marijuana?

A.   'Cause acid you, you can mess your brain up. Marijuana can't. Never did nothing to me.

Similarly a 16-year-old white male makes marijuana an exception:

A.   I usually don't lose my mind when I smoke pot. I still have control over myself, but just feel good. Most people can lose all control. I just feel good.

Q.   Did you kind of lose control with acid?

A.   I lost control; let me tell you.

Note in the above quote the emphasis on control. With marijuana, the daily users argue, they do not lose control. Also, note that not only is marijuana the exception but also "I" am the exception to "most people." This distinguishing factor is referred to by some subjects in terms of "handling it." A drug is viewed as acceptable for daily use if the individual can handle it.

Marijuana is seen by daily users, such as this 15-year-old white female, as something that is easily handled.

A.   Like I do, you can handle it, and I've never gotten in any trouble when I've gotten high and I don't think I ever will.

Any other drug legitimized in this manner can be deemed something they can handle. The subject argues that it is safe because he or she can handle it. In this case, it is the person's inability to handle the drug that is problematic, not the drug itself. Daily users of marijuana see themselves as persons capable of handling marijuana. Part of legitimizing the drug then, for personal and daily use, is making the user responsible for loss of control. With such ad hoc rules, any drug in daily or frequent use can justifiably be made an exception to cautionary rules. As long as "I" can handle it, "I" am not a "burnout." Consider an exchange with a 15-year-old white male:

Q.   So, you say there are some drugs that are pretty dangerous?

A.   Yeah.

Q.   Which ones are they?

A.   The ones I never do. Ha, ha, ha.

Q.   According to this, then that would be angel dust, tranquilizers, and heroin, that's all?

A.   Yup.

That control of usage is not only talked about but also acted upon by daily users is suggested by reports of abstaining (reports which were frequently confirmed through observations of the subjects in their schools, neighborhoods, and hangouts). One youth reports, for instance, that when he is with his girlfriend, he seldom smokes marijuana because he prefers to avoid intoxication while he is with her. Some report that they will not take drugs alone, others will exceed one or two joints per day only at special occasions such as parties or concerts, and many abstain when they wish to be in full control of their motor abilities—such as at athletic events, during examinations, when engaging in criminal activities such as burglaries, or amid phobias (for example, one youth reports a fear of heights that is intensified when he smokes marijuana). Nearly all of the frequent users also report giving up drug usage completely for periods lasting from several days to a few months at a time. They give reasons ranging from side effects such as headaches, hallucinations, or memory difficulties, to financial reasons ("It's too expensive" "Nobody had the money") to scholarship ("I had to buckle down in school"). In short, few subjects in our sample could be considered addicted.

When daily users gave up drug use for periods of time, they also delegitimized the drugs they had been using. Ad hoc rules once used were viewed as invalid. Marijuana or other once-legitimized drugs were no longer seen as an exception to the rules for addiction and loss of control. The delegitimized drug was redefined as harmful, based on a belief system again founded more in personal and direct experience than that of the random sample. A 17-year-old white male and an 18-year-old white female, both daily users of marijuana who decided to quit:

A.   Like I said, you get hooked on pot real bad and you want it and you keep needing it and your body wants it and you'd do anything to get the money for it.

A.   She's [mother] influenced me to stop. She's got a really bad addiction to reefer. And, you know, I, I still, I don't understand why she can't function without smoking every day constantly, and, I don't want that to happen to me. I don't want to become dependent or anything like that.

Friendship Patterns

Beliefs are not maintained in a vacuum. Youths work out and sustain the sorts of views just discussed through interactions with other youths. This study found that youths tend to have friends whose drug use patterns are similar to their own. Those who frequently use drugs have friends who do the same, and occasional users and nonusers also have peers with usage patterns like their own.

But the differences between the groups are not limited to drug use per se. Indeed, the very patterns of friendship appear to be different in comparing the more drug-involved subjects with those from the random sample. Members of the random sample typically reserve the term "friend" for persons who are known by name and who live in their own neighborhood or near their school. Most friends are from their own ethnic and social class background. Usually, they report only a few friends, and almost never more than a dozen. Ties to these friends often go back several years, and almost all randomly sampled youths can identify at least one "best friend."

Daily marijuana users differ on all of these criteria: they refer to large numbers of persons as friends, often cannot list all of their names, mention persons from a larger area and more diverse backgrounds, and make fewer references to "best friends." They also appear to be involved in several peer groups, these varying by activity, whereas members of the random sample are usually in only one group. For instance, one 16-year-old white daily marijuana user identified at least three different groups as "friends": One group is composed of individuals from his immediate neighborhood and that of his school, with whom he "hangs out"; a second consists of persons he has met at a local roller-skating rink, with whom he skates and "parties" at the rink; a third is made up of persons who reside across town, with whom he occasionally will "drink and get rowdy."

A ramification of these differences is the nature of interactions between friends. For the randomly sampled youths, friendship involves regular contact. A friend is someone with whom one has routine and face-to-face relations, which are said to terminate when mutual activities and interests cease. Among the heavier drug users, however, "friend" may be used to describe whole categories of persons similar to oneself in some way, and friends include persons with whom there has been little interaction or with whom contact has been broken. A 16-year-old white male:

Q.   Who do you usually hang out with?

A.   No one, really, I hang around with a lot of different people. There's no one person. Like, someone said that to me: "Who's your best friend?" and I said, "I don't have a best friend." I just hang around with like, Ira, Ivan at school. People at, where I work at: Olivia, and Ann, Eve . . . and Donna, and her boyfriend, Allen. And I usually hang out with whoever I see.

Q.   Do you have a particular group?

A.   No. I'm a popular person at school. Like a lot of people will, like think a lot of me or whatever. . . . I don't know why, but . . . and, I don't know, like I meet people, I just meet people through other people and it is just like, I see them and we get together and, like, later on it ends up we just start hanging out.

Similar activities are different in the two groups. For instance, school is seen as a place not only for learning, but importantly, for being with friends. For the randomly sampled youths, a key component of the school experience is talking with friends. Consider these descriptions of typical school days, by a 15-year-old white male and a 15-year-old black female:

A.   . . . I get, well, I get to school, well, I'm usually there a little early so I go to the library with my friends and we sit there and talk about what happened last night. And after that, I'd be to lunch. Go there to eat and then go to the library. And like do the homework like we've already had. Then, it will be either gym or study hall or typing and then go home.

Q.   Why do you go back to the library after lunch? Why don't you just hang out in the back of something?

A.   It's just too boring.

Q.   It's not boring at the library?

A.   After I get my homework done, it is, but usually there's some friends of mine that we sit at the same table and talk and do our homework.

A.   We just walk in before the bell rings in the morning. Everybody is always talking to each other, so we just go talk to our friends and say hello to everybody. You know when the bell rings you have three minutes, so we all talk in the halls and you see these dudes running down the school. Everybody is just fooling around. Then everybody is calm.

The daily marijuana users also speak of meeting others before and during school, but talking is less often cited as the primary activity, and the group of persons is usually larger. These adolescents emphasize that they get high with peers at school; and they appear to associate with a wider group than the small friendship circle found among the random sample. Consider the following typical day of a 13-year-old white female:

A. . . . Get up—six-thirty, get out and ready and everything. Catch the bus at seven, get there about twenty of eight, and everybody goes on the corner and has their morning cigarette. If somebody has pot, we get high before school.

Q. Does somebody usually have it?

A. Uh-hum. Yeah.

Q. And what happens at lunch?

A. Go there and eat. Go out, either go to the bathroom and have a cigarette, then go out in the back. Back of the school and get high or have another cigarette. That's what happens almost every day.

Several areas were utilized for marijuana smoking at school, despite attempts by school personnel to prevent or interrupt this activity. In each case, an area outside the school building was employed, and smoking also took place in the bathrooms.

Observers anticipated that frequent users took drugs in order to help them cope with school, or to escape from it. However, this appeared true among only a few of the subjects. Instead, drug use for the daily marijuana smoker appears to be a routine part of daily life. A 15-year-old white male describes his day:

A. I get up in the morning, smoke a cigarette, eat, get a phone call from a friend or something, go meet him some place, and usually have my own reefer, smoke a joint on the way or something and get down, probably go buy some beer and then just hang out the rest of the day.

In short, marijuana use for these daily users is an unexceptional activity. It is something they do with other people who also regularly use the drug.

Conclusion

This ethnographic study confirms findings that drug-abusing adolescents have turbulent family lives that go considerably beyond the experiences of other adolescents (Hendin et al. 1981; Brook et al. 1980; Brook et al. 1981). A key factor distinguishing their home environment from those of other youths is nonconventionality. Respondents suggest, however, that these circumstances had positive as well as negative dimensions because they often value nonconventionality, and see their experiences as resulting in skills and independence.

The findings disagree with others (for example, Jessor et al. 1980) in two areas (religion and work experience) where there were only minor differences between daily marijuana users and the random sample. This may have been due, however, to differences in the indicators used.

Young men and women have rules about usage versus addiction. Neither frequent drug users nor randomly sampled youths accept addiction or addicts, and both emphasize the importance of self-control. For the frequent drug user, however, this is seen in terms of choice of drug and of caution where there are perceived dangers from drug use.

Frequent users report larger and less intimate friendship groups than do other youths, and this is commensurate with findings of greater social isolation and normlessness among drug users (Paton and Kandel 1978; Miranne 1981), less overall interaction in groups of persons who are intoxicated on marijuana (Babor et al. 1978), and poorer interpersonal skills among marijuana users (Janowsky et al. 1979).

That few daily marijuana users appear to use drugs as a way of coping with school is consistent with findings that long-term marijuana use does not result in major impairment of intellectual function (Knights and Grenier 1976; Weckowicz et al. 1977). Instead, the use of marijuana appears to be tied to ambivalence about conventional goals, commitment to adventurousness, and to the ability of marijuana to serve as a social lubricant in facilitating interaction in groups.

Marijuana is used primarily to get high, to have a good time with friends, and to relieve boredom. Given these functions, it is not surprising that marijuana becomes an integral part of the daily lives of those who use it on a regular basis.

References

Babor, T.F.; Mendelson, J.H.; Gallant, D.; and Keuhnle, J.C. 1978. Interpersonal behavior in group discussion during marijuana intoxication. *The International Journal of the Addictions* 13(1):89–102.

Brook, J.S.; Whiteman, M.; and Gordon, A.S. 1981. The role of the father in his son's marijuana use. *Journal of Genetic Psychology* 138:81–86.

Brook, J.S.; Gordon, A.S.; and Brook, D.W. 1980. Perceived paternal relationships, adolescent personality, and female marijuana use. *The Journal of Psychology* 105:277–285.

DuPont, R. 1979. Marijuana: A review of the issues regarding decriminalization legalization. In Beschner, G. and Friedman, A. (eds), *Youth Drug Abuse.* Lexington, Massachusetts: Lexington Books.

Farley, E.; Santo, Y.; and Speck, D. 1979. Multiple drug abuse patterns of youths in treatment. In Beschner, G. and Friedman, A. (eds), *Youth Drug Abuse*. Lexington, Massachusetts: Lexington Books.

Feldman, H.; Agar, M.; and Beschner, G. 1979. *Angel Dust: An Ethnographic Study of PCP Users*. Lexington, Massachusetts: Lexington Books.

Hendin, H.; Pollinger, A.; Ulman, R.; and Carr, A. 1981. *Adolescent Marijuana Abusers and Their Families*. Washington, D.C.: NIDA Research Monograph 40.

Janowsky, D.S.; Clopton, P.L.; Leichner, P.P.; Abrams, A.A.; Judd, L.L.; and Pechnick, R. 1979. Interpersonal effects of marijuana. A model for the study of interpersonal psychopharmacology. *Archives of General Psychiatry* 36(7):781–785.

Jessor, R.; Chase, J.A.; and Donovan, J.E. 1980. Psychosocial correlates of marijuana use and problem drinking in national sample of adolescents. *American Journal of Public Health* 70(6):604–613.

Johnston, L.; Bachman, J.; and O'Malley, P. 1983. *Student Drug Use, Attitudes, and Beliefs*. Rockville, Maryland: NIDA.

Kandel, D., and Faust, R. 1975. Sequence and stages in patterns of adolescent drug use. *Archives of General Psychiatry* 32 (7):923–932.

Kandel, D.B.; 1975. Stages of adolescent involvement in drug use. *Science* 190:912–914.

Knights, R.M., and Grenier, M.L. 1976. Problems in studying the effects of chronic cannibis use on intellectual abilities. *Annals of the New York Academy of Sciences* 282:307–312.

Macdonald, D. 1984. Drugs, Drinking, and Adolescence. *American Journal of Diseases of Children* 138:117–125.

Miller, J.; Cisin, I.; Gardner-Keaton, H.; Harrell, A.; Wirtz, P.; Abelson, H.; and Fishbourne, P. 1983. *National Survey on Drug Abuse: Main Findings 1982*. Rockville, Maryland: National Institute on Drug Abuse: DHHS Publication No. (ADM) 83–1262.

Miranne, A.C. 1981. Marijuana use and alienation: A multivariate analysis. *The International Journal of the Addictions* 16(4):697–707.

Paton, S.M., and Kandel, D.B. 1978. Psychological factors and adolescent illicit drug use: Ethnicity and sex differences. *Adolescence* 13(50):187–200.

Penning, M. and Barnes, G. 1982. Adolescent Marijuana Use: A Review. *The International Journal of the Addictions* 17(5):749–791.

Petersen, R. 1980. *Marijuana: Research Findings*. Washington, D.C.: NIDA Research Monograph 31:120–132.

Schnoll, S. 1979. Pharmacological Aspects of Youth Drug Abuse. In Beschner, G. and Friedman, A. (eds), *Youth Drug Abuse*, Lexington, Massachusetts: Lexington Books.

Weckowicz, T.E.; Collier, G.; and Spreng, L. 1977. Field dependence, cognitive functions, personality traits, and social values in heavy cannabis users and nonuser controls. *Psychological Reports* 41:291–302.

7
Services for Adolescent Substance Abusers

Stanley Kusnetz

We just discovered that our child is using drugs. What do we do? Where can we turn for help? Who in the community will help us? These questions have a familiar and often futile ring. Parents who discover that their child is using drugs are likely to be confused and not to know how to respond or where to turn for help. Even trained professionals such as physicians, teachers, and clergy often have difficulty counseling these families and/or directing them to someone who can give them guidance.

In seeking professional assistance for a youngster with a drug problem there are many ways to proceed. Where to begin depends, of course, upon a number of factors, including the kinds of resources available in the community and the personal preferences of each family. Not to be overlooked is the importance of seeking assistance in a rational manner, knowing what potential resources are available and what questions to ask. Just as all physical illnesses are not the same and are not treated alike, "drug problems" are also different from one another and need to be diagnosed and assessed so that the most appropriate course of treatment can be determined. One cannot assume that because a youngster appears to have a "drug problem" he or she should simply be sent to a program that specializes in treating "drug problems." The problem is almost always more complex.

Diagnosis of the problem is essential in order to determine its extent and parameters. The various treatment agencies in the community must also be assessed in relation to the type and extent of treatment offered. It is important to find out what types of youngsters particular agencies are most successful in treating, and conversely, which youngsters do not benefit from the services provided by particular agencies. The following questions should be answered:

What are an agency's strengths and weaknesses?

To what extent are the parents involved?

What happens when a youngster completes the program?

Is followup or after care provided?

How much does the program cost?

If the youngster had a physical illness, it is likely that parents would know where to go to get help. They would expect a physician or another medical specialist to diagnose the youngster's problem and recommend a course of treatment. Unfortunately, few resources exist for the diagnosis and assessment of adolescent drug abuse and fewer still for the objective assessment of available treatment programs. Faced with the gap between what is needed and what is available, the concerned parent must be resourceful and willing to make a special effort in seeking resources and information. As parents attempt to locate the best possible services for their child, they should employ some of the same techniques they use in finding other types of information. The purpose of this chapter is to provide practical information about the kinds of treatment resources and services available to adolescent substance abusers and their families. The following are some of the possible sources of information and help that may be available.

Possible Resources

Family Physician

The family physician is usually the best first contact for the family. The physician should examine the youngster, after which the parents should be provided with an assessment of the problem. Some youngsters will confide in the family physician. However, not all physicians are adequately trained to treat drug abusers or knowledgeable enough about the resources available to make a recommendation for a particular drug problem. A recent study conducted by the American Medical Association shows that only 27 percent of the physicians polled felt competent to treat alcoholism (Kennedy 1985). Therefore, parents must be specific in questioning the doctor. If he/she cannot provide clear answers, they should ask for a referral to someone who can. Sometimes even though a doctor is not trained in this area, he/she will know of someone who specializes in treating adolescent substance abusers.

Clergy

Members of the clergy who have had the necessary training are often capable of helping families involved in a drug crisis. Some have had special training in pastoral counseling, including courses in psychology and counseling. Whether a family wishes to consult a clergyman will depend on how well they know him and the degree of confidence they have in him. One must be aware that some youngsters may relate well to the clergy, while others may not. As with the physician, if a clergyman cannot provide clear answers, referral should be sought to someone who can.

Friends

Parents may receive some help by talking about the situation with trusted friends and relatives. This source may be especially helpful if their friends or relatives have had drug problems in their own families. They may be able to recommend particular resources or people who can help. However, parents must be discreet in their choice of friends or neighbors in whom they confide. Friends and their children may gossip and this indiscretion could worsen the situation for the youngster and the family. It is also important to realize that the fact that a friend or relative has had a successful experience with a treatment program does not necessarily mean that the same program is appropriate for the youngster in question.

The Yellow Pages

The yellow pages of a telephone directory provide a list of potential treatment resources. Both evaluation and treatment resources may be listed under such headings as *Drug Abuse Addiction, Alcoholism, Information and Treatment, Substance Abuse, Counseling, Mental Health,* or *Psychological Services.* The listings may vary from one community to another but one or more of the above listings should be available in any yellow pages directory. After calling and making contact, parents can explain their needs and set up an appointment to learn more about specific programs.

The School Counselor

It is common for a youngster's drug problem to be discovered in school since school personnel see so much of the youngster and are in a good position to assess changes in behavior. Any trained guidance counselor, familiar with available community treatment resources and drug treatment programs, should be helpful in locating an appropriate treatment program for a drug abuser. Because the school's guidance counselor is likely to have had experience with a number of community resources, he or she may be particularly helpful in providing guidance as to the kinds of youngsters the various programs work for best.

Hotlines

Emergency telephone services that operate twenty-four hours a day are located in some cities and towns. Here, trained volunteers or paid staff take calls and make appropriate referrals. Calling an emergency hotline during a crisis can be an excellent beginning in approaching the problem of teenage drug abuse. To discover whether your area has a hotline, consult your local telephone directory or call the information operator.

Community Mental Health Clinics (CMHC)

Many parts of the United States are served by mental health clinics, usually under the auspices of the county or local government. These clinics offer a variety of services related to mental health and often offer services for drug and alcohol abuse. Typically, a mental health clinic with a substance abuse program will offer one or more of the following services:

Drug and alcohol information
Community education programs
Prevention and intervention programs in the community
Individual counseling
Group counseling
Family counseling
Drug use assessment
Crisis intervention
Referral

The counselors in a community health clinic, often knowledgeable about local treatment resources, can be very helpful to the parents in formulating a plan for the assessment and treatment of the youngster's problem. Nearly all CMHCs charge a fee, but these invariably are on a sliding scale. Most CMHCs are eligible for third-party insurance reimbursement.

State Drug/Substance Agency

If it is difficult to identify adolescent treatment services locally or to determine where to go for help from the sources listed here, parents can contact the state agency responsible for coordinating drug and alcohol treatment programs. These agencies, which exist in every state, are able to identify local treatment facilities and provide information about the suitability of these programs for particular individuals. A directory of state agencies, which includes their addresses and telephone numbers, is provided in the appendix at the end of this chapter.

Types of Services

Short-Term Inpatient Crisis Interventions

Some hospitals have established "chemical dependency units" to treat individuals who have had serious reactions to drugs or had overdose reactions. Depending on the problem, hospitalization may be required for a period of only a few days or may be necessary for several weeks. When treatment is completed, there is often followup counseling available, usually through the hospital's social services department, or a referral may be made to other modes of treatment for continued care and counseling. Costs are based upon the particular hospital's fee schedule and billing practices.

One impetus to the development of hospital-based drug abuse intervention was the upsurge in the illicit use of phencyclidine (PCP) in the middle and late 1970s when many youngsters required emergency inpatient treatment. PCP-induced psychotic episodes, resulting from high concentrations of PCP, are common in cities where this drug is sold (Lerner and Burns 1979). Hospitals often become the first line of treatment in those areas where PCP use has been common.

Inpatient Programs

These are usually hospital-based programs offering a greater variety of treatment services than crisis intervention and detoxification. Most of them provide both psychiatric and medical services. A typical inpatient program includes diagnosis of the severity of the youngster's drug abuse problem, individual, group, and family counseling and behavior modification. These programs are most appropriate for the youngster with dual psychiatric/drug abuse or medical/drug abuse problems requiring a controlled environment. Many inpatient programs for adolescent substance abusers are located in closed (locked) wards in a hospital. Youngsters referred to this type of facility are usually beyond the control of their parents. Because the hospital-based inpatient program is relatively brief (two months is average), further treatment in another mode is usually required after discharge. Since these programs are quite costly ($300 to $500 per day is not uncommon) third-party insurance coverage is usually necessary.

Outpatient Programs

These programs range from completely unstructured "drop-in" or teen "rap" centers located in store fronts to highly structured programs (Smith et al. 1979). They may be run by a municipal or state agency (as is the case with those programs affiliated with community mental health centers), or by organizations such as the YMCA or other privately run organizations. Some of these programs are free, but most have a fee for service, usually on a sliding scale. All of these programs offer at least one and often a number of the following services: individual counseling, group counseling, family counseling, educational services, remediation, vocational testing, vocational counseling, post-discharge followup, and, when appropriate, referral to other modes of treatment. A youngster will usually attend this type of program one or more times per week, spending one to three hours at each session, for periods ranging from several months to two or more years. Most (82.5 percent) adolescent substance abusers are treated in outpatient programs (NIDA 1983).

Day Care Programs

The youngster attends this type of program for more than four hours a day, usually five to seven days per week. Day care programs usually combine the elements of outpatient programs with additional or expanded rehabilitation services such as remediation, drug abuse education, recreation, and more extensive group and individual activities than can be offered in an outpatient program. As in outpatient programs, fees are usually based on a sliding scale, and a youngster can expect to spend from several months to two years, depending on the program and the youngster's needs.

Residential Treatment Programs (Other than Therapeutic Community)

Residential programs are generally structured to take the young substance abuser away from the environment where he/she uses drugs and away from the family in conflict. They attempt to provide a new, more wholesome environment where the youngster can learn more about his/her behavior, the potential consequences of this behavior, and why and how it should be modified. These programs, which generally vary from two to twelve months in length (some longer), are not as structured as therapeutic communities. Typically, such programs stress individual and group counseling, educational activities, recreation, and drug education. Many, particularly those located in rural areas, offer outdoor or wilderness experience incorporating a degree of challenge that requires cooperative behavior. The better of these programs, especially the shorter term ones, offer an extended period of aftercare consisting of periodic group and/or individual counseling. Parental involvement is often required during a youngster's stay in the program. These programs often organize self-help peer groups. Residential programs can cost up to $8,000 per month, so that third-party insurance coverage is often necessary.

Therapeutic Communities

TCs represent a process as well as a type of residential treatment and are *not* recommended for everyone. Less than 15 percent of all TC admissions graduate from treatment and over half leave treatment before 90 days (De Leon 1984). Most TCs are highly structured, non-permissive, drug-free residential settings, which serve as social learning systems. While there is wide variation from facility to facility, the daily regimen of the TC is intensive and includes encounter groups, group therapy, and/or counseling, tutorial learning sessions, remedial and formal education classes, residential job functions (cooking, cleaning, painting, repairs) and, in the last stages of treatment, provides employment in a regular occupation for clients who may then live outside the TC. Length of stay in TCs may vary from six to eighteen months and is often based on client needs and progress. Costs can be minimal or can range up to several thousand dollars per month, depending upon the facility.

Youngsters who can gain maximum benefit from the TC treatment approach are those who show antisocial or delinquent behavior (acting out, getting into fights with others, stealing, petty larceny). The TC provides a controlled structure where negative behaviors are not tolerated. TCs emphasize the setting of limits and promote development of the ability to make competent decisions.

Host Treatment Services

The "host" approach is founded on the principle of peer pressure. When a youngster enters the program, he/she is usually away from home for a minimum of fourteen days. The youngster is placed in the home of a peer who is further along in the rehabilitation process. The youngster attends programs at the agency during the day and goes to the host home at night to sleep. After the new client progresses in the rehabilitation program, his/her home may then become a host home and the youngster will be allowed to return to it while continuing to attend the program during the day. The average stay in these host programs is approximately one year. Costs are similar to those of other residential treatment programs.

Religious Treatment Programs

Some programs have treatment philosophies based upon religious principles. Supported by churches and clergymen, these programs are usually concerned with physical, mental, and social aspects of well-being, as well as having a major emphasis on "spiritual aspects." The treatment methods used are similar to those described for other settings. They aim to redirect a youngster through an intense learning experience that includes counseling, group therapy, recreation, education, and parent involvement. In addition, they attempt to help youngsters "develop a positive relationship with God." One of the largest treatment programs of this or any other type is Teen Challenge, a Christian organization with more than eighty independent treatment units. Costs are variable, depending upon the program and its sponsorship.

The Halfway House

Many communities support a halfway house as an alternative for those who may need to be housed in a location (with strict supervision) away from their own homes. The adolescent may be in school or work during the day or part of the day and return to the halfway house during the afternoon and evening where he/she will have meals and sleep. Halfway houses usually have small capacities (fifteen to twenty-five people), and while the length of stay will vary, the range of time in this setting is from one to four months. The halfway house is often used as a transition from a therapeutic community to the outside community or in conjunction with outpatient therapy. Costs vary according to how the halfway house is sponsored.

School-based Intervention

Some school systems have established special education programs for students who have been identified as substance abusers. These programs combine education with counseling, and for the most part, fit the middle ground between primary prevention and early intervention with youngsters who are beginning to have serious problems as a result of their drug use.

School systems are in an excellent position to help adolescent substance abusers. The school, first and foremost, is where the youngsters, except for dropouts, are for a significant part of their day. Additionally, schools have considerable control over the information that youngsters receive as well as influence over their attitudes.

Many school-based treatment programs do not require students to be drug free at the time they enter the program. These programs find it more advantageous to require young drug abusers (1) to be honest about the drugs they are using and (2) to work with counselors to reduce drug use and ultimately become drug free. Other school-based programs allow youngsters a certain amount of time to become drug free. However, these approaches are not readily accepted by many schools since illicit drug use is a criminal offense.

Alternative Activity Programs

Alternative activity programs are based on the principle that individuals will discontinue drug use when they find satisfaction and fulfillment from other sources. Any wholesome activity will do as long as the youngsters remain interested. The entire range of other possibilities for personal satisfaction can be considered when seeking alternatives. Single or related groupings of alternative activities when formalized comprise an alternative activity program.

One of the best known and widely replicated alternative programs is "Channel One," which was derived from an effort called the Gloucester (Massachusetts) Experiment. A grass-roots effort, it provides alternatives to drugs with an "emphasis on skill building." For example, students involved in the Gloucester Experiment built their own community resource center and completed an ambitious restoration of historical gravesites in the area.

Overview of Treatment Approaches

After finding out what kind of services exist, the next question might be: Which one is right for a particular youngster? The answer will depend largely on the problem the child is having, how long he or she has been on drugs, the type of drug(s) used, and personality traits. Unfortunately, however, a decision may have to be made based upon program availability. Outside of major urban areas there are few programs to choose from. Unless an inpatient or residential program is clearly called for, one may have to make do with what is available. Parents should check with other programs in the area and, if possible, visit more than one to get a better idea of the alternatives available.

All treatment programs have some form of initial interview. At this time parents learn more about the program's actual treatment setting and whether or not their youngster is right for the program. During the intake interview, rules, regulations, and goals of the program are described. It is important for parents to ask questions and, along with the staff member and youth involved, decide whether this program is appropriate. Parents should make sure they understand (1) what is being described; (2) what the costs will be; (3) the length of the program; (4) obligations for parents; as well as (5) the child's responsibilities.

Whatever treatment program a child enters, parents will most likely also be expected to attend counseling sessions. The emphasis on family is often crucial to the youngster's program. Good treatment programs all have one thing in common: they require *hard work on everyone's part*. The adolescent cannot do it alone. The parent cannot do it alone. The treatment program alone cannot make the difference. The adolescent, parent, and treatment program must work cooperatively.

A Closer Look at Nine Drug Treatment Programs

Most drug treatment programs are directed to older drug abusers who are addicted or debilitated (Blum and Richards 1979). In order to provide a better view of how typical adolescent drug treatment programs function and whom they serve, nine adolescent programs, identified as "good" programs by state authorities, are presented below. The programs do not by any means represent the entire range of adolescent drug treatment, but are presented in order to provide a background against which other programs can be seen and to offer a better understanding of some of the ways youngsters are treated for drug abuse. Although diverse in many ways, these programs share much in common. With two exceptions, the adolescent drug treatment programs presented are small, half of them serving thirty or fewer youngsters. Ages of youngsters served range from 11 to about 19 years of age. Most of the programs described have a preponderance of male clients, with Caucasians making up the greater proportion of those served. With one exception, all of the programs primarily serve their local areas (towns, cities, counties). The vast majority of the youngsters seen in these programs are multiple drug users, with alcohol and marijuana being the prime substances of abuse. Although fees charged vary considerably, ranging from zero to more than $800 per day, all programs are structured so that their services can be affordable through the use of a sliding fee scale based on need, third-party insurance, or a combination of both. All programs charging a fee claim that special arrangements can be made for the treatment of indigent clients.

Although there are many differences in the services offered, there are also many similarities. All of the programs presented make extensive use of group counseling. All programs also provide individual therapy and/or counseling. To some extent, all programs require parental and/or familial involvement at some point in the therapy process. Since these nine programs, like most adolescent drug treatment programs, have not been formally evaluated, it is not possible to determine their effectiveness in treating particular kinds of youngsters. Therefore, we can get only a general view of the programs, whom they serve, in what ways they serve, who they feel are served best and whom they have difficulty serving, or believe they serve least well.

Palmer Drug Abuse Program

The Palmer Drug Abuse Program, located in Houston, Texas, is an outpatient program with day care center capability. The basic service provided is counseling on an outpatient basis. However, there are satellite centers where clients can "come and hang out during the day and meet other people in the program." Palmer Drug Abuse Programs can be found in Texas, New Mexico, Arizona, California, Colorado, and Oklahoma. New centers are planned for Detroit, St. Louis, and Pittsburgh. Although distinctive in its own right, much of the Palmer Drug Abuse Program is patterned after Alcoholics Anonymous.

Approximately 95 percent of the clients reside in the city of Houston and its surrounding county. Youngsters from outside this area can be accepted, providing suitable living arrangements are made privately by the client. Three to four percent of the client population are from other areas of Texas and elsewhere in the United States, and approximately one percent is from outside of the United States. Most clients are self-referred or referred by family and friends. A small percentage are referred by various social agencies and the juvenile justice system. There are no charges made to either the youngster or the family. The criterion for entry to the Palmer Drug Abuse Program is only "the desire to live a chemically free life."

Program Philosophy. The program is structured around twelve phases or steps which are drawn from Alcoholics Anonymous. It is classifed as a self-help group program built upon client participation and interaction. In the words of the Palmer Drug Abuse Program director, "We try to encourage them [clients] to realize that God as you understand him is a force, or can be a force in your life. Our goal is to help people overcome chemical dependency, maintain sobriety, and live constructive lives without the use of chemicals." Program goals include motivating and encouraging teenagers to help them rebuild and replace lost confidence and thus increase self-esteem. "The drugs are a symptom of other problems. Children who take drugs generally have limited coping ability. Our role is to try and help youngsters to figure out and learn how to deal with the problems that they are facing, and how to enjoy life without the use of chemicals."

Most counselors in the drug abuse programs are former drug abusers who have recovered either through Palmer or some other self-help program. Approximately half of the counselors in the program are certified by the state of Texas as drug and alcohol abuse counselors.

Program Description. In the initial interview, a counselor will try to determine the youngster's level of motivation for change. The youngster is encouraged to participate in a series of weekly meetings as well as counseling sessions. In the first, as well as subsequent sessions, the youngster's problems are assessed in order to determine whether he/she is appropriate for the program or has needs that the program is not equipped to handle. If the latter is the case, there will be an attempt to make an appropriate referral.

The length and depth of an individual's program participation is based upon his/her needs and desires. Most clients stay involved for at least one year. A small percentage of clients has been involved for more than one year.

The Palmer Drug Abuse Program also organizes parent groups. The program director states, "When you are treating an adolescent substance abuser you must recognize that his or her problems involve the entire family. It is important to involve the family and we do." Many of the parents have their own substance abuse problems.

Under certain circumstances group counseling sessions will be held with parents and child. Parent meetings usually take place at the same time as the teenagers' meetings. As with the teenagers' meetings, the parent meetings are voluntary and anonymous. Parents also can receive individual counseling. All parents are expected to be involved in the program. "We won't say your teenager cannot come if you won't. We encourage involvement but not to the point where a youngster would not come because we push it too strongly. Basically, we expect parents to attend because they are part of the problem."

Who Does Best/Worst. The kind of client who does best in the Palmer Drug Abuse Program is the one who recognizes that he/she has a problem and is motivated to follow the structure provided. "It is the person looking for help, looking for some individuals to give him/her assistance." Older clients do better than the younger teenagers because "they have had more time to experience the negative consequences of drug abuse." The client who does the worst is the one who is "just not ready for help." Included among the clients who do poorly are those who are severely depressed and those who are unable to handle structured situations or are unwilling to take direction. Since this is a voluntary program, a youngster can stop treatment at any time. The youngsters who drop out early and present the most serious challenge are inhalant abusers and members of ethnic minorities. (It is felt by program staff that the latter is the case because of the overwhelming number of Caucasians in the program.) Youngsters whose families will not cooperate in treatment generally don't do well.

Bridgeback

Bridgeback, an outpatient program located in Los Angeles, California, serves approximately thirty youngsters at one time. Although the program is located in a juvenile justice center, youngsters can be referred from other sources.

Clients come to Bridgeback from a variety of sources: self-referral, other programs and agencies, the school system, and community groups. Most, however, come through court order, which makes about 80 percent of all referrals. The clients all come from Los Angeles. The program does not accept youngsters diagnosed as psychotic, more than mildly retarded, or those in immediate need of detoxification services. In these latter cases, appropriate referrals are made.

Although Bridgeback has a sliding fee scale, clients who cannot afford to pay are not charged. The program receives almost all of its financial support from the county.

Program Philosophy. According to the Bridgeback director, "One learns from those with whom one identifies. The program tries to provide role models, those young men and women who have acquired the emotional resources which have allowed them to respond constructively to the everyday pressures of life. The program attempts to guide clients by helping them search for and examine basic beliefs, attitudes, and habits."

Program Description. Client visits are scheduled on an average of twice a week, during which time the youngster participates in either group or individual counseling. A parent awareness group provides parents an opportunity to speak openly about their concerns and problems. The goal of these groups is to help parents learn how best to communicate with their children. Although parental participation is encouraged, it is not required. The staff consists of a supervisor, intake worker, and two counselors. Although a counseling degree is not essential to function as Bridgeback staff, extensive experience in counseling is a requirement.

Who Does Best/Worst. The youngster who does best is "one who wants to change. Those who recognize that they have a problem and sincerely want to correct it." Bridgeback staff do not feel that age, sex, or race has any bearing upon how well a person does in this program, although the younger clients improve more slowly because of their relative lack of life experience. The clients who do the worst are those with histories of violence, extensive drug usage, gang affiliation, and deep immersion in the drug culture.

Northwest Youth Outreach

Northwest Youth Outreach, a project of the YMCA in Metropolitan Chicago, was started in 1959 as an effort to work with youth in the northwest side of Chicago. Because of emergency needs, the program eventually focused on adolescent drug and alcohol abuse. This outreach and outpatient program provides a variety of resources to youths and their families. The program services approximately 340 young people residing in an area of approximately 60 square miles with a population of one and a half million people.

Clients of the Northwest Youth Outreach program are recruited from the surrounding neighborhood and community. The primary service area is Northwest Chicago and its surrounding suburbs, including two large adjoining townships.

The major point of entry to the program is through outreach activities conducted in the community. Northwest Outreach has two outreach teams comprised of five or six members who spend a portion of each day in the community at places where youngsters hang out: schoolyards, cafeterias, snack shops, parks, and street corners. When an outreach worker recognizes that a particular youngster appears to have a drug problem, he/she will try to form a relationship with that youngster and try to move the youngster into the formal structure of the treatment regime.

Community agencies also make referrals to the program. The director states, "Funded by a child welfare agency, we have referral mechanisms with the police, criminal justice system, mental health agencies, and the schools." The Northwest Youth Outreach program accepts youngsters both before and after court adjudication.

There are no fees charged for particpation in the program. However, participating families are asked for donations.

Program Philosophy. Northwest Youth Outreach is a community-based treatment program which reaches out and attracts youngsters in need of service without stigmatizing or labelling them. Chemical dependency is seen as a primary problem. The program believes that youngsters should be treated in their community so that comprehensive services can be provided not only to the youngster but also to those around him/her, including friends and family as well as systems such as school and police that affect him/her. Youngsters are given opportunities to participate in recreational activities and leadership training activities. The programs are oriented to develop self-awareness and social, coping, and problem-solving skills.

Program Description. Outreach is the key service provided by Northwest Outreach. According to the program director, "Outreach is a case-finding service, but it can also be seen as a direct treatment. What takes place in the informal setting is the same type of activity that takes place during individual counseling. Some of the best individual counseling takes place in someone's car or in the park." The outreach services is used to engage youngsters in treatment and to develop relationships between treatment staff and youth.

Approximately 70 percent of the youngsters in the formalized treatment program participate in some form of group. When a youngster is seen through an agency referral, the family must participate in an assessment process for at least one session. At any one time, 20 percent of the client population are involved in family therapy. Additionally, all youngsters are required to participate in individual counseling. Seventy percent of those in the program also participate in a recreational therapy program. Typically a youngster spends thirty to thirty-six weeks in the formal program with an additional four to six months of after care.

The treatment regime has four levels. Upon entry into the formal program, youngsters receive five consecutive weeks of education which include pharmacological aspects of substance abuse, disease concepts, family issues, and an introduction to self help. The second level, which lasts for six to twelve weeks, is a "discovery phase in which the youngster becomes aware of his/her alcohol and drug use through education and through individual meetings with a counselor." The program does a comprehensive assessment of the youngster. The youngster becomes familiar with the program and involved with other activities including those at drop-in centers.

In the third level, the abstinence phase, youngsters are encouraged to participate in self-help groups including Alcoholics Anonymous and Narcotics Anonymous and to participate more intensively in recreation and counseling groups. During level 2 they come to accept abstinence as a goal. At the same time, parents become involved in their own support groups. Northwest Outreach runs two parent group programs, one modeled after Tough Love, the other modeled after Families Anonymous. In level 4 the program focuses on other life skills that need to be developed. The staff works on decreasing the youngster's dependence on the program. "If he is involved in social and recreational activities, he now is involved as a leader. He begins helping other youngsters who are at a lower level of treatment." At the end of level 4, the youngster and members of his/her family or significant others participate in an achievement banquet. At any time during the program if a youngster should backslide or drop out but want to reenter the program, he/she may, most likely at a lower level.

The program's outreach staff need not be fully professionally trained or even have college degrees. However, they must be certified as either alcohol or drug abuse counselors. Staff who participate in the more formalized part of the treatment program generally have a minimum of two to three years' experience. Some are professionally trained social workers or persons with master's degrees in related fields.

Who Does Best/Worst. The Northwest Outreach staff feels that the youngster who is a chronic user and is invested in the drug culture is easier to work with than one who is not. "It is much easier for them to see the consequences of their use." Youngsters who do worst generally have had prior treatment involvements and are "treatment-wise." Some have been in and out of different outpatient and residential programs. "These are the type of kids who know the therapeutic talk, who know how to act in a therapeutic setting. They will frequently attempt to sabotage their own treatment or the treatment of others."

Northwest Outreach staff recognizes and expects that a good percentage of youngsters will drop out of the program for a period of time. Sometimes a youngster will reenter three or four times until he/she is ready to confront the issues seriously.

Corner House

Corner House is an outpatient program located in Princeton, New Jersey, a university town containing numerous corporate headquarters. The primary service area of Corner House is Mercer County. Ninety-two percent of all clients come from the city/county area with the remaining eight percent from within the state. The largest number of clients are self-referred or referred by family. Corner House also accepts referrals from community agencies and the juvenile justice system.

Clients are charged a sliding fee scale of between $1 and $50 per counseling hour. The fee charged depends upon income and the number of children in the family.

Program Philosophy. The goal of Corner House is to "provide caring and professional individual, family, and group counseling to adolescents and young adults." Drug and alcohol use is seen as essentially a symptom of a larger problem which is often buried deeply within the family. One of the first goals of staff is to establish a basis of trust in which the youngster can see that a problem exists and that something can be done about it. Much of the counseling concerns personal responsibility, values, and decision making. "The counselor strives to establish a feeling of trust and on that trust to establish motivation for treatment."

Program Description. Corner House is essentially an outpatient counseling program. All counselors are certified social workers. Additionally, there is a psychiatrist on the Corner House staff. Clients participate in individual as well as group counseling, and families are strongly encouraged to participate in family counseling sessions. Indeed, in cases where the staff considers it vital, family participation is a requirement of treatment. Typically, a client remains in the program for a period of three to eight months, although there are clients who remain as long as two to three years. If it appears that there is a serious psychiatric problem such as depression, the potential client will be referred to the staff psychiatrist for a diagnostic session. "If it is determined that a client is beyond our capabilities, he/she will be referred to an appropriate facility." Corner House does not accept clients who require detoxification. Referral services are considered an essential part of the program.

It is not an absolute requirement that a client be drug free at the time of discharge from the program. The counselors at Corner House look for improvement over a period of time in clients' ability to make responsible decisions for themselves, including decisions about using drugs or alcohol. It is recognized that some clients will backslide into drug usage, and in that case they can be readmitted the program.

Who Does Best/Worst. Corner House prefers to begin working with clients before they are heavily involved in drug usage. Motivation for change is recognized as the key to success. Since a large number of clients are self-referred, Corner House gets more highly motivated clients than other programs. Clients referred by parents, schools, or the juvenile justice system tend to be poorly motivated. The initial treatment goal is to establish a basis of trust and get the clients to see "that there is a problem and that something can be done about it."

The client who does best is "the one who is best motivated to control his/her drug use." For example, a youngster may be depressed because of family and/or school pressures and may begin to drink or use drugs, but may also be essentially concerned about working out the personal problem already recognized.

To a large extent success "depends on how involved an individual is in the drug culture. . . . Generally, the longer a person has been on any drug, the more likely it will be that we will have difficulty in working with him and the more time he will have to spend in the program."

Woodbridge Action for Youth

The Woodbridge Action for Youth, located in Woodbridge, New Jersey, contains an outpatient unit, an adolescent unit, and a prevention unit. The program is located in a blue-collar town that is undergoing change. The adolescents seen at this program are essentially from the older neighborhoods.

On a typical day, the Woodbridge Action for Youth day care program treats fifteen adolescents between the ages of 14 and 18. Fifty percent of those treated are from the township and 50 percent from the county and other areas of New Jersey that are within commuting distance.

The day care program charges are on a sliding scale ranging from $1 to $100 a week. Approximately 85 percent of all clients pay less than $15 a week for care. Under certain circumstances, the fee is waived entirely.

Program Philosophy. Woodbridge Action for Youth focuses on drug-related problems: interference with school, family, social lives, and the law. Abstinence is not required as a criterion for being in the program. The program director states, "We do accept the fact that at some point in their lives, clients may be able to drink recreationally. We are really not so strict in terms of abstinence as other programs, primarily because we can only see them for five hours a day . . . we can only control them for a certain amount of time. We work towards abstinence, but it is not a requirement to stay in the program."

Program Description. Clients, who come to the program for a total of five hours each day, are exposed to a combination of counseling, socialization, remedial education, and various other activities. There are several criteria for entry to this program: the prospective clients must agree not to be under the influence of drugs during program hours; they must agree to participate in all phases of the program; and their parents or guardians must agree to participate in the parents' group. Adolescents with a history of violent acting-out behavior or a history of severe psychiatric pathology are not accepted into the program. If detoxification is required, the youngster must complete such a program before he/she is accepted for treatment.

The first thirty days of the program are considered a probationary time during which clients are expected to demonstrate the motivation needed to participate in the program. If at the end of thirty days the youngster is still not adequately motivated, a meeting is held with the parents, the child, and other referral agency personnel. During this meeting, a recommendation may be made to transfer the youngster to another program, back to the school or the court, or simply to say that the youngster is not yet ready and suggest ways that he/she might be made ready to participate fully in the Woodbridge Program.

Family participation is required. In those cases where a youngster is self-referred and does not want his/her family to be involved in the treatment, the program will still provide treatment. "We will work with that youngster for a 'reasonable' period of time until he/she agrees to family counseling." Staff feel that the minimum amount of time that an adolescent should stay in the program is between six to nine months, with an additional six months of family counseling. The maximum amount of time the person can stay in the program is two years, and this length is rare.

Who Does Best/Worst. The youngster who does best has "some kind of active parental support." Youngsters over the age of 16 generally do significantly better than those who are younger. "Once they are 16 and over, they are easier to deal with because they are starting to feel the consequences of their own actions. Parents are beginning to force them to take responsibility. At age 14 and younger, it is hard to tell them that the gravy train is going to end soon, they don't understand that."

Another important factor in predicting treatment outcome is the length of time the youngster has been using drugs, and how invested he/she is in the drug culture. "The longer a youngster has been using drugs, the harder he is to treat." Another significant indicator is whether or not the youngster's family is abusing drugs or alcohol. "It is extremely difficult to work with a youngster whose parents are smoking pot. The child cannot see a distinction as to why the parents can smoke, are still working, and appear to be happy, but he or she cannot." The Woodbridge program estimates that at least 40 percent of all youngsters in the program have at least one parent who abuses alcohol, marijuana, or other drugs. Youngsters referred by the criminal justice system tend not to do as well as those from other referral sources.

Genesis House

Genesis House, located in Pampa, Texas, is a residential treatment center. Male and female clients are housed separately in two buildings located several blocks apart. A distinguishing feature of Genesis House is its extensive use of community facilities. All of the residents attend the local public schools and regularly participate in community athletic and recreational activities. Pampa is a small city of approximately 25,000 people located in the Panhandle section of Texas. Its population is made up mostly of farmers and industrial workers. Pampa is an old, stable town which believes in taking care of its own and has historically been supportive of Genesis House, as evidenced by the large number of volunteers who participate in the program by providing transportation, instruction to the clients, and other services.

Genesis maintains a census of fourteen youngsters, seven in each residence. Priority is given to youngsters who reside in the local area and surrounding counties, who account for 50 percent of the client population. The remaining space is used for referrals from other areas in the state. Between 50 and 75 percent of clients are referred by the Texas Youth Commission, which is part of the juvenile justice system. However, Genesis House will accept referrals from other agencies, school officials, and parents. Genesis House will not accept clients in need of detoxification. Clients with mild degrees of retardation or psychiatric disturbances will be accepted. Youngsters accepted by this program must be able to function in a public school.

Fees are on a sliding scale ranging from $1 to $26 per day. The referring agency will often pay the entire fee; otherwise the client's family is charged according to the ability to pay. A client will not be turned down if his/her family is unable or unwilling to support him/her in the program. The average family pays from $2.50 to $10 per day.

Program Philosophy. The Genesis House program is designed to change the adolescent's destructive behavior and substance abuse lifestyle through a highly structured residential program. Youngsters are given an opportunity to set achievable goals so that they will grow in self-esteem. "We want to turn their lives around and show them they are worthwhile people and that they can achieve without the use of drugs."

Program Description. This program provides a home-style residential atmosphere with a great deal of community involvement and interaction.

Clients attend the local high school and are required to complete at least one semester successfully as a condition of discharge. The high school offers a variety of educational programs and an appropriate course of work is chosen in consultation among the high school guidance counselor, Genesis House staff, and the client. Genesis House also provides a work readiness program in which clients are taught how to relate to employers, dress for job hunting, make job applications, behave in an interview, and present themselves and their skills in the best possible manner. Clients also participate in summer job programs. There is also a home skills program which includes landscaping, clothing care, decorating, and building maintenance such as painting and plumbing.

All clients are involved in regular in-house group and individual counseling. After the first month in the program, group counseling sessions take place at a minimum of twice a month and individual counseling once a month. Family counseling is available and is provided when the family is able and willing to attend sessions. When a client is referred by the juvenile justice system, the probation officer will maintain contact with both the client and the client's family.

Residents of Genesis House undergo screening for drugs only when the house supervisors suspect that drugs are being used. The average stay is from six to nine months, with six months being considered a minimum. A number of residents have stayed longer than nine months when this extension is dictated by treatment needs and untenable family situations. Clients cannot stay in the program past their eighteenth birthday.

Who Does Best/Worst. The client who does best at Genesis House is a person 16 years or older with an average IQ, who is able to express him/herself and state his/her feelings clearly. "We work best with the average normal youngster who just needs to be back on the right road." Genesis House finds that the most difficult clients to work with are passive youngsters and those who are retarded. "They are harder to reach and harder to motivate."

Additional problems are presented by the youngster whose parents abuse drugs and/or alcohol. It is estimated that upwards of 60 percent of the clients have smoked marijuana in the presence of or together with their parents.

The Bridge

The Therapeutic Center at Fox Chase, better known as The Bridge, is a residential treatment program located in Philadelphia, Pennsylvania, with a capacity of sixty to sixty-five clients. According to the director, "The goal of the program is to provide an atmosphere in which residents will feel comfortable, establish supportive peer relationships, take responsibility for themselves, and learn how to resolve problems. Staff provide guidance and direction as well as positive role modeling." The program aims to teach youngsters how to handle self, school, friends, and family.

Clients come to The Bridge through a variety of referral sources: self-referral, referral by family, schools, other community agencies, and the criminal justice system. Approximately 40 to 50 percent of clients are court referred.

Eighty-five percent of the residents are from the city of Philadelphia and surrounding communities. Fifteen percent are from New Jersey and from elsewhere in Pennsylvania. Occasionally some clients come from outside the states of Pennsylvania and New Jersey.

A per diem of $62.51 is charged to those in the residential program. This fee is usually paid by the referring agency or court. For those referred by self or family, a sliding scale applies. No one is turned away for lack of funds. Third-party insurance is also accepted when appropriate.

Program Philosophy. The program is founded on the belief that "drug/alcohol dependent adolescents can be helped to gain the motivation, the skills, and the external supports necessary for sober, independent, and responsible living." It is believed that the substance abuse problem is intimately connected to other problems. "It is one way that residents try to cope with or react to other problematic situations: esteem, social/emotional disturbance, marginal family structure, minimal academic achievement, inability to find or sustain employment, and negative peer relationships." The staff of the Bridge believe that adolescent substance abusers can be motivated to change and to learn skills which will help them to "develop an appreciation of their personal worth, learn how to make decisions, set goals, and accept consequences, learn how to cope, behave responsibly in difficult situations, communicate more effectively with their families, and develop honest, positive, and supportive friends."

Program Description. The criterion for entry to The Bridge program is that the resident must have alcohol and/or drug abuse problems. Because of facility limitations the program will not accept persons with severe physical handicaps. It will not accept applicants with serious psychological problems, suicidal tendencies, or a history of arson or other crimes which suggest that the youngster is a danger to self and/or others. Detoxification for potential residents is provided off-site. Upon entry all residents receive complete physical, dental, psychological, and educational assessments. The program is concentrated in five major areas:

1. Residents receive a minimum of ten hours of group therapy weekly and as much individual therapy as the staff feels is needed. Emphasis is upon reality and upon gaining awareness skills and strengths needed for responsible living.

2. A formal plan of family therapy is offered.

3. An education program provides residents with a minimum of 27 1/2 hours of classroom experience per week, including vocational guidance and development as well as job placement. The Bridge is licensed as a private academic high school in the states of Pennsylvania and New Jersey and residents complete credits for a high school diploma on the premises. Both regular and special education programs are offered.

4. The Bridge also offers a life skills development program which "provides residents exposure to, and instruction in, a wide spectrum of cultural, social, survival, athletic, and recreational skills. The purpose of the life skills development program is to help them learn how to organize free time and to become aware of alternatives to their present life style."

5. Additionally a full range of medical, dental, psychiatric, and psychological services is included.

A new resident moves through the program in four phases. In the initial four weeks, called the investment level, the resident "identifies personal strengths and gains self-confidence; identifies weaknesses/problems and begins to learn how to change them; and gains the motivation, trust, and support needed to change or to cope." A "big brother or sister" helps the new resident during this period of transition. The resident learns how addiction and drug abuse have impacted on life, family, friends, school, and work, and to appreciate how a new attitude and behavior will affect them.

In level 2, which ranges from two to three months, the resident assumes a leadership role within the community. He/she will "begin to share personal growth with younger residents and continue to help them address situations by offering support. During this time, family therapy is intensified." The goal of level 2 is to help the resident understand his/her responsibility and be able to ennumerate areas that need to be addressed with some or all family members.

During the two to four month period that comprises level 3, the resident begins to test new attitudes and behaviors. The goals are increased motivation and a new value system, as well as development of an external support system which will enable him/her to cope with problems and life situations in an appropriate manner.

In the final six to eight week period, the senior level, the resident finalizes educational and vocational goals, as well as the development of needed support systems. Following the senior level is graduation, which symbolizes the formal completion of the program.

Staff at The Bridge are trained, experienced, licensed, or certified in their specific areas of expertise.

Who Does Best/Worst. Residents 16 years of age and older generally do better than younger clients. This is thought to be due to the fact that older clients have experienced more of the negative effects of drug abuse and are more likely to "have hit rock bottom." Younger clients are less likely to consider their drug use or problems serious.

Psychiatric Institute of Montgomery County

The Closed Adolescent Unit of the Psychiatric Institute of Montgomery County is located in Rockville, Maryland, a suburb of the District of Columbia, and has a capacity of twenty youths. This hospital unit is designed to provide an intensive evaluation and treatment program for disturbed adolescents, particularly those whose psychiatric illness is complicated by alcohol and/or drug abuse.

The Psychiatric Institute reports that 77 percent of their clients come from the city of Rockville and surrounding counties. Because of the nature of the program, most clients are referred by parents, other family members, or physicians. Referrals are occasionally received through community agencies as well as the courts.

Clients are charged $418 per day in the closed (secure) unit or $365 per day in the open unit, plus additional professional charges, which average $700 per week, for a total of $3,626 (closed) or $3,255 (open) per week. The above charges do not include any prescribed medication or laboratory tests. Although there is no sliding scale, nearly all of the clients are covered by third-party insurance. The fee structure is adjusted on an individual basis in cases where families cannot afford the insurance co-payment, or when insurance has run out.

Program Philosophy. The Psychiatric Institute program focuses on adolescents who suffer from two concurrent problems: psychiatric illness and substance abuse or dependency. According to the program director, "Treatment of a psychiatric illness alone or substance abuse problem alone will not bring about recovery. Attention must be given to all problems simultaneously. The goal is to prepare the adolescent for continuing growth in a less restricted environment as quickly as possible. Our main goal is to help youngsters to the point where they see that there is a problem, something can be done about it, and there is something to learn about how to get there. We don't see ourselves as being able to cure what is a very serious chronic illness in a couple of months, but rather through therapy to help the family and the youngster understand problems and be in a better position to resolve them. We then refer the youngster to an outpatient or residential program depending on his/her best interests."

Program Description. Detoxification may be required prior to or during the early part of the evaluation phase, depending on the type of drug problem. Upon admission to the adolescent unit, the youngster and his/her family participate in an evaluation phase lasting approximately two weeks. This phase involves continued diagnostic assessment, including a medical history and physical examination, an assessment of daily living skills, and a social worker's evaluation of the adolescent's history and family relationships. The evaluation phase also includes a psychiatric evaluation of the nature and severity of the emotional disorders, and an evaluation of the youngster's ability and potential for self-expression, including his/her use of leisure time and social skills. Also accomplished during this period are a detailed drug and alcohol use history and an evaluation of the youngster's educational level and potential for learning. Other psychological testing is performed as appropriate.

During the evaluation phase, efforts are initiated to break through the youngster's tendency to deny that his/her substance abuse is a problem, or to deny that he/she has any problem at all. Should the evaluation phase show that the youngster can be helped by the treatment phase of the program, it will follow immediately. If not, an appropriate referral will be made.

An individualized treatment program is designed according to the needs of the youngster and family and is based upon the evaluation. Treatment is primarily composed of one-to-one counseling and traditional and confrontational group therapy.

As part of psychiatric treatment, the therapist educates the adolescent about his/her problems and about types of therapies and/or medications required for treatment. Therapies that encourage expression such as art, music, and drama are used as appropriate. A behavior modification program is used to help prepare the adolescent for learning ways to earn privileges and to feel rewarded for his/her efforts.

Youngsters also learn about the nature of their drug or alcohol problem and about the recovery process. The treatment program has been built around the recovery principles of such self-help organizations as Alcoholics Anonymous and Narcotics Anonymous. Patients attend meetings of AA and NA, as appropriate, during the treatment phase. While a drug-free lifestyle is encouraged on the inpatient unit, it is the viewpoint of the Psychiatric Institute that medications can be useful for treating patients. The family is involved in an intensive orientation program while the adolescent is in the hospital. Individual family therapy takes place once a week in addition to multi-family groups which also take place once a week while the patient is in the adolescent unit. Alanon meetings, lectures on drug and alcohol abuse, and parent peer groups are emphasized during this phase. The youngster is also enrolled in the "developmental school," which is a nonprofit special education junior/ senior high school located within the hospital.

The average client spends fifty-five days in the closed unit after which he/she is referred to either additional inpatient or to outpatient treatment as appropriate to his/her individual needs.

Who Does Best/Worst. The youngster who does best in this program is one who has an actively involved and supportive family group whose members are willing to listen and to work with staff. Youngsters who need a great deal of one-on-one therapy and who are unable to participate in group therapy programs do not do as well and are usually referred elsewhere after the evaluation period. The intensive evaluation period of this program helps to insure that only those youngsters who can benefit from the therapeutic services offered are accepted into the program and that others are referred to programs that would be more appropriate.

Rural Adolescent Model

The Rural Adolescent Model (RAM), located in a rural area of central Minnesota, combines a residential and day care program and serves up to fourteen clients. It is structured to meet the needs of rural communities and serves an area within a radius of approximately sixty miles. The residential program offered begins with a period of assessment followed by a period of residential treatment. A day program is offered to those completing the residential treatment program as well as to those for whom a residential treatment program is not appropriate or who have been evaluated and/or received primary treatment services elsewhere. The residential and day care programs are combined, the only difference being that those in the day care program return home to sleep. The residential and outpatient programs will be considered together as a total program because for most clients treatment begins in the residential setting and continues in the day program.

Geographically the program is in an area of marginal employment and marginal farming, with a very high unemployment rate. All clients are from within the state of Minnesota, and 29 percent of these reside in the agency's home county. The program generally limits acceptance to those youngsters living within a sixty mile radius of the program in order to involve their families better in the rehabilitation process.

RAM charges $135 per day in the residential program and $80 per day for the day care program. Third-party insurance covers part or all of the fees for approximately 40 percent of the families involved while the remainder of the fees are generally paid to the program through a state block grant.

Program Philosophy. RAM views chemical abuse as resulting from a variety of environmental factors. RAM staff believe that chemical abuse adversely effects the entire family, and therefore the entire family should be involved in the treatment process. Since in the rural community the families are usually geographically spread out, the agency makes an effort to provide family services in the family's community. The family is encouraged to become involved in community activities, including religious activities, which can offer a positive approach to their problems. Clients are also encouraged to learn and make use of the self-help principles of Alcoholics Anonomous.

A somewhat different approach is used in working with members of the American Indian community. A larger community/family group is involved in the rehabilitation process and local tribal leaders cooperate in obtaining community support.

Program Description. Typically a client will spend forty-five to fifty days in the Rural Adolescent Model program, twenty-eight days in the residential segment and twenty days in the day program. Some clients simply come for a ten to fourteen day evaluation in order to determine the potential treatment benefits of the program. If a youngster who has been referred for treatment completes an evaluation period, and it is felt by RAM staff that the particular youngster does not need full treatment services, the youngster would be sent home with a "contract, establishing what he/she should do to remain drug-free—including regular school attendance, weekly meetings with parents, and possibly a counselor involved in the case from the family's community, attendance at Alcoholics Anonymous meetings when appropriate, and criteria to govern chemical usage. Compliance with this contract is monitored through ongoing contact with the parents and other involved, helping professionals."

Treatment services include two daily group counseling sessions with individual counseling taking place at a minimum of every other day. There are two types of family counseling sessions available, one involving the client and his/her own family, the other involving several families together. During treatment the family meets with the youngster and RAM staff a minimum of ten times. In those cases where the family is reluctant to participate "we put tremendous pressure on the parents." The parents are told that the youngster will not improve without their involvement. The youngster is encouraged to call, write, or otherwise encourage his/ her family to become involved. Because of the potentially long distances that may have to be covered by families, effort is made to go into individual communities in order to hold multi-family meetings. These meetings are generally held at a church, school or some other neutral site.

The RAM provides a small one-room school, so that youngsters may keep up with their peers in the community school systems. The program also provides recreational opportunities and numerous educational seminars on drug abuse, alcohol abuse, sexuality, spirituality, and other topics of interest to an adolescent. Support groups including Alcoholics Anonymous are also provided at the facility.

Who Does Best/Worst. Clients who acknowledge the consequences of using drugs or alcohol do best in the program. The client who does best has a supportive family who acknowledge that they have been affected and are willing to do their part towards helping the situation. Since the goal is not only for the youngster to do well in the program, but also to continue to do well after leaving the program, it is felt that the key is high-quality family involvement and followup beyond treatment. The older adolescent appears to do somewhat better than the younger adolescent.

The youngsters who are most difficult to work with "come from a family who expects us to fix the kid and return him/her fixed to the family." In addition, the youngster who is immersed in the drug culture is often not motivated to change although every effort is made to induce him/her to take a good look at his/her behavior and become motivated to participate. Youngsters have to be responsible and help in the process. "We try to motivate them, but if we can't, we can't really help them." The decision to drop a client is made mutually by the youngster, the parents, and the referral agency. Occasionally a youngster might leave without permission, "but they would generally come back on their own in a short period of time, and usually but not always, are accepted back by the program." The clients who present the most serious challenge are those who have multiple problems in addition to chemical abuse— youngsters who have been sexually and/or physically abused and those who have anorexia and other psychiatric problems. Youngsters with such problems are accepted if the initial ten to fourteen day evaluation shows that they can benefit from the program offered.

Differences are also noted between those clients referred by the school and those referred by the criminal justice system. "The youngster who comes through school is more likely to be aware of the consequences of his abuse; he/she is more likely to acknowledge that there is a problem. The youngster who comes through the court too frequently is not as ready to acknowledge the consequences of chemical abuse. He has been there before and knows how to play the game."

Overview of Adolescent Substance Abuse Treatment Programs

What do adolescent programs look like? The adolescent programs described here receive the vast majority of their clients from within the cities or counties in which they are located. The most common referral sources are the courts and the schools although many youngsters volunteer for treatment or are referred by their families.

Few programs accept youngsters with serious psychiatric problems. With the exception of the Psychiatric Institute, which is hospital based, none of the surveyed programs accepts clients who are in need of detoxification.

Although there is considerable variation in the fees charged (ranging from zero to more than $3,000 per week) all programs make their services affordable, either through the use of a sliding fee scale based on need, third-party insurance payments, or a combination of both. All programs make special arrangements to treat indigent clients.

Program Comparisons. Although the programs have their differences, they also have many similarities. All of them make extensive use of group therapy. In addition, they all provide individual counseling. They also all require some parental and/or familial involvement in the program and attempt to provide family counseling and/or therapy where logistically possible.

Adolescent drug abusers coming to treatment present a multiplicity of problems which extend beyond drug use per se. All of the programs focus on what they call the "underlying problems" in the family milieu.

Of the programs surveyed, many make use of such self-help methods as Alcoholics Anonymous and Narcotics Anonymous. The self-help groups may meet at the program or the adolescents may be encouraged to attend AA or NA meetings in their neighborhoods.

Who Does Best/Worst. Adolescent programs tend to agree about the kinds of adolescents who do best and worst in treatment. The more successful youngsters recognize that they have a problem and are self-motivated to participate in the program. An actively involved and supportive family is also important. All of the programs find that older adolescents generally do better than younger ones because of the time they have had to experience the negative consequences of substance abuse. The older teenagers tend to be more mature, to have had life experiences they can use in problem-solving, and to be more motivated. Although the type of drug used is not felt to be a factor in predicting treatment success, the length of time a youngster has used drugs and has been immersed in the drug culture does appear to be predictive of treatment outcome. The greater the immersion in the drug culture, the poorer the prospect of a successful outcome (except for the contrary opinion of one program).

Without exception, the programs believe that the adolescent referred through the criminal justice system is less apt to have a successful outcome than one who is referred by other sources. Youngsters who have had numerous treatment experiences do more poorly than others. They often sabotage their own treatment and the treatment of others. Additionally, clients with histories of violence, extensive drug use, and gang affiliation do more poorly.

It was noted that adolescents coming from families in which the parents abuse alcohol or drugs do more poorly than adolescents with parents who do not abuse substances. In many of the families, marijuana has assumed a status similar to that of alcohol, is used casually, and is not considered a drug.

Motivation for change on the part of both the youngster and his/her family is the key to improvement. Although most programs will work with a youngster to increase motivation, there still must be that initial spark of readiness for change, a desire not only to stop using drugs, but also to change familial and social relationships. This spark must be present not only in the youngsters but also in their families. In the words of the director of Minnesota's Rural Adolescent Model, "We are not here for families that want to send their youngsters here and have us fix them. We are not going to do that." Both the youngsters and their families must be willing to take responsibility for their behavior. "We use all the skills we can to motivate the youngsters as well as attempting to motivate the family to understand and begin to change their behavior."

References

Blum, R. and Richards, L. 1979. Youthful drug use. In DuPont, R., Goldstein, A., and O'Donnell, J. (eds.), *Handbook on Drug Abuse*. Rockville, Maryland: National Institute on Drug Abuse.

DeLeon, G. 1984. *The Therapeutic Community: A Study of Effectiveness*. Treatment Research Monograph Series, DHHS Publication No. (ADM) 84–1286. Rockville, Maryland: National Institute on Drug Abuse.

Kennedy, W. 1985. Chemical Dependency: A treatable disease. *The Ohio State Medical Journal,* February.

Lerner, S. and Burns, R.S. 1979. Youthful phencyclidine (PCP) users. In Beschner, G. and Friedman, A. (eds.) *Youth Drug Abuse: Problems, Issues and Treatment.* Lexington, Massachusetts: Lexington Books.

National Institute on Drug Abuse. 1983. *National Survey on Drug Abuse: Main Findings 1982.* DHHS Publication No. (ADM) 83—1263. Rockville, Maryland.

Smith, D.; Levy, S.; and Striar, D. 1979. Treatment services for youthful drug users. In Beschner, G. and Friedman, A. (eds.), *Youth Drug Abuse: Problems, Issues and Treatment.* Lexington, Massachusetts: Lexington Books.

Appendix 7A
Directory of State Substance Abuse Coordinating Agencies

Alabama

Department of Mental Health
200 Interstate Park Drive
P.O. Box 3710
Montgomery 36193
(205) 271–9209

Alaska

Office of Alcoholism and Drug Abuse
Department of Health and Social Services
Pouch H–05–F
Juneau 99811
(907) 586–6201

Arizona

Office of Community Behavioral Health
Arizona Department of Health Services
1740 West Adams
Phoenix 85007
(602) 255–1152

Arkansas

Arkansas Office on Alcohol and
Drug Abuse Prevention
1515 West 7th Avenue, Suite 300
Little Rock 72202
(501) 371–2603

California

Department of Alcohol and Drug Abuse
111 Capitol Mall
Sacramento 95814
(916) 445–1940 or 322–8484

Colorado

Alcohol and Drug Abuse Division
Department of Health
4210 East 11th Avenue
Denver 80220
(303) 331–8201

Connecticut

Connecticut Alcohol and
Drug Abuse Commission
999 Asylum Avenue, 3rd Floor
Hartford 06105
(203) 566–4145

Delaware

Bureau of Alcoholism and Drug Abuse
1901 North DuPont Highway
Newcastle 19720
(302) 421–6101

District of Columbia

Health Planning and Development
1875 Connecticut Avenue, N.W.,
Suite 836
Washington 20009
(202) 673–7481

Florida

Alcohol and Drug Abuse Program
Department of Health and Rehabilitative
  Services
1317 Winewood Boulevard
Tallahassee 32301
(904) 488–0900

Georgia

Alcohol and Drug Section
Division of Mental Health, Mental
  Retardation and Substance Abuse
Georgia Department of Human
  Resources
47 Trinity Avenue, S.W.
Atlanta 30334
(404) 894–6352

Hawaii

Alcohol and Drug Abuse Branch
Department of Health
P.O. Box 3378
Honolulu 96801
(808) 548–4280

Idaho

Bureau of Substance Abuse
Department of Health and Welfare
450 West State Street
Boise 83720
(208) 334–4368

Illinois Illinois Department of Alcoholism and
  Substance Abuse
100 West Randolph Street, Suite 5–600
Chicago 60601
(312) 793–3840

Indiana Division of Addiction Services
Department of Mental Health
429 North Pennsylvania Street
Indianapolis 46204
(317) 232–7816

Iowa Iowa Department of Substance Abuse
505 Fifth Avenue
Insurance Exchange Building, Suite 202
Des Moines 50319
(515) 281–3641

Kansas Alcohol and Drug Abuse Services
2700 West Sixth Street
Biddle Building
Topeka 66606
(913) 296–3925

Kentucky Alcohol and Drug Branch
Bureau for Health Services
Department of Human Resources
275 East Main Street
Frankfort 40621
(502) 564–2880

Louisiana Office of Prevention and Recovery from
  Alcohol and Drug Abuse
P.O. Box 53129
Baton Rouge 70892
(504) 922–0730

Maine Office of Alcoholism and
Drug Abuse Prevention
Bureau of Rehabilitation
State House Station #11
Augusta 04333
(207) 289–2781

Maryland	Maryland State Drug Abuse Administration 201 West Preston Street Baltimore 21201 (301) 383–3312
Massachusetts	Division of Drug Rehabilitation 150 Tremont Street Boston 02111 (617) 727–8614
Michigan	Office of Substance Abuse Services Department of Public Health 3500 North Logan Street Lansing 48909 (517) 373–8603
Minnesota	Chemical Dependency Program Division Department of Human Services Centennial Building, 4th Floor 658 Cedar St. Paul 55155 (612) 296–4610
Mississippi	Division of Alcohol and Drug Abuse Department of Mental Health Robert E. Lee Office Building, 11th Floor Jackson 39201 (601) 359–1297
Missouri	Division of Alcoholism and Drug Abuse Department of Mental Health 2002 Missouri Boulevard P.O. Box 687 Jefferson City 65101 (314) 751–4942
Montana	Alcohol and Drug Abuse Division State of Montana Department of Institutions Helena 59601 (406) 449–2827
Nebraska	Division of Alcoholism and Drug Abuse Department of Public Institutions P.O. Box 94728 Lincoln 68509 (402) 471–2851, Ext. 5583

Nevada

Bureau of Alcohol and Drug Abuse
Department of Human Resources
505 East King Street
Carson City 89710
(702) 885–4790

New Hampshire

Office of Alcohol and Drug Abuse
    Prevention
Health and Welfare Building
Hazen Drive
Concord 03301
(603) 271–4627

New Jersey

Division of Narcotic and Drug Abuse
    Control
129 East Hanover Street
Trenton 08625
(609) 292–5760

New Mexico

Drug Abuse Bureau
Behavioral Health Services Division
P.O. Box 968
Santa Fe 87504
(505) 984–0020, Ext. 331

New York

Division of Substance Abuse Services
Executive Park South
Box 8200
Albany 12203
(518) 457–7629

North Carolina

Alcohol and Drug Abuse Section
Division of Mental Health and
Mental Retardation Services
325 North Salisbury Street
Raleigh 27611
(919) 733–4670

North Dakota

Division of Alcoholism and Drugs
North Dakota Department of
Human Services
State Capitol
Bismarck 58505
(701) 224–2769

Ohio

Bureau of Drug Abuse
170 North High Street, 3rd Floor
Columbus 43215
(614) 466–7893

Oklahoma

Alcohol and Drug Programs
Department of Mental Health
P.O. Box 53277, Capitol Station
4545 North Lincoln Boulevard
Suite 100 East Terrace
Oklahoma City 73152
(405) 521–0044

Oregon

Mental Health Division
2575 Bittern Street, N.E.
Salem 97310
(503) 378–2163

Pennsylvania

Drug and Alcohol Programs
Pennsylvania Department of Health
P.O. Box 90
Harrisburg 17108
(717) 787–9857

Rhode Island

Department of Mental Health,
Mental Retardation and Hospitals
Division of Substance Abuse
Substance Abuse Administration Building
Cranston 02920
(401) 464–2091

South Caolina

South Carolina Commission on
Alcohol and Drug Abuse
3700 Forest Drive
Columbia 29204
(803) 758–2521 or 758–2183

South Dakota

Division of Alcohol and Drug Abuse
Joe Foss Building
523 East Capitol
Pierre 57501
(605) 773–3123

Tennessee	Alcohol and Drug Abuse Services Tennessee Department of Mental Health and Mental Retardation James K. Polk Building 505 Deaderick Street Nashville 37219 (615) 741–1921
Texas	Drug Abuse Prevention Division Texas Department of Community Affairs 2015 South IH 35 Austin 78741 (512) 475–2311
Utah	Division of Alcoholism and Drugs 150 West North Temple, Suite 350 P.O. Box 2500 Salt Lake City 84110 (801) 533–6532
Vermont	Alcohol and Drug Abuse Division 103 South Main Street Waterbury 05676 (802) 241–2170 or 241–1000
Virginia	State Department of Mental Health and Mental Retardation P.O. Box 1797 109 Governor Street Richmond 23214 (804) 786–5313
Washington	Bureau of Alcoholism and Substance Abuse Washington Department of Social and Health Services Mail Stop OB–44W Olympia 98504 (206) 753–5866
West Virginia	Division of Alcohol and Drug Abuse State Capitol 1800 Washington Street, East, Room 451 Charleston 25305 (304) 348–2276

Wisconsin	Office of Alcohol and Other Drug Abuse 1 West Wilson Street P.O. Box 7851 Madison 53705 (608) 266–3442
Wyoming	Alcohol and Drug Abuse Programs Hathaway Building Cheyenne 82002 (307) 777–7115, Ext. 7118
Guam	Department of Mental Health and Substance Abuse P.O. Box 8896 Tamuning 96911
Puerto Rico	Department of Addiction Control Services Box B–Y, Rio Piedras Station Rio Piedras 00928 (809) 763–5823
Virgin Islands	Division of Mental Health, Alcoholism and Drug Dependency P.O. Box 7309 St. Thomas 00801 (809) 774–4888
American Samoa	Public Health Services LBJ Tropical Medical Center Paga Pago 96799
Trust Territories	Health Services Office of the High Commissioner Saipan 96950

8
Secondary Prevention: A Pragmatic Approach to the Problem of Substance Abuse among Adolescents

Jerome F. X. Carroll

Whereas primary prevention is intended to prevent the occurrence of a disease or disorder, secondary prevention aims to detect the problem in its early stages of development. It seeks to provide an appropriate therapeutic intervention to avoid further deterioration and to promote healing and recovery. When these concepts are applied to youngsters who have already had experience in using drugs, secondary prevention seems to have some clear advantages over primary approaches.

In attempting to reach the potential or novice user, earlier primary prevention efforts in the 1970's typically took a "total and permanent abstinence" or proscriptive approach to the use of all psychoactive substances. For the most part, they relied on the use of "authoritative, scientific information" to convince adolescent audiences that the use of these substances inevitably leads to serious negative psychobiosocial consequences. Studies done at this time indicate that these early approaches were not very successful, especially with adolescents who had already started using drugs at an early age (Swisher et al. 1971; De Lone 1972; Swisher 1974; Stuart 1974; Wolk and Tomanio 1974; Brown and Klein 1975; Bry 1978; Dembo et al. 1978; Blizard and Teague 1981; Schiler 1981; Nathan 1983). What seems to be needed is more diversity in our prevention strategies, especially greater emphasis on secondary prevention.

There are some obstacles to the application of the total abstinence primary prevention approach. For example, our society permits and even encourages (through advertising) the use of a variety of licit psychoactive substances by both adults (and adolescents) in order to "feel better," socialize, go to sleep at night, get going in the morning, get through the day, look and feel younger, be sexy, and so on (Irwin 1973; Chafetz 1974; Zinberg et al. 1975; Floyd and Lotsof 1977; Portnoy 1980). Those who yield to this form of social pressure and use socially sanctioned clinical substances are not generally perceived as sick or disturbed (Harding and Zinberg 1977; Jalali et al. 1981; Hilliker et al. 1981; Milgram and Pandina 1981; Iutcovich and Iutcovich 1982). Unfortunately, this sanctioned marketing of licit psychoactive substances tends to obscure the dangers associated with the misuse of such substances and thereby indirectly supports the experimental use of substances by adolescents who are inclined to imitate their elders.

Another obstacle for the total and permanent abstinence position is the fact that for many adolescents, the consumption of alcohol and/or marijuana has become a rite of passage to adulthood, and as such, it constitutes an integral part of their social scene (as it does with some adults). Adolescents making this transition are not likely to accept an adult-imposed double standard: "Do as I say, but not as I do."

What is needed at this juncture is a pragmatic approach—one which is more closely aligned with the reality of particular situations and the norms and lifestyles of particular kinds of adolescents. The pragmatic approach being advocated is to shift our prevention emphasis from primary to secondary strategies. This chapter identifies three specific goals for a secondary prevention program, and offers a number of suggestions for achieving these goals and avoiding some of the problems which have curtailed the success of primary prevention programs.

No one prevention strategy can hope to stop adolescents effectively from *experimenting* with and/or *using* various substances, especially alcohol and marijuana. A more realistic, potentially achievable goal would be to seek to disrupt developing substance *abuse* behavior patterns as early as possible, before serious and irreversible damage is done. Thus, the basic secondary prevention goal is to identify those adolescents who are in the incipient stage of substance abuse and to encourage and assist them to seek help in coping with their drug and other problems in living.

In a secondary prevention program, peers can play a vital role. While prevention specialists are not likely to be very successful in persuading adolescents to urge their peers to immediately and permanently abstain from alcohol and/or other drugs, peers could be convinced to assist their friends (or family members) to get help whenever they begin to experience difficulties as a result of substance use.

The recent broadcast and printed media ads conveying the message "Friends don't let friends drive drunk" illustrates the essence of a sound secondary prevention approach. This differs from the typical primary prevention message which would likely read, "Friends don't let friends drink and/or use drugs."

Three Major Objectives for a Secondary Prevention Program

There are three major secondary prevention objectives for adolescents:

1. To teach adolescents how to identify the early signs of substance abuse, that is, how to distinguish "use" from "abuse";

2. To teach adolescents how to assist their substance-abusing peers (and family members) to recognize and accept that they have a substance abuse problem and need treatment; and

3. To teach them where their substance-abusing friends (and family members) can go for help for their problem.

General Principles for Achieving the Three Objectives

Teaching Adolescents How to Identify the Early Signs of Substance Abuse

Both the National Council on Alcoholism (1972) and Palisano (1980) have developed criteria to assess the seriousness of an individual's alcohol problem (see below). These criteria could be widely disseminated and discussed with adolescents (and adults) in a variety of social settings, which would increase the likelihood of identifying an incipient alcohol abuse problem. The individual:

Drinks alone while at home or in public.

Drinks more heavily than usual when in trouble or under pressure.

Has blackouts, or is unable to remember what happened while drinking.

Misses work frequently, particularly on Fridays, Mondays, and days following holidays.

When drinking with others, tries to have a few extra drinks when others will not know it.

Changes jobs repeatedly, especially to successively lower levels.

Wishes to continue drinking after friends say s/he has had enough.

Exhibits marked personality or behavior changes after drinking.

Pays little attention to personal appearance or hygiene.

Feels guilty about his/her drinking.

Refuses to admit excessive drinking and becomes annoyed if the subject is mentioned.

Has persistent family or job difficulties.

Avoids family or close friends while drinking.

Gets arrested for drunkenness.

Has often failed to keep promises made to self re: controlling or cutting down on drinking.

Experiences physical problems, such as early morning nausea and the shakes, loss of appetite, nerve pain, and muscle weakness, especially in the legs.

Can no longer drink as much as s/he once did.

A similar approach can be used to reach some adolescent drug users. References to "work" in the above criteria would simply be changed to "school," for example, misses class frequently, particularly on Fridays, Mondays, and days following holidays.

Since marijuana is the second most commonly abused substance by adolescents, specific guidelines for identifying abuse of this substance are provided. Weller and Halikas (1980) for example, provide four criteria for distinguishing marijuana abuse from marijuana use:

Adverse physiological and psychological drug effects: toxic deliriums or anxiety reactions, health problems, blackouts, or subjectively defined addiction or dependence.

Control problems: unsuccessful attempts to stop, inability to limit use, early morning use, or binge or bender use.

Behavior problems: arrests due to behaviors when high, traffic violations, job problems, fighting, or lost friends.

Adverse opinions: being told marijuana is being used too much, family objections, or guilt feelings.

The following dimensions should be considered when attempting to assess the seriousness of a marijuana user's problem (Carroll 1981):

Age: the younger and less mature the user, the greater the danger of negative consequences from use.

Psychophysical status: the individual's mental and physical state of well-being is very important. The less emotionally stable the person is and/or the poorer his/her physical health (especially people with heart disorders and lung problems), the greater the danger incurred from the use of marijuana.

Pattern of use: using marijuana in conjunction with other more potent psychoactive substances such as alcohol, PCP, or amphetamines, and/or using marijuana alternately as a substitute for other more potent psychoactive substances in a complex pattern of multiple substance abuse. Such usage patterns are considered potentially more harmful than the occasional use of moderate amounts of marijuana.

Motivation for use: when marijuana is being used repeatedly as a nearly exclusive means of coping with stress, unpleasant situations, difficult problems, unacceptable impulses, or bad feelings, for example, loneliness, inadequacy, boredom, fear.

Frequency, amount, and duration: daily or almost daily use of three or more joints or their equivalent for at least one month, or using heavy amounts of marijuana on binges (staying very high for days at a time, which may also include losing consciousness or suffering blackouts).

Evidence of negative psychobiosocial consequences: physical or mental health deteriorates, job performance or school work declines noticeably in quality, and family and social relationships are seriously impaired due to use. For example, grade averages may suddenly decline, or the adolescent may dramatically change his/her style of interacting with parents, becoming more withdrawn, secretive, noncommunicative, and argumentative.

Smith (1984), while not condoning or encouraging the use of psychoactive substances by adolescents, provides the following five guidelines to distinguish use from abuse for those adolescents who insist on using marijuana despite society's best efforts to prevent such use:

1. Use would be moderated. Because of marijuana's potency, no more than four or five joints per week.
2. Use would be limited to after school and weekends. Students should not use marijuana before or during school; use during school hours interferes with learning.
3. Marijuana, especially potent varieties, would *not* be used before driving motor vehicles. Driving skills suffer as a result of impaired judgment and gross motor coordination brought about by marijuana use.
4. Adolescents would be discreet in their use. Though police are often tolerant about personal use, brazen behavior invites legal entanglements.

5. Multiple drug use, especially of street-quality drugs, is hazardous.

These guidelines can be utilized in a variety of ways. For example, they could be included in a general health or wellness curriculum. They could also be used to stimulate discussion in small groups in schools or community-based programs for adolescents. They could also be used in programs designed to instruct teachers and parents about marijuana abuse.

Teaching Adolescents How to Assist Those Abusing Substances to Recognize the Need for Treatment

This is the most challenging of the three prevention objectives. Anyone who has ever attempted to confront a friend or relative with his/her need for substance abuse treatment knows that the individual will deny that there is a problem and will often resist advice and recommendations. The denial system of the adolescent is buttressed by the fact that s/he typically has not experienced the full negative psychobiosocial consequences of an adult addiction. Nevertheless, since peer pressure is *the* strongest social force for most adolescents, mobilizing the power of this dynamic force to assist those in need of help makes good common sense.

To the extent that adolescents can be taught the behavioral signs of incipient substance abuse and dependence, they will be better prepared to confront their peers in need of assistance. What they will then need is effective instruction in the art of providing effective feedback to a friend in trouble with substance abuse when that friend will be disinclined to hear the feedback.

Existing community-based substance abuse treatment programs and self-help groups could provide staff for instructional purposes at little or no cost. This would constitute good public relations for them and would also be likely to generate potential referral sources for their programs, since many families with a substance-abusing adolescent also have one or more other family members with a substance abuse problem. The National Institute on Drug Abuse (NIDA) and the National Institute on Alcoholism and Alcohol Abuse (NIAAA) could also play a vital role by developing a national resource pool of experts able to provide such training.

Treatment staff and recovered persons performing twelfth step work assisting other addicted men and women to get sober through AA or NA have considerable knowledge and skills for successfully confronting the denial typical of most substance abusers. Adolescents could be taught how to confront denial by such experts, especially those who are recovered, since adolescents would likely perceive them as possessing inherently valid knowledge, because they have "been there." Preferably these recovered staff instructors should be relatively young and familiar with the youthful substance abuse scene and argot.

One of the best teaching devices is role playing. After a demonstration of the basic principles and strategies for confronting an adolescent, trainees could practice what they have learned through role playing. Through feedback from other role players and observers or via videotape, the adolescents receiving such training should be able to acquire the skills needed.

Adolescents receiving training should be volunteers; they should not be pushed or lured into undergoing such training. Interested adolescents could be enlisted through an appeal similar to that used for cardiopulmonary resuscitation (CPR) training: the promise of being trained to save lives. This training need not be offered exclusively in the schools. For example, churches and youth groups could also be utilized as training centers for this purpose (Eiseman 1974; Bry in press).

One bonus of such training programs is that the rate of substance abuse for the trainees is typically reduced to a level below that of their peers. In addition, it is highly probable that those receiving this training will be better able to cope with substance abuse in both their families of origin and their future families.

Teaching Adolescents Where to Go for Help

The same programs and organizations which provide instructors for confronting denial could also be utilized to accomplish the third objective. Local substance abuse agencies and organizations should know the various treatment options located in their geographic area. Their knowledge of the full spectrum of "continuity of care," as well as their expertise in assessing the depth and breadth of a substance abuse problem are precisely what is needed to accomplish the third objective.

Specific information could be dispensed through various media, including formal lectures, posters, spot advertisements on radio and TV, telephone hotlines, and others. Ideally, access to this information should guarantee privacy and anonymity to those seeking help, much like information and assistance with birth control.

Existing substance abuse treatment programs will have to consider what adjustments they will need to make if a large-scale secondary prevention program is initiated. As pointed out in chapter 7, relatively few adolescent programs exist compared to those available for adults. To the extent that a nationwide secondary prevention program would be successful, the need for treatment facilities and programs would become more acute. Treatment providers and prevention specialists, therefore, should work together in planning and implementing the proposed strategies.

How to Organize, Implement, and Evaluate a Secondary Prevention Program

Secondary prevention programs should be planned, implemented, and evaluated by a broad spectrum of participants, including adolescents and local community representatives (Brody 1975; Swisher 1979).

Generic Programs

The prevention program should be *generic* in character, rather than substance-specific. Considerable evidence now exists to indicate the predominance of *multiple substance abuse* (MSA): the sequential and/or concurrent abuse of several psychoactive substances, typically alcohol and some other drug or drugs (Carroll et al. 1977; Marjot 1979; Carroll et al. 1980; Lowman 1981–1982; Simpson and Lloyd 1981; Croughan et al. 1981; Ottenberg and Carroll 1982; Benzer and Cushman 1983). This is especially true for youthful substance abusers who readily switch from one substance to another and/or who constantly search for drugs that provide the best high (Beschner and Friedman 1979; Greene 1980; Carroll 1980a; Carroll et al. 1980; Santo and Friedman 1980).

The phenomenon of MSA, plus substantial clinical and research evidence that the personality dynamics and psychopathology of drug abusers and alcohol abusers are more similar than different (Carroll 1980b; Carroll et al. 1981; Carroll et al. 1982), would seem to argue cogently for a generic prevention strategy. Rather than placing emphasis on a particular substance, generic prevention strategies focus on addressing the major underlying problems associated with substance abuse (for example, low self-esteem, abuse of substances by family members and/or peers, serious family conflicts and problems, and frustrating and stressful learning or work environments) and the multitude of environmental factors that support and sustain substance abuse. Generic prevention programs, therefore, should be equally well received regardless of what substance(s) adolescents may have used.

Ecological Emphasis

The proposed secondary prevention program should also be *ecological* in character, meaning that it should attend to both individual *and* environmental factors and their interrelationships. A growing appreciation of the ecological perspective has been slowly gaining momentum within the substance abuse field, which for the most part is still dominated by the "disease" and "intrapsychic" points of view (Halleck 1970; Bowes 1974; Nelson 1974; Nelson et al. 1975; Carroll 1975; Norem-Hebeisen and Lucas 1977; Dembo et al. 1978; Dembo 1979; Crisp 1980a,b; Schwartz 1981; Payton 1981).

In such a program, the role of individual pathology (for example, depression, anxiety) and inadequate coping skills (for example, in forming intimate relationships, decision-making, acting assertively) would be stressed. Also emphasized would be the significance of negative role modeling, peer pressures, and societal forces which frustrate the fulfillment of basic human needs and the realization of potential (for example, racial and sexual prejudices, unemployment).

An ecological perspective is particularly important in substance abuse prevention, since numerous external environmental factors have been correlated with substance abuse (Nelson 1974; Bowes 1974; Nelson et al. 1975; Dembo et al. 1978; Dembo 1979; Payton 1981). Role modeling of substance abuse by significant others (especially parents and older siblings) and peer pressure in particular have received considerable attention (Meier and Johnson 1977; Evans et al. 1978; Gritz 1978; Evans et al. 1979; Perry et al. 1980a,b; U.S. Department of Health and Human Services, ADAMHA, NIDA, 1981). Any treatment strategy or prevention program which fails to address the adolescent substance abuser's principal ecosystems (for example, family, school, peer social network) can, at best, expect only limited success.

Honesty

Another recommendation for a sound secondary prevention program is that it adhere scrupulously to scientific ethics and traditions regarding the interpretation of published research findings. This means that when scientific data contrary to one's point of view have been published in the literature, this information must be faced and presented in an honest and straightforward manner. For example, the contradictory claims concerning marijuana's effect on the immune and reproductive systems, as well as the scientific studies rejecting claims of brain damage with low to moderate levels of marijuana use, would be presented to adolescents in a marijuana-oriented prevention program.

This admonition also means that a presenter must take care not to overgeneralize, exaggerate, distort, or conceal the existence of scientific data in order to convince his/her audience to abstain from some substance. Whatever the short-term gains to be realized through such attempts, the long-range costs associated with a sense of betrayal, outrage, and distrust of the older generation by adolescents are simply not worth it.

It is a well-established psychological fact that a two-sided argument is superior to a one-sided argument when a presenter is delivering a message that runs counter to his/her audience's belief (Baron and Byrne, 1981). Thus, if a prevention specialist wishes to diminish the incidence of substance abuse among adolescent substance users, s/he will be more persuasive by covering both sides of the argument (for example, in discussing legalizing marijuana or allowing 18-year-olds the right to purchase and use alcohol.)

Alternatives to Fear Induction

Secondary prevention programs should not rely upon fear as a principal dynamic for achieving compliance with the program's objectives. Fear alone is of limited value in effecting lasting behavioral change (Janis and Feshbach 1953). No matter how charged the message with forebodings of imprisonment, disease, mental illness, and so on, most young substance users assume these dire consequences will not happen to them—someone else perhaps, "but not me." This clinical observation was borne out by a recent study of students (grades 7–13) concerning their use of marijuana (Goodstadt et al 1984).

In confronting a substance abuser with the negative psychobiosocial consequences of his/her abuse, other messages must also be communicated. For example, instilling a sense of hope, communicating a genuine sense of concern and acceptance, and providing support and encouragement for constructive behavioral changes in the direction of sobriety and self-fulfillment are also important ingredients.

The presenter, therefore, must do more than criticize the pattern of substance abuse, since doing only that would likely be perceived as merely "dumping" or playing "psychiatrist" or "parent." The adolescent substance abusers must also perceive genuine caring and concern.

Multidimensional, Tenured, Integrated Programs

In the past, most school-based prevention programs were unidimensional (for example, designed to enhance self-esteem), transient, "one-shot" experiments conducted by "outsiders." This gave the programs an artificial, foreign quality, which contrasted sharply with other school programs that were continuous and well integrated into the curriculum and presented by school faculty. To be successful, prevention programs must have some degree of tenure; should be multidimensional in scope; should be well integrated into the environment; and wherever possible, should enlist faculty, students, and community representatives to do at least some of the instructing and training.

To be well integrated, secondary prevention programs must blend with the various settings in which they are based and interface well with the treatment centers to which the serious substance abusing adolescent can be referred. This can be readily achieved by enlisting the aid of staff from local treatment agencies in the planning and implementation of the prevention programs. In that way, the entire referral process can be expedited, a key ingredient in secondary prevention.

Multidimensional prevention programs recognize that addiction and substance abuse have multiple causes. To counter this, prevention programs must address a variety of issues, over time, in an interrelated manner. In this respect, secondary prevention programs should be blended into a curriculum which also provides for some primary prevention programming. This could be accomplished by stressing wellness programs in the elementary and junior high schools. Such programs would be directed toward affective education, enhancing communication and decision-making skills, and so on. As the student matures, secondary prevention should play a greater role, especially in identifying early signs of emotional distress and substance abuse.

Examples of School-Based and Community-Based Secondary Prevention Programs

An excellent example of secondary prevention in a school-based program is the Lincoln School in Montgomery County, Pennsylvania (Ottenberg et al. 1985). In effect, the school operates a day treatment center for adolescents with multiple problems, including drug and alcohol abuse. Referrals are made to the Lincoln School from the local school district, the courts and probation system, and the local family and youth services agencies.

The program's operative principles combine the values, traditions, and practices of a therapeutic community with the principles and practices of B.F. Skinner's operant conditioning. Thus great emphasis is placed on creating a positive, therapeutic milieu wherein caring, responsible concern for self and others, open communication, personal growth, and a sense of community are promoted. A token economy for recognizing and reinforcing (rewarding) positive behavior is also employed. Violence of any kind is strictly prohibited. Other proscribed behaviors include possessing or using any drug(s) on school grounds, coming to school high, displaying drug paraphernalia or symbols, leaving the facility without proper permission, and using foul, sexist, or racist language.

The program's staff includes certified teachers provided by the Norristown Area School District, drug and alcohol counselors, and volunteers. All have been thoroughly trained and educated concerning drug and alcohol abuse by adolescents. Many of the staff live in Montgomery County. The staff tends to mirror the demographic characteristics of the students.

The Lincoln School provides the following clinical services: individualized treatment planning; individual, group, and family counseling; art and recreational therapy; crisis intervention; and discharge planning. Regular lectures and discussions are provided on substance abuse by in-house and outside speakers.

The program satisfies the definition of a secondary prevention program in that it provides an effective therapeutic intervention early on in the addictive process. It teaches the students how to recognize the early signs of substance abuse, as well as how to constructively confront the substance-abusing adolescent (and adult). It also informs them where they can turn for help with their problems.

The program is also involved in primary prevention in that it seeks to provide constructive and interesting alternatives to substance use for students not abusing substances. It focuses on building self-esteem, improving family relationships, and acquiring the skills needed to be an effective decision-maker.

Other school-based secondary prevention programs (Alternatives, Inc., Hampton-Newport News, Virginia; Rites of Passage in Philadelphia, Pennsylvania; the Phoenix School Program in Montgomery County, Maryland: and New York City's SPARK program) have been described by Cohen (1985).

Feldman and his colleagues (1985) have provided a detailed description of a community-based secondary prevention program, the Youth Environment Study (YES) program operating in the San Francisco Bay area. To ascertain the needs and problems confronting youthful substance abusers in this area, YES conducted ethnographic research (that is, had its staff make direct observations and contacts with youth by immersing themselves in the youth subcultures of the area). The staff relied on introductions by individuals trusted by youth and/or hung around until some natural, "fortuitous incident" presented itself (for example, helping a young man who had accumulated many parking tickets to cope with the court system) as their principal means of gaining access to the youth subcultures.

Significantly, Feldman et al. repeatedly cautioned against focusing solely on substance abuse problems. They noted that substance abuse problems typically are "enmeshed in a complex of other and often more important issues and problems." The YES program also stressed meeting young people in their respective communities through activities they found interesting (athletics, music and dance, and various forms of arts and crafts). YES services included crisis intervention, client advocacy, referral, supportive individual counseling, group counseling where appropriate (for example, Latino males were described as being adverse to group counseling), and assisting in the arrangement for special events (for example, block parties, exhibits, and entertainment).

The appreciation of an ecological perspective shown by the YES staff and its unique ethnographic approach to needs assessment distinguished this project from any other which this author has encountered. To a great extent, the YES project is an embodiment of the secondary prevention approach advocated by this author.

Other community-based secondary prevention projects are described by Cohen (1985); they include the Community Coordination of Drug Abuse Control (CCODAC) in Boise, Idaho; Channel One, derived from a local program in Gloucester, Massachusetts; and the Alternative Pursuits Project in Hampton-Newport News, Virginia. These programs share a common nonpsychiatric perspective of substance abuse by youth and a deep commitment to redirecting young people into alternative, constructive, and responsible activities. Typically, community leaders and adolescents are involved with project staff in conducting community needs assessments, identifying community resources, and planning and implementing projects designed to empower youth, enhance their self-esteem, improve their social relationships, and involve them in meaningful social service to their communities.

Evaluation and Accountability

The need for evaluation and accountability in prevention has been widely and repeatedly addressed (Schaps et al. 1981; Klee and West 1982; Kim 1982; Glynn 1983). Two suggestions are offered to insure a valid assessment of a program's effectiveness. One, broaden the spectrum of people charged with evaluating prevention programs by including consumer representatives (adolescents), self-help groups such as AA and NA, community-based representatives, and experienced clinicians. Two, abandon absolute standards in favor of relative standards. For example, instead of counting any instance of substance use subsequent to participation in a prevention program as a "failure" discern whether there has been a relative increase or decrease in use. Employ measures such as "number of days without use," "number of days inebriated or high."

Finally, the time at which assessment is done is particularly important. Convenience and funding limitations often dictate when and which followup measures will be taken. Good common sense is needed to recognize that after a prevention program ends many significant psychosocial events will occur which can influence outcome measures. Determining the extent to which outcome variables reflect the efficacy of a particular intervention, rather than factors external to the program, has always been, and probably always will be, one of the most difficult challenges to meet.

Analyzing Resistance to Secondary Prevention

Secondary prevention concerns itself primarily with youngsters who are already using drugs, some regularly. Therein lies both the strength and weakness of this approach. Because secondary prevention strategists do not condemn all forms of unsanctioned substance use, they can more readily engage adolescents in a meaningful, honest dialogue about the types of substances that are used and about how to decrease such use and eventually become drug free. While this approach is likely to be effective in reaching some adolescents, it can engender considerable anger and resistance from other quarters, including parents, school authorities, and politicians, who may not fully understand why it is necessary to use different approaches. This further supports the argument for enlisting a broad spectrum of experts in the planning, implementation, and evaluation of secondary prevention programs.

Some people will misunderstand secondary prevention strategies and feel that the prevention specialist is condoning or even encouraging substance use by adolescents. Anyone contemplating a secondary prevention program should be prepared to address this issue patiently and repeatedly. Coping with these attitudes may constitute either a hindrance or an opportunity, depending on one's resources and situation. Perhaps the best way to educate the public would be to provide graphic, concrete illustrations of the difference between use and abuse. Such education should also include informing people where they can turn for help when they are confronted by a substance abuse problem.

Prevention programs generally have to face the reluctance of some parents to acknowledge substance use and abuse by their adolescents. Fearful images of an uncontrollable, incurable disease destroying their offspring, coupled with the specter of unrelenting self-accusations of failure as a parent, can generate considerable denial and resistance. Furthermore, teaching parents the distinction between use and abuse will ultimately demand a more knowledgeable approach and diagnostic evaluation of their adolescent's involvement with substances. Many parents would find it simpler to take the absolute position that the use of substances is unacceptable no matter what the circumstances, even if that risks cutting off honest communication with their offspring. To help overcome such resistance, special training materials need to be developed (such as video cassettes, film strips, and movies) which would clearly illustrate the futility and cost of insisting on a rigid and absolute proscription.

Some school administrators may also resist a secondary prevention program, since it requires honestly admitting that there may be widespread substance abuse problems in their schools. Such admissions may have serious negative political consequences in certain communities. In selling secondary prevention programs to the schools, therefore, the lasting gratitude of parents whose adolescents will be spared the serious devastation associated with an undetected, untreated addiction through the implementation of a secondary prevention program should not be overlooked. The promise of such appreciation could serve as an important counterpoint to the fear of acknowledging substance use and abuse in the schools.

Prevention specialists might best seek to implement such programs at the school district level, which would not place any particular principal in the position of being the only principal with these kinds of problems in his/her school district. Providing school administrators with concrete evidence of parental approval of secondary prevention programs implemented in other schools would also help overcome politically based resistance.

Primary Prevention's Place

The suggestion to use secondary prevention does not mean that primary prevention should be abandoned. Much can be learned from different prevention strategies that have been initiated in recent years:

1. Programs designed to enhance self-esteem (Eiseman 1974; Botvin and Eng 1980; Iverson and Roberts 1980).

2. Programs designed to increase interpersonal competencies (Wolk and Tomanio 1974; Botvin et al. 1980; Kearney and Hines 1980).

3. Programs that teach adolescents how to resist social pressures to use substances (Hurd et al. 1980; McAlister et al. 1980; Perry et al. 1980a,b) and how to make sound decisions (Botvin et al. 1980; Kearney and Hines 1980; Smith 1983).

4. Programs designed to enhance awareness of feelings and appropriate expression of feelings (Mathews 1975; Safford et al. 1975; and Blizard and Teague 1981).

5. Programs designed to teach stress management (McAlister et al. 1979).

6. Programs which employ positive identification figures, including the use of older adolescents as teachers or role models for younger adolescents (Evans et al. 1978; Spitzzeri and Jason 1979; Hurd et al. 1980; Iverson and Roberts 1980; McAlister et al. 1980; Perry et al. 1980c; Evans et al. 1981). Smart et al. (1976), however, caution that the use of peers as instructors does not always yield lower rates for substance use.

Regardless of what age group is targeted, primary prevention programs should also be multidimensional in character, be extended over time, and be fully integrated with other school and/or community services. For example, the more promising primary approaches cited above could be developed into a sequence of courses to be offered over a span of several years. Each of the objectives, taken at face value, would seem to be conducive to good mental health which would aid in reducing substance abuse.

Stressing one type of prevention does not mean other prevention strategies need to be abandoned, but that under certain circumstances they may be relegated to a less intensive focus and be allocated fewer resources. Thus, some training in identifying the early signs of alcohol and/or drug abuse could be included in primary prevention programs; and primary prevention strategies should be part of secondary prevention programs, as illustrated by the Lincoln School program described above.

Summary

There is a growing awareness that multiple strategies are needed to prevent youngsters from using or becoming more seriously involved with drugs. Emphasis in this chapter has been on secondary prevention which has, up to this time, been given less attention than primary prevention.

The three major objectives of a secondary substance abuse prevention program for adolescents are

1. to teach adolescents how to identify the early signs of substance abuse;

2. to teach adolescents how to assist their peers to recognize and accept the fact that they need treatment; and

3. to teach adolescents where they can refer their friends in need of treatment.

A list of early signs of alcohol and marijuana abuse was provided to illustrate the first objective. Suggestions were offered for achieving the second and third objectives, with particular emphasis on working closely with existing community-based treatment programs, including self-help groups such as AA and NA.

Information was also provided on how best to organize, implement, and evaluate secondary prevention programs, including generic programs suitable for the multiple substance abuse dominant among adolescents. An ecological frame of reference was recommended, as was honesty and evenhandedness in presenting scientific facts to adolescents. Those initiating prevention programs should avoid the tendency to rely too much on fear induction as the principal means of effecting behavioral changes. Multidimensional, tenured, integrated programming was advised. Specific illustrations of school and community-based secondary prevention programs were provided. Finally, the need for evaluation and accountability was stressed. Two suggestions were provided to improve this process: utilizing a broad spectrum of experts for purposes of evaluation, and using relative rather than absolute standards.

Resistances to secondary prevention programming were identified, including widespread misunderstanding and failure to appreciate the value of distinguishing substance use from abuse, parental fears and denial, and school administrators' reluctance to confront directly the widespread substance use and abuse in their schools. Primary prevention is not to be neglected, especially among pre- and early adolescents. Specific primary prevention strategies for use along with secondary methods were cited (for example, increasing personal competencies and teaching adolescents how to resist peer pressure to use substances). Where appropriate, primary and secondary prevention strategies may be combined.

References

Baron, R.A. & Byrne, D. 1981. *Social Psychology: Understanding Human Interaction.* 3rd ed. Boston: Allyn & Bacon.

Benzer, D. & Cushman, P. 1983. Alcohol and benzodiazepines: Withdrawal symptoms. *Alcoholism: Clinical and Experimental Research* (3): 243–247.

Beschner, G.M. & Friedman, A.S., eds. 1979. *Youth Drug Abuse: Problems, Issues and Treatment.* Lexington, Mass.: Lexington Books.

Blizard, R.A. & Teague, R.W. 1981. Alternatives to drug use. An alternative approach to drug education. *The International Journal of the Addictions* (2): 371–375.

Botvin, G.J. & Eng, A. 1980. A comprehensive school-based smoking prevention program. *The Journal of School Health* 50(4): 209–213.

Botvin, G.J.; Eng. A.; & Williams, C.L. 1980. Preventing the onset of cigarette smoking through life skills training. *Preventive Medicine* 9(1): 135–143.

Bowes, R. 1974. The industry as pusher. *Journal of Drug Issues* 4(3): 238–242.

Brody, L.G. 1975. Drug program development at the community level: An integrative strategy. *Addictive Diseases: An International Journal* 1(4): 455–464.

Brown, E.H. & Klein, A.L. 1975. The effects of drug education programs on attitude change. *Journal of Drug Education* 5(1): 51–56.

Bry, B.H. 1978. Research design in drug abuse prevention, review and recommendations. *The International Journal of the Addictions* 13(7): 1157–1168.

Bry, B.H. 1985. Substance abuse in women: Etiology and prevention. In A.U. Rickel, M. Gerrard & I. Iscoe (eds.) *Social and Psychological Problems of Women: Prevention and Crisis Intervention*. New York: McGraw-Hill/Hemisphere. In press.

Carroll, J.F.X. 1975. "Mental illness" and "disease": Outmoded concepts in alcohol and drug rehabilitation. *Community Mental Health Journal* 11(4): 418–429.

———. 1980a. Uncovering drug abuse by alcoholics and alcohol abuse by addicts. *The International Journal of the Addictions* 15(4): 591–595.

———. 1980b. Similarities and differences of personality and psychopathology between alcoholics and addicts. *American Journal of Drug and Alcohol Abuse* 7(2): 219–236.

———. 1981. Perspectives on marijuana use and abuse and recommendations for preventing abuse. *American Journal of Drug Alcohol Abuse* 8(3): 259–282.

Carroll, J.F.X.; Malloy, T.E.; Hannigan, P.C.; Santo, Y.; & Kendrick, F.M. 1977. The meaning and evolution of the term "multiple substance abuse." *Contemporary Drug Problems*, Summer: 101–133.

Carroll, J.F.X.; Malloy, T.E.; Roscioli, D.L.; & Godard, D.R. 1981. Personality similarities and differences in four diagnostic groups of women alcoholics and drug addicts. *Journal of Studies on Alcohol* 42(5): 431–440.

Carroll, J.F.X.; Malloy, T.E.; Roscioli, D.L.; Pindjak, G.M.; & Glifford, J.S. 1982. Similarities and differences in self-concepts of women alcoholics and drug addicts. *Journal of Studies on Alcohol* 43(7): 725–738.

Carroll, J.F.X.; Santo, Y.; & Hannigan, P.C. 1980. Description of the total client sample, analysis of substance use patterns, and individual program descriptions. In S.E. Gardner (ed.), *National Drug/Alcohol Collaborative Project: Issues in Multiple Substance Abuse* (DHEW Publication No. (ADM) 80–957). Rockville, Maryland: National Institute on Drug Abuse.

Chafetz, M.E. 1974. Prevention of alcoholism in the United States utilizing cultural and educational forces. *Preventive Medicine* 3: 5–10.

Cohen, A.Y. 1985. Drug treatment in school and alternative school settings. In A.S. Friedman & G. Beschner (eds.), *Treatment Services for Adolescent Substance Abusers*. Rockville, Maryland: NIDA (DHHS Publication No. (ADM) 85–1342).

Crisp, A.D. 1980a. Making substance abuse prevention relevant to low-income black neighborhoods. *Journal of Psychedelic Drugs* 12(1): 13–19.

———. 1980b. Making substance abuse prevention relevant to low-income black neighborhoods II: Research findings. *Journal of Psychedelic Drugs* 12(2): 139–156.

Croughan, J.L.; Miller, J.P.; Whitman, B.Y.; & Schober, J.G. 1981. Alcoholism and alcohol dependence in narcotic addicts: A prospective study with a five-year follow-up. *American Journal of Drug and Alcohol Abuse* 8(1): 85–94.

DeLone, R.H. 1972. The ups and down of drug-abuse education. *Saturday Review* 55(46): 27–32.

Dembo, R. 1979. Substance abuse prevention programming and research: A partnership in need of improvement. *Journal of Drug Education* 9(3): 189–208.

Dembo, R.; Burgos, W.; Babst, D.V.; Schmeidler, J.; & La Grand, L.E. 1978. Neighborhood relationships and drug involvement among inner city junior high school youths: Implications for drug education and prevention programming. *Journal of Drug Education* 8(3): 231–252.

Eiseman, S. 1974. An approach to primary prevention of drug abuse among children and youth—parental influence. *Journal of Drug Education* 4(1): 27–35.

Evans, R.I.; Henderson, A.; Hill, P.; & Raines, B. 1979. Smoking in children and adolescents. National Institute on Child Health and Human Development. In U.S. Department of Health, Education and Welfare, *Smoking and Health. A report of the Surgeon General* (DHEW Publication No. (PHS) 79–50066). Washington, D.C.: U.S. Government Printing Office.

Evans, R.I.; Rozelle, R.M.; Maxwell, S.E.; Raines, B.E.; Dill, C.A.; Guthrie, T.J.; Henderson, A.H.; & Hill, P.C. 1981. Social modeling films to deter smoking in adolescents: Results of a three-year field investigation. *Journal of Applied Psychology* 66(4): 399–414.

Evans, R.I.; Rozelle, R.M.; Mittelmark, M.B.; Hansen, W.B.; Bane, A.L.; & Havis, J. 1978. Deterring the onset of smoking in children: Knowledge of immediate physiological effects and coping with peer pressure, media pressure, and parent modeling. *Journal of Applied Social Psychology* 8(2): 126–135.

Feldman, H.W.; Mandel, J.; & Fields, A. 1985. In the neighborhood: A strategy for delivering early intervention services to young drug users in their natural environments. In A.S. Friedman & G. Beschner (eds.) *Treatment Services for Adolescent Substance Abusers.* Rockville, Maryland: NIDA (DHHS Publication No. (ADM) 85–1342).

Floyd, J.D. & Lotsof, A.B. 1977. If we could make it so: Drug education for exceptional children. *Journal of Drug Education* 7(1): 63–70.

Glynn, T.J., ed. 1983. *Research Issues 33: Drug abuse prevention research* (DHHS Publication No. (ADM) 83–1270). Rockville, Maryland: U.S. Dept. of Health and Human Services, ADAMHA, National Institute on Drug Abuse.

Goodstadt, M.S.; Sheppard, M.A.; & Chan, G.C. 1984. Non-use and cessation of cannabis use: Neglected foci of drug education. *Addictive Behaviors* 9: 21–31.

Greene, B.T. 1980. Sequential use of drugs and alcohol: A re-examination of the stepping-stone hypothesis. *American Journal of Drug and Alcohol Abuse* 7(1): 83–99.

Gritz, E.R. 1978. Smoking: The prevention of onset. In National Institute on Drug Abuse, *Research on Smoking Behavior* (NIDA Research Monograph

17, DHEW Publication No. (ADM) 79–581). Washington, D.C.: U.S. Government Printing Office.

Halleck, S.L. 1970. The great drug education hoax. *The Progressive* 34(7): 30–33.

Harding, W. & Zinberg, N. 1977. The effectiveness of the subculture in developing rituals and sanctions for controlled drug use. In B. Du Toit (ed.), *Drug rituals and altered states of consciousness*. Rotterdam, The Netherlands: A.A. Balkena.

Hilliker, J.K.; Grupp, S.E.; & Schmitt, R.L. 1981. Adult marijuana use and Becker's social controls. *The International Journal of Addictions* 16(6): 1009–1030.

Hurd, P.D.; Johnson, C.A.; Pechacek, T.; Bast, L.P.; Jacobs, D.R.; & Luepker, R.V. 1980. Prevention of cigarette smoking in seventh grade students. *Journal of Behavioral Medicine* 3(1): 15–28.

Irwin, S. 1973. *A rational approach to drug abuse prevention*. Madison, Wisconsin: Stash Press.

Iutcovich, J.M.; & Iutovich, M. 1982. Just for fun: Alcohol and the college student. *Chemical Dependencies: Behavioral and Biomedical Issues* 4(3): 167–185.

Iverson, D.C. & Roberts, T.E. 1980. The juvenile intervention program: Results of the process, impact and outcome evaluations. *Journal of Drug Education* 10(4): 289–300.

Jalali, R.; Jalali, M.; Crocetti, G.; & Turner, F. 1981. Adolescents and drug use: Toward a more comprehensive approach. *American Journal of Orthopsychiatry* 51(1): 120–129.

Janis, I.L.; & Feshbach, S. 1953. Effects of fear-arousing communications. *Journal of Abnormal and Social Psychology* 48: 78–92.

Kearney, A.L.; & Hines, M.H. 1980. Evaluation of the effectiveness of a drug prevention education program. *Journal of Drug Education* 10(2): 127–134.

Kim, S. 1982. A uniform progress and evaluation reporting system for alcohol and drug abuse prevention agencies: Two examples. *Journal of Drug Education* 12(4): 309–323.

Klee, T.E. & West, M. 1982. *Prevention Program Evaluation: A Funding Model for Prevention Programs*. Harrisburg, Pennsylvania: Office of Drug and Alcohol Programs.

Lowman, C. 1981–82. Alcohol use as a indicator of psychoactive drug use among the nation's senior high school students. *Alcohol Health and Research World* 6(2): 41–46.

Marjot, D.H. 1979. Annotation: Alcohol, alcoholism and drugs. *British Journal on Alcohol and Alcoholism* 14(2): 69–73.

Mathews, W.M. 1975. A critique of traditional drug education programs. *Journal of Drug Education* 5(1): 57–69.

McAlister, A.L.; Perry, C.; Killen, J.; Slinkard, L.A.; & Maccoby, N. 1980. Pilot study of smoking, alcohol and drug abuse prevention. *American Journal of Public Health* 70(7): 719–721.

McAlister, A.L.; Perry C.; & Maccoby, N. 1979. Adolescent smoking: Onset and prevention. *Pediatrics* 63(4): 650–658.

Meier, R.F. & Johnson, W.T. 1977. Deterrence as social control: The legal and extra-legal production of conformity. *American Sociological Review* 42: 292–304.

Milgram, G.G. & Pandina, R.J. 1981. Educational implications of adolescent substance use. *Journal of Alcohol and Drug Education* 26(3): 13–22.

Nathan, P.E. 1983. Failures in prevention: Why we can't prevent the devastating effect of alcoholism and drug abuse. *American Psychologist.* 38(4): 459–467.

National Council on Alcoholism. 1972. *The Modern Approach to Alcoholism.* Little Ferry, New Jersey: Employee Communications.

Nelson, G. 1974. New laws are needed to regulate the drug industry. *Journal of Drug Issues* 4(3): 243–248.

Nelson, S.H.; Wolff, B.; & Batalden, P.B. 1975. Manpower training as an alternative to disadvantaged adolescent drug misuse. *American Journal of Public Health* 65(6): 599–603.

Norem-Hebeisen, A.A. & Lucas, M.S. 1977. A developmental model for primary prevention of chemical abuse. *Journal of Drug Education* 7(2): 141–148.

Ottenberg, D.J. & Carroll, J.F.X. 1982. Combined treatment of alcoholism and drug addiction. In J. Solomon & K.A. Keeley (eds.), *Perspectives in Alcohol and Drug Abuse: Similarities and Differences.* Boston: John Wright.

Ottenberg, D.J.; Olson, G.R.; & Schiller, B.D. 1985. The day treatment center: An alternative for adolescent substance abusers. In A.S. Friedman & G. Beschner (eds.), *Treatment Services for Adolescent Substance Abusers.* Rockville, Maryland: NIDA (DHHS Publication No. (ADM) 85–1342)

Palisano, P. 1980. Alcoholism: Industry's $15 billion hangover. *Occupational Hazards* 1981. 42(9): 54–58.

Payton, C.R. Substance abuse and mental health: Special prevention strategies needed for ethnics of color. *Public Health Reports* 96(1): 20–25.

Perry, C.L.; Killen, J.; Slinkard, L.A.; & McAlister, A.L. 1980a. Peer teaching and smoking prevention among junior high students. *Adolescence* 15(58): 277–281.

Perry, C.L.; Killen, J.; Telch, M.; Slinkard, L.A.; & Danaher, B.G. 1980b. Modifying smoking behavior of teenagers: A school-based intervention. *American Journal of Public Health* 70(7): 722–725.

Perry, C.L.; Maccoby, N.; & McAlister, A.L. 1980c. Adolescent smoking prevention: A third year follow-up. *World Smoking & Health* 5(3): 40–45.

Portnoy, B. 1980. Effects of a controlled-usage alcohol education program based on the health belief model. *Journal of Drug Education* 10(3): 181–195.

Safford, P.L.; Deighan, W.P.; Corder, L.K.; & Miller, W.S. 1975. Training teachers for drug abuse prevention: A humanistic approach. *Journal of Drug Education* 5(4): 335–349.

Santo, Y. & Friedman, A.S. 1980. Overview and selected findings from the National Youth Polydrug Study. *Contemporary Drug Problems* 9(3): 285–300.

Schaps, E.; DiBartolo, R.; Moskowitz, J.; Palley, C.S.; & Churgin, S. 1981. A review of 127 drug abuse prevention program evaluations. *Journal of Drug Issues* 11(1): 17–43.

Schiler, P. 1981. Information, teaching and education in the primary prevention of drug abuse among youth in Denmark. *Bulletin on Narcotics* 33(4): 57–65.

Schwartz, S. & Bodanske, E.A. 1981. Environmental strategies for primary drug abuse prevention programs. *Journal of Prevention* 1(3): 188–198.

Simpson, D.D. & Lloyd, M.R. 1981. Alcohol use following treatment for drug addiction. *Journal of Studies on Alcohol* 42: 323–335.

Smart, R.G.; Bennett, C.; & Gigliotti, R.J. 1976. Are drug education programs effective? *Journal of Drug Education* 6(4): 305–311.

Smith, T.E. 1983. Reducing adolescents' marijuana abuse. *Social Work in Health Care* 9(1): 33–44.

———. 1984. Reviewing adolescent marijuana abuse. *Social Work* 29(1): 17–21.

Spitzzeri, A. & Jason, L.A. 1979. Prevention and treatment of smoking in school age children. *Journal of Drug Education* 9(3): 189–208.

Stuart, R.B. 1974. Teaching facts about drugs: Pushing or preventing? *Journal of Education Psychology* 66(2): 189–201.

Swisher, J.D. 1979. Prevention issues. In R.L. DuPont, A. Goldstein, & J. O'-Donnell (eds.) *Handbook on Drug Abuse*. National Institute on Drug Abuse. Washington, D.C.: U.S. Government Printing Office.

———. 1974. The effectiveness of drug education: Conclusions based on experimental evaluations. In M. Goodstadt (ed.), *Research on Methods and Programs of Drug Education*. Ontario, Canada: Addictions Research Foundation.

Swisher, J.D.; Crawford, J.; Goldstein, R.; & Yura, M. 1971. Drug education: Pushing or preventing? *Peabody Journal of Education* 55: 68–75.

U.S. Department of Health and Human Services, ADAMHA, NIDA. 1981. *Adolescent Peer Pressure: Theory, Correlates, and Program Implications for Drug Abuse Prevention*. DHHS Publication No. (ADM) 83–1152. Washington, D.C.: U.S. Government Printing Office.

Weller, R.A. & Halikas, J.A. 1980. Objective criteria for the diagnosis of marijuana abuse. *Journal of Nervous and Mental Disorders* 168: 98–103.

Williams, M. & Vejnoska, J. 1981. Alcohol and youth state prevention approaches. *Alcohol Health and Research World* 6(1): 2–13.

Wolk, D.J. & Tomanio, A.J. 1974. A community-school problem-solving approach to the drug situation. *Journal of Drug Education* 4(2): 157–168.

Worden, M. 1984. Traditional prevention efforts don't work. *U.S. Journal of Drug and Alcohol Dependence* 8(3): 16.

Zinberg, N.E.; Jacobson, R.C.; & Harding, W.M. 1975. Social sanctions and rituals as a basis for drug abuse prevention. *American Journal of Drug & Alcohol Abuse* 2(2): 165–182.

9

Adolescent Drug Abuse: The Parents' Predicament.

Leslie H. Daroff
S.J. Marks
Alfred S. Friedman

Introduction: "Not My Child"

Our society tends to hold parents responsible for the behavior of their adolescent children. Some jurisdictions even punish parents by levying fines against them if their children are involved in drug abuse, are not attending school, or are refusing treatment. But in reality, many thousands of parents feel powerless to control their children's behavior or to cope with the myriad problems generated by their youngsters. The fact that their child is using drugs is, for most parents, very difficult and painful to accept. This pain of the parent adds to the emotional complexity of the problems associated with adolescent drug use.

To begin with, few parents are ready to believe that their own child is using drugs. They have a tendency to disbelieve or deny the symptoms of drug use in their children and to interpret even obvious indicators in other ways. Many parents attribute the abrupt changes in their child's behavior and personality to "adolescence." As a result, it is common to find that a youngster's drug problem has gotten quite serious before the parents take any action on their own or seek professional help. Most parents believe that they have raised their children with love, guidance, and support, so that the children should have developed the personal values and self-assurance needed to resist peer pressure to use drugs. A parent may believe tentatively that the teenager is using drugs but doesn't confront the teenager. The child may see the parent's reluctance to confront the problem even though the youngster may be inwardly yearning for help.

One of the frequent questions that parents ask is "How can I tell if my child is on drugs?" Parents are often looking for a simple guide to recognizing physical and/or behavioral signs. There are booklets providing this information, but, in spite of what has been said above, one should be careful not to jump to conclusions. For example, there are many reasons other than drugs why youngsters might have bleary eyes. It could possibly be because they stayed up late at night talking on the telephone to a boyfriend or girlfriend, or watched a late television show, or couldn't sleep because of personal concerns. The more important factor for parents to consider is the quality of their relationship with their children and whether or not open communication is possible. If the relationship is solid, it is probably unnecessary to play medical detective.

Generally, parents should be advised to communicate openly with a child when there is any evidence of drug use. They should express their concerns for the child's health and future, and encourage the youngster to get help from someone who has more knowledge about these matters. It is likely that the youngster will deny using drugs regardless of the evidence. Typical responses are: "It's not mine; I'm holding it for a friend of mine." "I tried it once and didn't like it."

When the evidence becomes too obvious to ignore, parents either find that they do not know what to do or else they take actions that escalate the tensions that already exist in the family. The first reaction of many parents to teenage drug use is panic. However, panic usually does not help the situation and can very well complicate it. The authors surveyed seventy-eight mothers of adolescent drug abusers to find out how they reacted when they first discovered that their children were using drugs. The mothers reported that they

> Expressed concern for the effects of drug use on his/her life (89 percent)
>
> Gave reasons against drug use (84 percent)
>
> Withdrew privileges (55 percent)
>
> Threatened to discipline or punish (54 percent)
>
> Argued with (or yelled) at him/her (53 percent)
>
> Punished him/her (46 percent)
>
> Threatened to get rid of him/her (kick out of the house) (32 percent)

None reported that they did or said nothing.

Forty percent discovered the drug use when they found illicit drugs or drug paraphernalia in the adolescent's room. Only 11 percent found out by being notified by school personnel. Sixty-three percent of the mothers reported that their drug-abusing children "never" confided in them regarding their use of drugs, and another 28 percent reported that the children only confided in them "occasionally" or "seldom." Fifty-six percent of these mothers reported that they understood "nothing" or "little" about why their child was using drugs.

Other specific problem behaviors of the drug-abusing youngsters which were reported by the mothers were

He/she is difficult to talk to (78 percent)

His/her behavior warrants checking up on (71 percent)

He/she does what he/she pleases without consideration for me (69 percent)

He/she ignores house rules (68 percent)

He/she doesn't let me know where he/she is or what he/she is doing (67 percent)

He/she is distant and aloof (60 percent)

He/she doesn't respect me (59 percent)

His/her behavior frightens me (53 percent)

Findings of another research study (Glickman and Utada 1983) show a dramatic degree of misunderstanding, disagreement, and conflict between parents and their adolescent children who are seriously involved in drug abuse. The young drug abuse clients reported the following attitudes and reactions from at least one of their parents to them and their behavior, indicating a severe degree of family conflict.

Objects to my friends (77 percent)

Is disappointed in me (69 percent)

Complains too much (64 percent)

Doesn't trust me (63 percent)

In addition, at least half of the clients reported that their parents had negative perceptions of each of at least ten items of client behavior. Adolescent drug users have also been reported to perceive their parents as having less influence on them than their peers (Jessor 1975), and to perceive less shared authority and poorer communication in their families, compared to adolescents who do not use drugs (Cannon 1976).

Whether to take drugs is a choice that most children are going to have to make at some point in their lives. One of the most important elements in a family to counteract drug abuse is honesty. Parents should explore methods of fostering an atmosphere in which honesty is rewarded and communication with children is open. If a child honestly admits to using drugs, it should not prompt an extreme reaction from the parents or automatic punishment. If parents create a situation in which honesty brings only emotional upheaval, then the children certainly are not going to be honest. This does *not* mean that parents must give permission to use drugs. They still must say, "You don't have my permission to do that." It is important that the adolescents know what parents' rules, limits, and expectations are. If children feel that they can come to parents from the beginning, not only with their questions but also with their mistakes, it can avoid later crises when the choices become limited (when the youngster gets suspended from school, or the parent receives a phone call that the youngster has been admitted to a hospital emergency room with an overdose).

The following suggestion can be offered to parents who suspect that their teenage youngsters are using illicit drugs: there should be open discussion and an open atmosphere in the family about the pros and cons of drug use and, particularly, marijuana use. If there is good, open communication and if the parents do not overreact, do not get too uptight and do not moralize or threaten too much, the results of communication will be more positive.

Parents who confront the situation in an honest, open manner, talking about their own helplessness, guilts, fears, and angers, are more likely to gain the youngster's trust and have some influence on his/her drug taking. At times, parents need to be persistent and tenacious in order to succeed in their attempts to resolve disagreements, resentments, and impasses which prevent understanding and communication with their children. Some parents attempt to discuss their concerns in a calm and rational manner (as indicated by the majority of mothers referred to above) but are met with an unreasonably hostile response from their offspring. It is sometimes very difficult for a parent to know how to react, or what to do. The advice that the National Institute on Drug Abuse (NIDA) has for parents who think that their children are abusing drugs is as follows:

> In a straightforward way, tell your child about your concern and the reasons for it: taking drugs is harmful to one's physical, mental, and social well-being. Tell your child that you are opposed to any drug use and you intend to enforce that position. WHAT YOU SHOULD TRY TO BE IS: *Understanding* ("I realize you're under a lot of pressure from friends to use drugs."); *Firm* ("As your parent I cannot allow you to engage in harmful activities."); *Self-examining* ("Are my own alcohol and drug consumption habits exerting a bad influence on my child?"). WHAT YOU SHOULD NOT BE IS: *Sarcastic* ("Don't think I don't know what you're doing."); *Accusatory* ("You're lying to me."); *Stigmatizing* ("You're a terrible person."); *Sympathy-seeking* ("Don't you see how much you're hurting me?"); *Self-blaming* ("It's all my fault.").

Such statements tend to make the child defensive and likely to tune you out. (NIDA 1984a, pages 4–5)

Confronting a Painful Situation

A typical urgent phone call comes into a drug treatment clinic, from an anxious and confused mother. She has just been cleaning the child's room, and has come across "pills," "joints," a bag of "grass," or "'liquor." Initially, she may simply want some advice—whether she should tell her husband, whether they should confront the child, whether they should ignore it, whether they should take the child somewhere for help or whether they should contact others (clergy, school personnel). The counselor should try to reduce the anxiety and let the parent know that this is a serious but not necessarily an emergency situation. One must be careful in trying to diagnose by telephone because the situation is often different from the view of it that the parent has. The parent should be encouraged to discuss the situation with the spouse, so that they can make a united effort. Frequently, mothers are afraid to inform their husbands. "Oh, no, I couldn't tell my husband; it would kill him," or "I could never tell my husband, he would throw our son out in the street, or beat him up," or "My husband and son would come to physical blows."

Making the initial decision to address the problem is particularly difficult because it forces parents into a myriad of painful feelings and self-realizations. They are likely to feel that they have failed as parents and lost control of their children; that their own weaknesses are reflected in their children's "bad behavior"; that the child they have known and loved has become a stranger. How and why did this happen? "What's the matter with me/us?" It is only natural for parents to resist and defend themselves against looking at such implications until the drug problem has escalated into a very serious situation.

In addition to painful self-reflection, love and concern can lead to overwhelming grief, disappointment, and despair, as well as concerns about the child's physical and mental state and his or her ability to function in the future. Other emotional responses that parents frequently have are anger, embarrassment, and outright hostility toward the youth. While anger with the child's lying and rule breaking surrounding drug use may be appropriate and expected, open hostility among family members is a condition which was probably years in the making.

With this backlog of feelings, when parents confront their child on the issue of his or her drug use the encounter is often a very charged, emotional event complete with angry words, accusations, and counter-accusations. Such a scene usually results in further deterioration in the communication between parent and child and in everyone's feeling worse than before. The frequency of this type of disturbing interaction may well be greater than was indicated by the 53 percent of the mothers surveyed above who "argued with (or yelled) at him/her."

Mixed, Ambivalent, and Contradictory Feelings of Parents toward Their Adolescent Children

Parents have both positive and negative feelings toward their adolescent children who are using drugs. They want to protect and take care of them in certain ways, and they love them and are concerned for their welfare. But they also can get angry and even feel hostile towards them at times. They may want to get rid of the burden and responsibility, especially when the drug abuse problem becomes acute or has been going on for a long time. Many parents feel that it is not appropriate to admit having such negative and hostile feelings toward their own child, or to admit that they sometimes feel like getting rid of the child and the problem. They cannot handle these feelings in an honest, appropriate, or constructive way, and talk only about their positive feelings and concerns for the child. But children are very sensitive to the negative feelings and can pick them up very quickly. Some parents do not handle such ambivalent feelings constructively because they are in conflict—wanting to hold onto the child forever and to keep the child dependent on them, but at the same time wanting to get rid of the problem. One such mother, a divorced single parent, gave her 16-year-old drug-abusing son a deadline to leave home and be out on his own when he graduated from high school. However, she could not tolerate the idea of her son's not graduating from high school, and she needed him in certain ways particularly because she was divorced. He worked hard after school, earned money for drugs, but failed his courses in school, although he was very bright and had made good grades in the past. At 19 years of age he was still at home, still in school and his mother was still battling with him daily over his drug use and still trying periodically to get him to move out.

Parental Guilt and Self-Blame

Most parents have expectations about their children's leading successful lives. If the children fail, the parents may feel that they haven't prepared them appropriately, or haven't been good parents. A parent may feel ashamed or humiliated when a child fails or gets into trouble for example, being a self-destructive drug abuser, or getting into trouble with the school authorities or the law. Some adolescent drug abusers may take some pleasure in humiliating their parents.

Parents who take the position that "It must be my fault because of my parenting," generally feel helpless to do anything about the situation. If they confess these feelings to their youngster, it may help them to relieve the guilt feelings, but it may not help the youngster to change his/her behavior and stop using drugs. It is best if parents keep an open mind and approach the problem objectively and non-defensively, trying to understand how they may have contributed to the problems that led to the youngster's becoming seriously involved with drugs.

Sometimes both drug-abusing adolescents and their parents feel guilty about the problem. However, guilt feelings and self-blame do not necessarily result in improvement. In the following case, both the mother and the drug-abusing adolescent daughter blamed themselves.

An Italian Catholic mother, who had worked hard all her married life and supported her three daughters after her husband had died, was ashamed of her 22-year-old daughter, who had been on PCP and other drugs since she was 12 years of age. The daughter had overdosed, made eight suicide attempts, and the last time almost succeeded. The daughter knew how ashamed her mother was that the neighborhood people knew about her drug use and that she had given birth to a child out of wedlock. Her mother had been quite satisfied to raise the grandchild for the past five years while her daughter continued to use drugs. The daughter had expressed to her therapist genuine feelings of guilt at having embarrassed her mother publicly and stated that her mother didn't deserve to be hurt this way. She had recently had an abortion when she became pregnant a second time and had not been able to bring herself to confess to her mother about the pregnancy and abortion. The reason the daughter gave for her most recent suicide attempt was that because she felt guilty she could not tell her mother that she was going to have an abortion. At the same time, she seemed oblivious to the fact that her suicide attempt may have hurt and embarrassed her mother as much or more than the pregnancy and abortion. The mother said that she felt that she had failed as a parent to her daughter. Both mother and daughter felt ashamed and guilty. But having these feelings, while better than being indifferent, callous, or hostile toward each other, was not sufficient to improve the daughter's behavior or the relationship.

Some parents of adolescent drug abusers do not blame themselves or try to explore an understanding of the problem objectively. Many of these parents have been programmed all their lives to avoid blame. They tend to project the blame onto others—society, the school, the police, or their youngster. Having such guilt feelings would be too painful and uncomfortable, and they automatically defend themselves from experiencing such feelings.

It is not easy for the family to explore objectively how other family members might be involved, unwittingly, in the continuation of a youngster's drug abuse, nor to find ways as a family to improve the situation. Such an effort often requires the help of a professional third party, a family therapist who is experienced in working with such families.

You Are Not Alone

Because of the difficulties and suffering that they endure with adolescent drug problems and their need for support, many parents have banded together and developed organizations to help them deal with their uncertainties about the need to act and to find ways to assert their responsibility and authority. A publication entitled, "Parents, Peers and Pot II: Parents in Action," (NIDA 1984b) encourages these parental and community efforts and describes approaches that parent groups can take. Parent groups in some communities set up appropriate uniform curfews and party rules so their children and their friends will follow the same parental guidelines. Some parent groups function on a political and community level to counter the dissemination of illegal drugs and drug paraphernalia. Other parent groups have assisted youth groups to organize and promote drug-free alternatives, programs, and activities for themselves. Parent peer groups also help to dispel the sense of isolation of parents who must cope with the drug abuse of their adolescent offspring. The sharing of common experiences, values, and rules for their children, and ways of enforcing the rules, creates a common bond; it strengthens each parent's confidence in coping with the problem, which otherwise might loom as too overwhelming. One organization, *United Parents of America, Inc.,* promotes a school policy whereby parents will be called as soon as any drug or alcohol use is suspected, without fear or threat of legal suit.

> Parents working together can help each other. As a group, they can set rules for their children's behavior, make these rules clearly known, and be consistent in enforcing them. If you work with the parents of your children's friends in setting these rules, you will spend less time arguing about curfews, parties, chaperones, and other issues, and have more time to spend with your children in constructive or fun activities. (NIDA 1984b, page 7)

We know that parents have had to bear the brunt of the problem, or at least a large share of the burden of the problem, of teenage drug abuse. Also, parents, no matter how good their intentions, often get caught up in the problem and become part of it. It may seem paradoxical, therefore, to say that the problem, in many cases, cannot be solved without the input of the parents and their resources and efforts. Parents in parent-organized communities no longer feel quite so powerless in regard to the drug use of their adolescent children.

Why Teenagers Use Drugs

A basic question that parents generally ask is, "Why do youngsters take drugs?" There are probably as many reasons why individuals take drugs as there are people who take them. The youngsters who use drugs heavily are usually using them for more reasons than just to go along with the group, or to rebel against parents. Drug abuse may serve a youngster's personal needs (pleasure, recreation, relief from tension or boredom, self-medication, or need for peer socializing).

To understand fully what adolescent drug use is all about and how to prevent or treat it, one must look at it in the full context of a teenager's life. Teenagers, probably more than any other age group, tend to have feelings of low self-esteem and inadequacy. As they struggle to achieve an identity, they frequently doubt whether they are going to make it in life. Upon experimenting with drugs, some youngsters are likely to find that they blur these negative feelings, at least temporarily. Many parents are unable to recognize or relate to the challenging and anxiety-laden aspects of modern adolescent development. They neither understand nor know how to deal with such adolescent behavior as rebellion, drug and alcohol use, sexual promiscuity, and school failure. Adolescents often distrust their parents and people who could be of help and turn to chemical solutions in an attempt to "feel better fast."

Psychoactive drugs take away depression, anxiety, or tension, or produce euphoria. Thus, some youngsters end up taking drugs to escape from uncomfortable or painful feelings. It is difficult for parents to identify with or understand why or how adolescents might be self-medicating. A typical response might be "What has my boy got to be depressed or anxious about? He doesn't have a mortgage to pay, he doesn't have car payments, he doesn't have to go to work or work at something he doesn't like." Problems of the adolescent are often minimized or discounted. If a sensitive youngster is disappointed in love, the frustration may be discounted and the full impact never really understood: "Oh, that's puppy love and you'll have a hundred other loves." Yet the adolescent might feel that the world is coming to an end. There are school pressures and the pressures to choose a career and make important decisions for their future lives. Like all human beings, adolescents have their pressures, their depressions, their anxieties, their losses, their fears; and it is sometimes difficult for others to know what toll these hardships may take.

A Generation Gap

It is generally recognized that there is a gap between the attitudes of adults and the attitudes of adolescents regarding the use of drugs. Nowlis (1969) concluded that there is some contradiction when so many adults react with moralism, anger, and punitiveness on hearing of youth drug abuse when it is adults "who are the main consumers of tranquilizers, pep pills, addictive sleeping pills, brain-damaging drugs like alcohol, and cancer-producing agents like cigarettes." Dr. William Pollin (1984) reports that tobacco, which is openly sold for profit, is the deadliest of all addictive drugs. Smoking cigarettes results in the death of more people than injecting heroin. It follows that parents who smoke cigarettes are not in the best position to be effective in warning their children of the harmfulness of drugs like marijuana. One survey showed that 25 percent of all women over the age of thirty were receiving prescriptions for amphetamines, barbiturates, or tranquilizers, with the proportion approaching 40 percent for women of higher-income families (Cohen 1971). Excluding alcohol, coffee, and cigarettes, Cohen estimated that "over 50 percent of the total American population over thirteen years of age has at least tried some powerful mind-altering drug via prescription or on the illicit market" (page 16).

Friedman and Santo (1984) found that 99 percent of parents in PTA groups disapproved of use of marijuana by their children, compared to 47 percent of high school seniors who disapprove; 30 percent of the parents responded that there should be different standards for adults and young persons regarding the use of drugs and alcohol. Only 9 percent of the parents said that parents should refrain from use of alcohol if they disapprove of use of marijuana by their children. The reasons that the parent group gave for not wanting their child to smoke marijuana were, in order of frequency of response, as follows:

It is harmful to the mind (impairs mental functioning) (88 percent).

It interferes with performance of school work or with functioning in other important serious life tasks (87 percent).

It interferes with the development of good, mature personality (79 percent).

It impairs positive motivation, drive, or ambition (induces apathy) (78 percent).

The child could get arrested, get into trouble with the law or with school authorities (75 percent).

Modern-day parents should be familiar with what has been learned about drugs. Children will pay more attention if they know their parents are well informed, and it helps to counteract some of the less reliable information that they learn from their peers. What are some of the reliable scientific facts that parents can tell their youngsters about the dangers of using drugs like marijuana? For example, it is true that recent research has shown that there are more serious, long-term, harmful physical and mental effects from heavy use of marijuana than had been known earlier. It is known that impaired lung function, similar to that found in cigarette smokers, follows the extended use of marijuana. The research also suggests that there may be serious effects on the human reproductive system. More directly relevant for youngsters is the fact that acute marijuana intoxication interferes with mental functioning and may impair the learning and thinking processes. It is, thus, an impediment to classroom performance. In addition, marijuana use has effects on perception and motor coordination and therefore may affect driving performance, increasing the likelihood of automobile accidents.

Young people tend to believe that they cannot be seriously harmed by drugs. It is not easy to frighten them away from using drugs. It is therefore essential that parents have the facts, and not try to use "fire and brimstone" tactics, and do not threaten or moralize too much.

An argument that youngsters throw at parents is "Well, you yourselves drink and smoke." If the parent(s) use illicit drugs it becomes even more difficult to present an argument against their use. Parents who are social drinkers might emphasize that it takes a certain amount of development and maturity to be able to use alcohol in a responsible manner.

The Family Role in Adolescent Drug Abuse

In adolescence there is a search for family stability. When a family breakup occurs through divorce or when the parents are living together but emotionally divorced or there is an atmosphere of unremitting tension or quiet dispair in the family, the teenager's anxiety intensifies and there is more likelihood of using drugs. Teens may miss the protection and warmth of the family and the support that they had during childhood. Involvement in drug use could be a signal that the youngster is having difficulty moving toward a more independent status.

There can be problems in the family relationships or in the child's perception of the parent-child relationship of which the parents are not aware. As a matter of fact, it has been found that approximately one half (49 percent) of adolescent clients who enter treatment for drug abuse report that "family problems" are one of the main reasons they apply for treatment. Included in the category of family problems are family crises in the areas of health, mental health, death, and so on; lack of family interest and support in schoolwork; chronic family disruptions; and runaways (Friedman et al. 1980).

Some adolescents exaggerate the seriousness and importance of family problems and minimize the seriousness of their own drug abuse problems. The parents of these youngsters tend to see the situation quite differently: the worst problem is their adolescent child's drug abuse, without which they claim the family would manage reasonably well.

However, serious involvement in drug use has been found to be influenced by family relationship factors and the quality of parent-adolescent relationships. The degree of severity of abuse is significantly related to such family factors as the religious background and educational level of the parents, the disruption and dissolution of family structures, certain family constellation factors, and the number and types of problems which the adolescent clients perceived to be present in their families (Friedman et al. 1980).

Newcomb and his colleagues (1983) concluded that parents, particularly the mother, are a powerful modeling influence for their children, either encouraging or discouraging drug use. When the mothers are cigarette smokers and/or moderate drinkers, teenage children are more likely to use a variety of drugs (Miller and Cisin 1983). Unconventional parents, excessively passive mothers, lack of perceived closeness to parents by adolescents, and drinking and drug use patterns of parents are all factors which have been found to be positively correlated with drug use (Kandel 1982; Brook et al. 1980; Jessor and Jessor 1977). These reported characteristics are, however, not true of all families in which adolescents use illicit drugs and they can also be found in some families where the adolescent members do not use illicit drugs.

Families of adolescent drug users differ significantly from families in which the adolescent offspring either do not use drugs or have used marijuana only experimentally. In contrast to experimental drug users or non-users, adolescents with serious drug problems come from families with the following characteristics:

> There is more discrepancy between how the parents would ideally like their children to be and how they perceive them actually to be (Alexander and Dibb 1977).

Parents are perceived as having relatively less influence than peers. Both parents are perceived to be more approving of drug use (Jessor 1975).

Offspring perceive less love from both parents, particularly from fathers (Mellinger et al. 1975; Streit et al. 1974).

There is less shared authority and poorer communication in the family (Cannon 1976; Hunt 1974).

There is less spontaneous problem-solving in structured family interaction tasks (Mead and Campbell 1972).

High levels of perceived parental support and perceived positive parent-child relationships have been found to be related to low levels of drug use in adolescents in several studies (Blum 1972; Bethards 1973; Streit et al. 1974). Cooper and Olson (1977) noted that high school students who reported little or no drug use also reported that they perceived a high degree of parental supportiveness in their families and that they experienced high personal esteem; whereas low perceived parental support and low self-esteem were related to frequent drug usage.

In his family therapy work, Reilly (1978) found nine dysfunctional family interaction patterns to be characteristic of families with substance abuse members, which he postulated could maintain and exacerbate drug abuse. These characteristics are not unique or specific to substance abuse families, but tend to occur more regularly and in more extreme or intense form in these families.

Negative interaction (family members give negative messages when they communicate: criticism, put-downs, complaints, and nagging).

Inconsistent limit setting or structuring by parents.

A cry for help or attention by the substance abuser revealing drug use and related problems as a way of getting a particular response such as attention from parents.

Global or massive parental denial (they manage not to see what is going on). They fail to relate to either the evidence of substance abuse or to accidents and other signs which indicate that the problem is getting worse.

The use of drugs by offspring provides vicarious gratification which parents need either consciously or unconsciously.

Use of drugs and alcohol as self-medication or as a disinhibitor by the substance abusing member who needs this aid for expressing or acting out reactions or feelings such as destructiveness or violence.

Difficulty in expressing anger between parents and children (unexpressed rage). There is no appropriate continuum of expression, resulting in either no expression or violence.

Irrational parental expectations of the substance-abusing child, who is perceived in terms of the parents' feelings about a grandparent or other relative, and is not seen as a real person for him or herself.

"Incredible language." Family members make statements, such as promises about their behavior in the future, that are so unrealistic they cannot be believed.

Obviously, one way to try to solve family problems is to work directly with the family. It is not just the adolescent drug abuser, but the parents and other family members who need help. Aside from other problems that may exist in the family, the impact on the parents' lives resulting from their adolescent child's drug abuse is often devastating. The youngster's drug-related problems (difficulties at school, involvement with police, erratic and sometimes violent behavior) themselves create a family crisis.

Also, it obviously would help the situation if family members would try not to blame each other for problems. Each family member should try to adopt an objective and non-defensive stance, and to search their own attitudes and behavior for any possible way that they could be contributing to the maintenance of the adolescent's drug abuse.

What Is Real Help?

Several frantic phone calls came into the drug treatment clinic one day from the mother of an 18-year-old girl. The mother wanted to know what to do about her child who was not coming home at night. According to the mother, her daughter was apparently using and selling drugs, and behaving in such a way as to cause a tremendous amount of stress and anxiety for the family. The parents were bending over backwards in trying to be helpful, but they were fearful of the complications and concerned that they might be pushing the girl to suicide (the ultimate threat).

The therapist talked about some of the things the parents might do. While it would probably be inappropriate to confront their daughter in a threatening way, she could nevertheless be confronted in a supportive and loving way. The parents could let her know how concerned they were and also how painful and disruptive the experience was for them, not just because they cared about her but because they cared about their own lives and couldn't continue to live like that. If the daughter really wanted to live a disruptive lifestyle—she was over 18—there might be little the parents could do. They might have to accept that reality but point out to the daughter that she would have to set up her own residence because they could not approve of her behavior. The situation would still worry the parents, and would continue to be very painful, but her departure would cut down the level of stress in the home. It was important to be supportive but also firm (in terms of setting limits and by insisting that the daughter go into treatment), because she was showing that she needed help by the nature of her behavior.

Many young drug abusers manage to keep their drug problem secret. Those who let it become public knowledge, or at least known in the family, are often asking either for limits and control or for help, no matter how much they say they are not. This mother was urged to get everybody in for a family session and the girl was scheduled for individual counseling.

Another type of phone call that comes into a drug abuse treatment clinic is a call from a parent wanting help or advice on how to handle the problem of an adolescent who has gotten into trouble. He may have stolen something from the house, and one parent knows about it and is trying to protect the child from being restricted or punished by the other parent. Or he may have had a run-in with the law related to drugs and his parents are trying to keep it a secret from other relatives and to avoid the legal consequences of the offense. The parents may be trying to avoid restrictions that the school has placed on drug and alcohol users. The parents may have been repeatedly rescuing their youngster. When parents collude with a child to protect him or her from the consequences of his/her actions, they teach a lesson that isn't true. In the larger world, outside the family, there are consequences to human actions. For some adolescents, the parents' continuous rescuing only results in the youngster taking more chances and provoking a more serious problem. For these adolescents it appears that there is a tendency, albeit not conscious, to continue testing the relationship and the situation, until they miscalculate and end up either with a serious overdose or in court. Even though adolescents assert that they don't want limits put on their behavior, they feel safer in a milieu in which they know what the limits are and know the limits are enforced. There is a point at which the parents are going to have to face the inevitable and tell their youngster that past rescuing has not improved the situation and that they are going to have to let the youngster face the consequences of his/her actions. Of course, it is helpful if the parents get the youngster into counseling or treatment before they cut off the rescuing.

Many parents cannot emotionally tolerate seeing their children face any kind of pain or disappointment. They never teach them how to deal with loss. When a goldfish dies, rather than let the child mourn the goldfish, they take the dead one out and go to the store to replace the fish so the youngster doesn't have to experience the loss. A parent must be willing to admit that it's all right to have a depressed day, a happy day, an angry day, to feel sad, or to cry. People learn from what they experience.

Children learn how to fall down in the process of learning to walk. If they are held all the time, they do not learn balance. And if they are not permitted to walk on their own, the muscles atrophy and they never walk. Emotional strength needs to be exercised in the same way. If one is carried emotionally throughout life, then one never develops the ability to cope with difficulties.

We have seen literally hundreds of parents who continue to give money to their adolescents which they know is being spent to buy illicit drugs. They are afraid that if they stop giving money, their youngster will steal and get in trouble with the law. Also, it is often a way of holding on to their relationship with their youngster as they are afraid of losing the relationship.

Another question that parents ask: If our child has started smoking grass and drinking beer, isn't it better to let him continue on condition that he only use these substances in the house? These parents think that by allowing a youngster to use drugs in the home, he or she is less likely to use them on the street or in the school yard, and less likely to be picked up by the police, or to get into some other trouble. They accept the problem as a fait accompli, and are looking for a way to contain it. They are not thinking of the future implications of the message that although they disapprove, they are trying to make a compromise because they feel helpless. Their mixed feelings of disapproval and helplessness are conveyed to the child. Their chances of being obeyed are not enhanced.

Don't promise things or make threats that you can't keep. Don't buy your children's obedience. All you do by giving all the time is teach your children how to take. In substance-abusing families, we see that often language doesn't mean anything. Kids lie all the time and parents threaten all the time, but they often make ineffective threats. "If I catch you doing this again, I'm throwing you out of the house, or I'm going to beat you up. Or, I'm going to turn you over to the police." A threat doesn't mean anything, if you're not going to carry it through. And if the threat is carried out, it often only leads to more drug abuse on the part of the teenager. Something that is most difficult for parents to face and understand is that a child who is very seriously involved in drugs over a long period of time may be committing a kind of passive suicide.

Listening

Adolescents often feel that they are not heard, listened to, or adequately regarded by their parents. When that happens they feel rejected. Parents are often not aware that they have a tendency to shut children out. Michele Marks, the daughter of one of the authors of this chapter, put it this way: "Parents should listen to their children's problems but not just to give their advice. I like it when I can go to my parents and they share their experiences with me. It makes me feel closer to them. I'm sure many other kids would love for their parents to open up to them, not feel that their parents are above them. Kids can gain a lot from talking, not getting lectures, from their parents. A discussion or retelling of a parent's earlier experience when the parent was young can help their kid much more when it comes to living their lives."

Thirteen-year-old Connie is an example of how an unexpressed hidden fear of an adolescent can lead to disturbed and rebellious behavior. Her father was a fire-fighter, and her mother was not in very good health. Connie was afraid that her parents would die soon and therefore she could not talk to them about her problem and was upset and angry. She had no living relatives to go to if her parents were to die. She began hanging out more with a group after school and, like the others, used marijuana. She stayed out late some nights, and her school performance worsened. Connie's parents were making an effort to listen and understand what was making Connie's performance change. They discovered that she was using drugs, but they had not been able to elicit the underlying fear. Seeking help, the family went to a family therapist who was able to help the family understand what was really bothering Connie. When Connie was reassured, she began to return to her earlier, more cooperative behavior. Fortunately, Connie was reached early before her drug use became a serious problem.

Why is it that parents have difficulty listening to their adolescent children? Why is it that many adolescents feel they are not being heard or understood by the parent? Some parents have defenses or barriers that make it difficult for them to hear or understand certain attitudes or feelings. Some interrupt or block out the adolescent's expression of unacceptable attitudes.

Parents must not only understand the content of what the adolescent is expressing or trying to express, but also the feelings associated with the content. This often means encouraging the adolescent to say more about and explain further his or her feelings and attitudes relating to a particular issue at hand. To learn how to be a good listener, a parent must be able to adopt a non-judgmental attitude and a non-defensive stance. It does not mean that the parent has to agree with everything the adolescent is saying, or even to take it all as being factual or accurate. One can listen with sensitivity and empathy, accepting the child's right to his or her feelings, without accepting the child's behavior. Also, in ruling out a particular behavior the parent should be careful not to give the impression of rejecting the child.

Some teenagers are impatient, intolerant, and eager to act; they have no time for thoughtful consideration. They test and challenge. They frequently respond to parents and other authority figures with irritation, argument, and denial. They may also become moody and depressed—overly serious and with a dark outlook on life. The challenge for their parents and teachers, and other older people who deal with them, is to change the mood from anxious intensity, despair, and anger to a more positive and thoughtful climate.

Parents faced with such challenging situations should ask themselves, "Can we listen to our child's complaints and anger (especially when directed at us) with an open mind? Do we have the capacity to listen with understanding to ideas, activities, and values that are antagonistic to our own?" This is illustrated by the following brief excerpt from a family therapy session. The parents and the other children of this "blended" family (including two children from the mother's previous marriage and three children from the father's previous marriage) were admonishing Jeanne, a 13-year-old drug user, that she should make every effort to "adjust" to the situation, like everyone else:

Jeanne:	"I hate you all." (To the stepmother and her two children.) "I don't want to be around you. I want to stay in my own house where I'm comfortable, I don't want to talk to you."
Therapist:	"That's all right. At least you got it out."
Father:	"Do you know how you are hurting us? Do you know how much pain you caused for your mother? You've got to adjust."
Therapist (to Father):	"Let her express herself."

Jeanne:	(Turns away from parents, the back of her head faces them and she talks to wall.)
Stepmother:	"Turn around, if you want to talk."
Therapist:	"That's okay, as long as she keeps talking. Let her talk away from you; make an attempt to listen."

By the end of the session the parents weren't just asking her to adjust, they were listening. Later that evening Jeanne hugged her stepmother: "I want you to know I don't just hate you." Once she was able to express her hatred, she could begin to give it up. She had been allowed to express her feelings. Her parents and her brother and sisters had accepted her statements, and no one had criticized her for them.

It is, of course, easier for the therapist to be patient with a rebellious, challenging adolescent since the therapist has to deal with this situation for only one hour a week. It is much harder for parents living with the child to respond with the objectivity and patience of a therapist. Expressions of adolescent disrespect and hatred can be tolerated in a therapy room, but are too difficult for many parents to deal with at home.

"I hate you; I have always hated you." Most parents consider such a statement from their child as inappropriate and may refuse to listen to it or punish the child for saying it. A red flag goes up when a child expresses disrespect, hostility, challenge, or hatred. Nevertheless, usually the best thing the parent can do in the situation is to listen to the negative expressions and try to understand more about why the child feels that way. There is likely to be fear, anxiety, and confusion behind the anger. Most parents can do this only after they have been helped to learn how to control their own feelings, since the tension of a rebellious and disturbed adolescent is wearing on the parent.

Parents can even take advantage of the child's hostile and provocative expression to improve the relationship. An appropriate response by a parent might be: "I didn't know that you hated me that much. Obviously, it upsets me a great deal and hurts me, and even makes me angry at you. But it's more important that we find out why you have been hating me and then to see whether there is something we can do to improve the situation between us."

This is a lot to ask of a parent: to accept hostility, deflect anger, foster positive feelings, and try to restore the teenager's trust. Parents are to be forgiven if they cannot hold to this objective, understanding model. Nevertheless, it can be a goal toward which parents strive.

Acceptance, Approval, and Disapproval

A genuinely compassionate attitude on the part of the parent creates a facilitating atmosphere. This does not mean that the parents should give unconditional approval to anything their child does. Adolescents tend to respond to the need for immediate results or gratification, while parents often look at the larger picture, and at what will be the best for the adolescent in the long run. It is generally best not to approach the behavior of adolescents from a judgmental or disapproving point of view, but only to point out what may work better for the adolescent's life.

It is sometimes helpful if the parent has a capacity for humor and the ability to tap into the liveliness and natural exuberance of the teenager. The adolescent who has learned to laugh at what angered, embittered, or frightened him or her, or caused shame or guilt, is likely to be showing improvement.

Adolescents may question how useful it is to confide in parents or to talk over such issues as whether to smoke marijuana. Times are different from when the parents were teenagers and social attitudes are different. Parents have not been in the same situations as their children and have not had to make the same decisions. A parent can say, "I did not have all the same experiences that you have been having lately, but I knew what it was to be disappointed or frustrated, or angry at my parents or unhappy or confused. Those are human conditions that we all share." Parents do not have to have the answers at all times, and it is sometimes better to empathize with feelings rather than acting and sounding as if one has the answers at all times.

It is important to communicate in order to keep the conversation or dialogue going, to remember when one was a teenager with frustrations, confusions, and impulsiveness, and to share what you felt and did during adolescence. However, it is not easy for some parents to share their adolescent experiences and problems in a frank, open way.

Differences Between Firmness and Punishment

Can you stop your adolescent child from using drugs through punishment? Generally, the temporary withdrawal of privileges is more effective, as a disciplinary measure, than harsh types of punishment, especially with older adolescents. For young children who are misbehaving, temporary restraint is better than harsh retaliation, and most parents know this.

The older adolescent needs more explanation of the parent's actions. Firm and consistent limit setting, which is often sufficient for the younger adolescent, will be less often sufficient for the older one unless accompanied by reasonable discussion and explanation. Teenagers desire and need the respect of their parents. They are struggling themselves to become responsible men and women.

Almost everyone agrees that parents have to be in charge. Parents have to provide direction, give guidance, and sometimes must exercise discipline. There is less unanimity of opinion regarding the use of punishment. Some parents seem to know how to use punishment judiciously and constructively and other parents don't. In general, it is wise to think twice about imposing punishment and to be careful not to do it in the heat of anger. For example, if an adolescent has been refusing to behave as considered appropriate by the parent, or has been disrespectful or challenging, the parent might say, "I want you to go to your room and stay there for a while." In some families, as stated above, this may work reasonably well. The alleged "punishment" may actually serve more as a cooling-off mechanism for both parent and child than as an unpleasant experience or a threat to the teenager. It could possibly have the effect of teaching the teenager to avoid in the future the types of misbehavior that led to the punishment. In other cases, it might engage the teenager and the parent in an adversarial relationship or cut off communication. The teenager might become more angry because of having the punishment imposed. As a result, he/she might continue the misbehavior in the future but try to do it in a more covert way to lessen the likelihood of being caught. Or the teenager might retaliate against the parent in a different way.

There are some parents who appear to be successful in teaching their adolescents to maintain adequate self-control and acceptable behavior without resorting to punishment. While it is doubtful that adequate control of a 4- or 5-year-old can be achieved without exercising some restraint or punishment, procedures that make it possible to maintain adequate control of adolescents without punishment are to be desired. However, there are other risks or dangers which the parent must watch for in the no-punishment situation. Has the parent achieved this degree of control by inducing too much guilt or too much fear, thus severely constricting the child's spontaneity, or by putting too great an emotional burden on the child?

When there is anger, it may work better for some parents to say, "I'm aware that I am angry at you now and I don't think you and I can deal with this problem constructively at this time. I suggest that we put it aside for now but I would like to talk with you about the problem in an hour from now." After the cooling-off period, the parent will be better able to control any impulsive or emotional reactions and to understand the teenager's side of the situation. This break also gives the youngster time to reflect and consider his/her own motivations and actions. Sometimes an adolescent is unintentionally being rebellious and provocative in a search for secure and realistic boundaries, and actually wants this rebellious behavior controlled by the parent. If the parent can explain the limits, boundaries, and rules in a clear, firm, and consistent way, and feels reasonably confident of the usefulness and justice of his/ her position, rather than feeling insecure or guilty about depriving the youngster, it is likely that it will make some positive impression on the teenager, even if it doesn't solve the problem immediately.

How To Be a Good Parent

There are plenty of readily available books on how to be a good parent. Reading one or two such books can be a worthwhile investment of a parent's time. However, such reading can be of limited value. The advice given is more appropriate for preventing the development of serious problems in parent-child relationships than for eliminating or solving the problems after they have already developed. Many parents feel that it is easy to give the advice, but not so easy to apply it effectively in a real-life situation. The advice often does not seem to fit the parent's unique family situation, or the actions and attitudes recommended by the book do not fit the particular parent's values or personality.

While recognizing the limited value of such advice, there is nevertheless some point to presenting here the following brief synopsis of one such approach to positive parenting. In his systematic approach to "Confident Parenting," Silberman (1982) suggests that parents accept a view of their children's needs which balances the "executive" and "caring" roles of parents:

> The executive role involves all those parental tasks which directly let a child know that he or she is under the influence and direction of an adult who is *in charge*. When parents are doing their executive job, they meet children's need for advice, coaching, choices, direction, discipline, limits, religion, responsibility, role models, structure. . . . Children are reassured by having parents who make decisions about the directions their lives are taking and the rules by which they must live. . . . Children get valuable practice early in life on not getting their own way all the time and being confronted with demands for responsible behavior. . . .
>
> The caring role involves things parents express and do to let a child know that he or she is accepted, nurtured, supported, and loved. When parents are doing their caring job, they meet children's needs for acceptance, attention, communication, encouragement, friendship, fun, love, material things (food, money, clothes), patience, protection, respect, time, trust, understanding. . . . The degree to which parents have the power to reinforce their children's behavior, both through rewards and penalties, depends upon children's feelings that they are valued. . . . When children feel continually rejected, they become immune to paren-

tal reinforcements. . . . Children cannot weather the frustration caused by their own limitations and failures without parental support. . . .

Parents need to perform both roles to have *influence* over their children's behavior. Often, parents see these two roles conflicting with each other. Therefore they tend to favor one over the other *or* jump back and forth between them, totally confusing the child. It is important *and* possible to blend the two roles into one approach to parenting. [pp. 6–8]

If the parent-child relationship has developed reasonably well, the adolescent should need a lesser degree of each of the executive and caring parental functions than he/she needed at an earlier age. But the adolescent's strivings and demands for autonomy and independence can be deceptive, and he or she still needs a fair amount of parental direction as well as nurturing and caring.

In his discussion of how parents should implement their executive role in an assertive and confident manner, Silberman presents the following table of parental responses ("authority styles") which is helpful in differentiating between "nonassertive, aggressive, and assertive stances toward children" (pg. 39):

Nonassertive	*Aggressive*	*Assertive*
You:	You:	You:
are evasive	blow up in anger	persist
beg	get into power struggles	listen to children's point of view
act flustered	endlessly argue	
try to "make things do"	accuse	reveal honest feelings
are confusing, unclear	discredit children's thinking	give brief reasons
let yourself be treated unfairly	trick, tease, put down	politely refuse to do something
worry about being popular	give harsh punishments	empathize
are afraid of upsetting children	nag	carry out reasonable consequences
blame yourself	withhold information about what you expect	make clear, direct requests

References

Alexander, B.K. and Dibb, G.S. 1977. Interpersonal perception in addict families. *Family Process* 16: 17–18.

Beschner, G.M. and Friedman, A.S. 1985. Treatment of adolescent drug abusers. *Journal of the Addictions* 20(6 & 7): 971–993.

Bethards, J. 1973. Parental support and the use of drugs. *Humbolt Journal of Social Relations* 1: 26–28.

Blum, R.H. 1972. *Horatio Alger's Children*. San Francisco, California: Jossey-Bass.

Brook, J.S.; Lukoff, I.F.; and Whitman, M. 1980. Initiation into adolescent marijuana use. *Journal of General Psychology* 137: 133–142.

Cannon, S.R. 1976. *Social Functioning Patterns in Families of Offspring Receiving Treatment for Drug Abuse*. Roslyn Heights, New York: Libra Publications.

Cohen, A.Y. 1971. The journey beyond trips: Alternatives to drugs. *Journal of Psychedelic Drugs* 3: 16–21.

Cooper, D.M. and Olson, D.H. 1977. Perceived parental support and self esteem as related to adolescent drug use. Minneapolis: Multi-Resource Center.

Friedman, A.S.; Pomerance, E.; Sanders, R.; Santo, Y.; and Utada, A. 1980. The structure and problems of the families of adolescent drug users. *Contemporary Drug Problems*, Fall.

Friedman, A.S. and Santo, Y. 1984. A comparison of attitudes of parents and high school senior students regarding cigarette, alcohol and drug use. *Journal of Drug Education* 14 (1).

Glickman, N. and Utada, A. 1983. Characteristics of Drug Users in Urban Public High Schools. Rockville, Maryland: Project Report to National Institute on Drug Abuse, Grant No. H81 DA 01657.

Hunt, D.G. 1974. Parental permissiveness as perceived by the offspring and the degree of marijuana usage among offspring. *Human Relations* 27: 267–285.

Jessor, R. 1975. Predicting time of onset of marijuana use: A developmental study of high school youth. In Lettieri, D., ed., *Predicting Adolescent Drug Abuse: A Review of Issues, Methods and Correlates*. Washington, D.C.: DHEW Publication Number ADM–76–299, National Institute on Drug Abuse, U.S. Government Printing Office.

Jessor, R. and Jessor, S.L. 1977. *Problem Behavior and Psychosocial Development: A Longitudinal Study of Youth*. New York: Academic Press.

Kandel, D. 1974. Inter- and Intragenerational influences of adolescent marihuana use. *Journal of Social Issues* 30 (2): 107–135.

———. 1982. Epidemiological and psychosocial perspectives on adolescent drug abuse. *Journal of the American Academy of Child Psychiatry* 21 (4): 328–347.

Mead, D.E. and Campbell, S.S. 1972. Decision-making and interaction by families with and without a drug abusing child. *Family Process* 11: 437–498.

Mellinger, G.D.; Somers, R.H.; and Manheimer, D.I. 1975. Drug use research items pertaining to personality and interpersonal relations: A working paper for research investigators. In Lettieri, D.J., ed., *Predicting Adolescent Drug Abuse: A Review of Issues, Methods and Correlates*. Washington, D.C.: DHEW Publication Number ADM–76–299, National Institute on Drug Abuse, U.S. Government Printing Office.

Miller, J.D. and Cisin, I. 1983. *Highlights from the National Survey on Drug Abuse: 1982*. Rockville, Maryland: National Institute on Drug Abuse, DHHS Publication Number ADM–83–1277, U.S. Government Printing Office.

National Institute on Drug Abuse. 1984a. *Parents: What You Can Do About Drug Abuse.* Washington, D.C.: NIDA, U.S. Government Printing Office, DHHS Publication Number ADM–1267.

———. 1984b. *Parents, Peers and Pot II: Parents In Action.* Washington, D.C.: NIDA, U.S. Government Printing Office.

Newcomb, M.; Hula, G.; and Bentler, P. 1983. Mothers' influence on the drug use of their children: Confirmatory tests of direct modeling and mediational theories. *Developmental Psychology* 19: 714–726.

Nowlis, H.H. 1969. *Drugs on the College Campus.* Garden City, New York: Anchor Books.

Pollin, W. 1984. ADAMHA News, November. Washington, D.C.: U.S. Department of Health & Human Services Vol x, No11, p. 1.

Reilly, D.M. 1978. Family factors in the etiology and treatment of youthful drug abuse. *Family Therapy* 2: 149–171.

Silberman, M.L. 1982. *Confident Parenting: Assertive Relationships with Children.* Ardmore, Pennsylvania: The ARC Program.

Silberman, M.L. and Wheelan, S.A. 1980. *How To Discipline without Feeling Guilty: Assertive Relationships with Children.* New York: Hawthorn Books.

Streit, F.; Halsted, D.; and Pascale, P. 1974. Differences among youthful users and nonusers of drugs based on their perceptions of parental behavior. *The International Journal of the Addictions* 9(5): 749–755.

10
The Family Scene When a Teenager Uses Drugs: Case Vignettes and the Role of Family Therapy

Arlene Utada
Alfred S. Friedman

The purpose of this chapter is to show the effect on a family when an adolescent becomes a drug abuser, to elucidate how the parents may have been implicated in the development of the problem, and to present the rationale for family therapy. One of the methods utilized in the chapter is the presentation of three case vignettes about actual families in which drug abuse problems occurred.

Each year hundreds of thousands of families in the United States are challenged, distressed, and sometimes torn apart by a teenage family member using drugs. Parents, adolescent substance abusers, and the other family members are caught in a desperate situation that may escalate into a major crisis in the life of the family. Many of these families may be confronted with recurring crises over a period of years. What is perhaps most disconcerting about this situation is the likelihood that the parents themselves unwittingly contributed to the development or the escalation of the drug problem.

Although the fact that there are many harmful illicit drugs readily available to young people makes possible the drug abuse problem, the problem cannot be explained solely by this fact. One might say that even with the availability of the substances young people should be more enlightened or exercise more self-control or, at the least, should have been frightened away or deterred from use of these harmful substances. There is also the role of the family to consider in the development of this problem: Why have the parents not been effective in raising children or adolescents so that they do not become involved in substance abuse? The family has a lot at stake; it is the entity that often is hardest hit by the drug abuse problem—sometimes even devastated—when it happens to an adolescent member of the family. Some parents may actually experience more suffering from the youngster's involvement in drug abuse than the adolescent abuser experiences himself or herself.

The parents unfortunately are in the front-line trenches in this battle against drug abuse and usually have the main responsibility for dealing with and solving the problem. Why this is so needs further explanation. The parents may feel that they didn't create this problem but that it was imposed upon them: if it were not for the fact that their youngster came under the influence of the wrong friends; if it were not for the government's failure to adequately control the large-scale trafficking in drugs; if it were not for a deterioration in the social and moral values of our society. . . . On the other hand, if the problem is explained by the fact that this has become a drug-using society, and that using drugs has become a rite of passage for all adolescents, why have half the adolescents not tried drugs at all, and the majority who have experimented with drugs have only used them infrequently or occasionally at a party? Why have only approximately 10 percent become so seriously and heavily involved in regular substance abuse or addiction that it has become the central theme in their lives, and has negatively affected their development and careers, and the lives of their families? It is reasonable that the effort to understand the problems of this 10 percent should include not only the study of the adolescents as individuals, but the study of the families, and certain situations and conditions in the histories of these families, and the histories of the particular child growing up in these families.

Thus, blaming the peer group, or blaming the larger society, the schools, the churches, or the drug enforcement agencies, is not very realistic. No one or any single cause is to blame; not the parents, not the grandparents, not the peer group. All are caught up together in a complicated situation and the solutions are not easy to find. In many cases the ways that the parents have contributed to the development of the problem are subtle and hard to see. Was it just that they did not listen to the youngster in an understanding enough way, or they didn't pay enough attention, or were rejecting, or too strict or controlling, or not firm enough, or too permissive, or too indulgent? The parents need the help of someone not directly and emotionally involved in the family situation, who can perceive objectively what happens in the family, is skilled and wise and experienced, will listen with understanding and discernment, and will intervene in constructive ways that the family can accept and respond to.

Even relying on a psychiatrist or on the expertise of a specialized drug treatment program to solve the problem is not sufficient. The family almost inevitably has to be actively involved in the solution, since it may well have been part of the problem. The problem needs to be understood within the framework of the family, and in terms of the dynamics of the system of relationships and interactions that have developed in the family. Every family is unique in regard to the constellation of interrelationships that have developed during its history, and these relationships operate at more than one level. For example, one family can be described as having "pseudo-mutual" relationships: the family members appear on the surface to get along with each other, to be loyal and unified, to defend each other against outsiders; but this is partly a facade kept up at the price of suppression of resentments and hostilities felt toward each other. Another family may be openly argumentative and conflictual, but with deeper ties of affection and love than the first family. Given this and even greater degrees of complexity of each family's system, it requires time and understanding on the part of a skilled family counselor or therapist to enter into the various levels on which the family interrelationships are operating. From such empathic understanding one may find some clues for helping the family change its pattern of interactions or some of the attitudes and feelings that the members have toward each other.

There is a growing awareness that parents are not only inextricably involved, but that for the future welfare of the child it is essential that parents become involved in whatever treatment process is recommended. Adult drug abusers have more independent control of their life situations than young drug abusers. Most youngsters, even after successfully completing an inpatient or residential treatment program, must return to their families and the living conditions they were in when they used drugs.

Some adolescents abuse drugs to gain attention in a family that otherwise ignores them. Family therapists who specialize in treating substance-abusing young people have found that the families of their patients often are conflictual or disengaged, or lack open communication, mutual respect, reasonable organization, and close, loving relationships. The parents and children often are alienated and the parents may be poor models, or may be overly controlling. In such cases, expert assistance may be needed. The drug use itself is of deep concern but cannot be treated outside the context of these other factors.

Researchers (Friedman et al. 1980; Kandel 1974) found that initial use of illicit drugs by adolescents is related to parent-child relationships. Adolescents who feel close to their families are less likely than others to begin using illicit substances. Conversely, the children of parents who are perceived as maintaining strict controls and parents who tend to disagree about discipline are more likely to begin using illicit drugs. Use of drugs by parents has also been found to be an important predictor of adolescent drug use.

Findings produced by the National Youth Polydrug Study (Friedman

1980) show the relationship between family factors and adolescent drug abuse:

> Adolescents whose parents had drug problems, alcohol problems, psychiatric problems, or problems with the law are more heavily involved in drug abuse than adolescents whose parents were not reported to have such problems.

> There is a significant positive correlation between the number of problems reported in families and the number and types of drugs used by the adolescent offspring.

High school students who use drugs spend more time with peers who have similar drug use behavior patterns and are more likely to be estranged from parents and other adults than students who do not use drugs (Friedman 1983).

Absence of parent, lack of parental closeness, unconventional parents, excessively passive mothers, lack of perceived closeness to parents, and drinking and drug use patterns of parents have been positively correlated with drug use (Jessor and Jessor 1977; Brooke et al. 1980; Kandel 1982).

Families of adolescent drug users differ significantly from families in which the adolescent offspring either do not use drugs or have used marijuana only experimentally. In contrast to experimental drug users or nonusers, adolescents with serious drug problems come from families with certain characteristics:

> Parents are perceived as having relatively less influence than peers. Both parents are perceived to be more approving of drug use (Jessor 1975).

> Offspring perceive less love from both parents, particularly fathers (Streit et al. 1974; Mellinger et al. 1975).

> Less shared authority and poorer communication characterize the family (Hunt 1974; Cannon 1976).

> Less spontaneous problem solving occurs in structured family interaction tasks (Mead and Campbell 1972).

The following verbatim report of an individual ("one-to-one") interview with an adolescent drug abuser reveals clearly and in detail how this young client perceives his father's attitudes and behavior as the primary cause of his drug abuse.

Why do you think that you started using drugs?

"Well, I guess in my family my dad was always very, I would probably call it overbearing. He was always trying to control my life and he was always pushing very hard on school work. While I did very well in school he was never quite satisfied with it. I didn't really express resentment towards that early on, I started to express it more later as I got older. But I couldn't really do anything about it by the time I started to express myself. So I started to use drugs to escape from the bad feelings that I had, the problems that I couldn't express or that I couldn't deal with, my feelings towards him. I needed to escape from the difficulties I had dealing with people as a result of my upbringing. I hadn't been exposed to the situations where I had to open up and be vulnerable, I just escaped uneasiness and difficulties."

What were some of the feelings that you were trying to escape?

"Uneasy, just anger basically I guess and resentment later, because I hadn't expressed the anger at first. It was not just that I was angry at him for wanting me to do well in school. I was angry with him for not being satisfied when I did do well in school. He always seemed to be trying to be overly controlling my life at home and otherwise."

How did you use drugs? How did they help you?

"Well, I would just retreat into my own little world. I would go up into my room. They would generally be just watching TV or something at night. I would put on music and turn the lights down and get high and I wouldn't have to think about it. For me, drugs helped me get more along, help me be more comfortable with myself, because I didn't have to face the feelings that I had inside."

What kinds of feelings did you have?

"Sad I guess, because he hadn't given me what I wanted. And because he hadn't given the rest of my family what they wanted. I also had a lot of fear. He wasn't showing any signs of changing, and I didn't want it to go on like that but I couldn't really do anything about it and I had some guilt for not doing or saying anything about it."

How often did you use drugs?

"Pretty much every day since I've, well when I first started I used it about

every week for the first six or eight months, then I started doing marijuana every day for about the next few years. That took away the bad
feelings without really taking away my ability to function as much as
alcohol."

How did drugs effect your relationships with others?

"When I got high, I was more self-centered. It helped me withdraw into
myself, so I didn't make it a point to go out in public, not to be seen
in situations where people would be looking at me or noticing my eyes
or noticing that I was high. And it made me uncomfortable in public not
just among adults but among other kids my age. That's just one of the
effects."

Did you use drugs more by yourself or with other people?

"Mostly, with a select group of close friends, who I could trust not to
get down on me for doing it or notice me, just paying special attention
to me cause I was high. After awhile I started doing it a lot alone, just
sitting in my room playing guitar and getting high. It made me withdraw
even more."

How have drugs affected different aspects of your life?

"They [drugs] made it hard for me to function with people a lot more
than probably would have happened if I had not taken up the drugs.
They definitely interfered with my ability to work at school, not so much
at first because I would do my work and then get high, but later as I
started getting high I enjoyed doing work while I was high, or thought
I enjoyed it. I did enjoy doing it more but I didn't do it as well. They
[drugs] kept me from dealing with my family as well, because they made
me want to forget about everything and not deal with it, just get high,
and forget about my problems. Yeah, not deal with things, a lot easier
to get high and forget it."

What kind of person are you? How do you see yourself?

"Quiet, thoughtful I suppose, but I don't have very strong feelings one
way or the other that I like to admit to myself. I don't like to show my
emotions. It's just been so long since I've been able to express my true
feelings to anybody or even myself that I kinda forgotten. I don't think
I was really ever able or willing to express my feelings to my family since
early childhood, I don't think I ever really."

Did you have trouble expressing feelings to your mother?

"Less trouble I suppose, because she was not the object of control that my dad represented for me. She wasn't so much the authoritarian figure, so it was a lot easier to express myself to her. You know, I would express my emotions concerning my father to my mother, but they never really got relayed to him with the same intensity that I felt. I guess I didn't always express them to her in the same intensity."

Did you feel that you were more a failure or success when you were using drugs?

"It [drug use] definitely made my family see me as a failure. At first I didn't want to admit to myself that I was. My school work was suffering, or my summer employment would be suffering from it, but it became pretty obvious after awhile. Definitely it caused me to drop out of school."

Do you think that the fact that your friends and acquaintances and other people your own age around you used drugs had any influence on your starting or continuing to use them?

"Yeah, one of my father's complaints at the beginning when I first started using drugs was that I was valuing my acquaintances more than I valued my family. I guess I was rebelling against him and against all structures more than I even knew, without basically thinking about why I was doing it, I was just going to my friends because they shared some of the same feelings I had that definitely had an effect on me socially. Pretty much all we would do after I started getting high was getting high when we were together. When we were together it naturally spurred us to get high."

How did drugs affect your relationships with girls?

"The problems that I had dealing with people were further injured by the drugs. I guess that I used it to withdraw into myself so I wouldn't have to face people. I always had problems dealing with girls more than guys. I didn't go around with as many girls as other guys so I certainly wasn't exposed to them. Anyway, I definitely had problems meeting girls. I thought I could deal with them more openly and equally because of drugs.

"The first girlfriend was very into drugs. We would always get into it. That's how we met, at parties getting high, and that, our relationship was based almost totally on sex and drugs. That didn't really work cause a relationship can't last on those for too long healthfully. So I kinda ended it. After that, well, I still dated girls that were using drugs, but they weren't using drugs as heavily as she was. The next girl I went out with was not into drugs as far as other people were concerned. She was very straight, she would drink once in awhile, but she was really concerned with her schooling."

Do you think that school had anything to do with you using drugs?

"School was just another authority for me, I was at that time really rebelling against my father and all the structure that he imposed on me. I hadn't objected out loud, not to him. School was just another thing to rebel against and I was looking for anything that was there to rebel against. I was up for rebelling and drugs just helped me to rebel against authority. It was something I could do. I could do things that were strictly against their regulations and all."

How did your family react when they found out that you used drugs?

"They were aware of my abuse and they were scared that I was going to get caught and screw up my future. They were very angry with me for doing it, even though I made all these rationalizations to them about how all my friends do a lot more. I was very discreet about it [drug use] and only did it at times, very late at night, and only did it when I wouldn't be caught. They were still pretty gullible back then, but they were very angry with me. My dad more vocal about it than my mother."

What's your folks' attitude now?

"If I were to tell them that I was still using it everyday I don't think they would probably let me stay in the house, they would probably want me to get out. They told me if I really wanted to smoke everyday and wanted that to be my lifestyle then they would be much happier if I got out of the house. I pretended not to want to do that and stayed in the house just to please them, which is basically what I have done since I started smoking. That's their attitude. They don't want me to do it and they are willing to support me if I don't do it; but if I want to do it, they would rather have me doing it out of the house."

Have you been doing it?

"With one exception I haven't done it in the last nine weeks or so. So it's been a drastic change in my life. At first I wasn't really sure, that I wanted to stop at least for a while. I wasn't really sure how long I would want to stop, I mean after the second week I was talking it over with them and saying I wanted to be able to get high every once in a while. But then after five weeks I got high again and I wasn't really enjoying it. I didn't really know what to do because I was all alone again and I was high for the first time in awhile, I felt guilty about getting high, about ruining the chance that I had started for myself. I didn't really enjoy it at all."

What do you want to get, if anything, from coming here for treatment?

"A better attitude I guess towards drugs, and towards dealing with my problems, that's basically all."

Do you feel like you are getting something out of the family therapy?

"Yeah, a lot more of the family therapy than the group therapy, cause I don't feel comfortable with the group yet and I don't really talk a lot. Family therapy stirs up the problems that already exist and makes us talk about them and deal with them. When we go home the problems are still there but it's helpful to get them out in the open, realize what they are, and try to face them. So it's been helping."

Today, most adolescent drug treatment programs (outpatient, residential, and hospital settings) provide family services. Increasingly, programs have come to realize that adolescent substance abuse impacts severely on the family and that the whole family may need assistance to cope with the problem.

Most families who come with or bring an adolescent member for drug abuse treatment see this adolescent as the only or main problem in the family. Their attitude is that the adolescent needs to be treated or controlled so that the family can get some relief from the problem, but not that the whole family needs treatment. If they agree to attend any family sessions they are likely to see their role as providing information about the behavior of the young client to the client's therapist. The family therapist however may view the adolescent drug abuser as an integral part of a dysfunctional, disturbed, or disorganized family. It follows from this view that the family needs to change. In some families it appears that the drug abuse behavior of the adolescent may serve the function, whether intentionally or not, to maintain the family homeostasis or status quo. For example, if the parents are in a state of emotional divorce, or have a very conflictual marital relationship, it may appear that the parents need to stay together to cope jointly with the continuing family crises posed by the adolescent's drug abuse problems. This deflects the parents from facing the problem of their relationship, and avoids the greater danger of the family breaking up. Or in another family it may appear that a parent needs to keep an adolescent dependent in such a way that the adolescent does not become self-sufficient and independent enough to move away from the parents. A mother may believe that she continues to give her adolescent child money to buy drugs so that he or she does not steal, and thus to avoid the risk of the child's going to jail. At the same time this parental behavior may operate to keep the child tied to the parent.

Even if it is assumed that the family was not significantly involved originally in the development of the adolescent's drug problem, the family can, with expert guidance, help the drug abusing youngster to overcome the problem. This may develop into a long-term endeavor, in the more severe cases, requiring patience, firmness, persistence, and tolerance of frustration on the part of the parents. For this reason the parents often need the support of a professional during the process.

A central concept of family therapy is to work with and attempt to change the family system rather than the individual family members. The family, rather than the identified drug-abusing client, is the main focus of treatment. In some cases, the emotional atmosphere is so consistently negative or pathological in the family that it is necessary to treat teenage drug users in a different living milieu, away from the family. Inpatient or residential treatment may also be needed by young clients who require a maximum degree of structure and control for their drug abuse and other problem behavior. The parents themselves may welcome the separation from the youngster, since it promises temporary relief from recurrent crises and behavior that they may feel helpless to control. In situations like these, the adolescent client is treated separately until it is determined that family interaction should begin. Where possible, programs have youngsters and their families participate in the same sessions, to help prepare them for the youngster's return home.

Not every family is available to participate in family therapy, and some are not willing to be involved. There are some families who are afraid of what might be exposed. In a recent case in our drug abuse treatment clinic, it was difficult to get the mother and the 15-year-old daughter, the drug client, together for a session. The mother showed up alone for the first scheduled family session, and stated that she was afraid to meet together with the daughter. She was very angry at her daughter's behavior, and was concerned that if she expressed her anger, it would be harmful to her daughter and would complicate the situation further. The daughter had started in individual counseling and was cooperating with the treatment. But she was adamant about not having joint sessions with her mother. It turned out that the mother had undergone major surgery several months earlier, and the daughter was afraid that if the anger between her and her mother were allowed to surface it could conceivably kill her mother. In such a situation the family is not ready for family therapy. Often family members need professional help and support on an individual basis before they are ready to face joint family sessions. It is possible that, in the case example cited, the mother and daughter could, after adequate preparation, have several joint sessions in which they could reach a better mutual understanding and a more satisfactory relationship.

Many adolescent drug abuse clients resist the idea of involving their parents and other family members in treatment. They want to be in control of what is talked about in the therapy or counseling sessions, to tell their side of the story or to withhold information about their questionable behavior. They are often also afraid of confrontation with their parents. Thus, they need to be reassured that the therapist is not going to side with the parents against them. Parents are also afraid of what the adolescent might reveal in the family therapy sessions: a parent's questionable behavior, a family secret, or problems in the parents' marital relationship.

It is important to get the parents working together to reinforce the family's generational hierarchy. At the same time, it is necessary to find appropriate ways to join and support the adolescent. Each side should be helped to recognize what is legitimate in the other's position.

The therapist looks for possible ways that the family problems, the negative aspects of the family system to which the adolescent drug abuser is reacting, can be changed so that the more positive and functional tendencies of the adolescent can emerge and be facilitated. Also, the therapist looks for potential assets and strengths that can be developed and actualized in each family member, and facilitates the adolescent's developmental need for individuation and differentiation.

One of the family situations in which it is easiest to see how the parents have contributed to the development of the problem is where they have been poor role models, particularly if one of them has been a substance abuser himself or herself (most often an alcoholic father). This inevitably has caused a serious problem in the history of the family and in the childhood development of the adolescent.

One example of such a family, recently seen by the authors, was a split family in which the parents had been divorced for six years and the father was currently involved in cocaine abuse. The mother, 36 years of age, was living with the only child, a 13½ year old daughter. The girl, Amy, was attractive, rather heavily made up with cosmetics, physically well developed, large for her age, giving the impression of being 15 or

16 years of age. She was quite popular in school. Some of the mother's complaints about the girl were: "Her behavior and attitude is getting worse, and she is failing in school. She rigged her school report card before she showed it to me. I had asked her in advance what grades I should expect to see, so that I would not be taken too much aback. She doesn't come home from school when she should. She lies to me all the time."

It appeared that Amy didn't have much self-restraint and was repeatedly asking her mother to buy things for her, to give her money, to permit her to go places and to do things. One day last week, Amy had telephoned her mother at work five times insisting that her mother agree to let her do something. The mother, who was busy at work, felt she couldn't take the pressure any more, "caved in," and agreed in order to get Amy off her back. Later, the mother was angry and reneged on a promise she had made to let Amy go skating on the weekend. "It's an impossible situation. I get angry at her every day. I'm 'lamming' off at her all the time. We never agree on anything or reach any conclusions."

The mother's inability to be consistent and firm with her daughter and to stand up to her was discussed. The mother admits that she "parentifies" Amy, needs her to help make decisions about the mother's own life, and this gives up to Amy a lot of power and authority. The mother has always related to and used her older sister this way. It was pointed out that it will not be best for Amy in the long run to be conditioned to be so unrestrained, demanding, and aggressive.

During the preceding two sessions the daughter had been saying repeatedly, with intense feeling, that she hated her mother and wished she had a different mother. It appeared, when this was explored, that the girl was becoming preoccupied and somewhat obsessed with this idea. It would come to mind during school hours and would interfere with her concentrating on schoolwork. The therapist decided to use a paradoxical prescription and give the girl the assignment of scheduling two minutes every hour, including school hours, to think about how much she hated her mother, and then to take five minutes after school each day to write down how much she hated her mother. The girl readily accepted this assignment, and managed to follow the prescribed behavior during the subsequent week.

Amy had also been saying in an angry, surly, belligerent way that she could not tolerate living with her mother any more, that she wanted to go live with her father (who had much more money, a large house, and so on) and his new family. The mother said: "He splits, turns her against me. I told him that I rather she not see him. He has disappointed her once too often. I bear her pain. But she telephones him when she has an argument with me." The mother had told the therapist separately on the telephone that the father really doesn't want Amy to come and stay at his house for any length of time, but that he tends to misrepresent and to lead her to believe that he wants her. The mother also expressed that she took it as a personal insult to herself that Amy wanted to stay with her father.

The therapist took the position that it might be good for Amy to have the opportunity to learn from the actual experience how it would be to stay with, or live part time with, her father's family rather than to fantasize about it and idealize it. The therapist encouraged the mother, who was afraid to let the girl go, to take a chance and let her go on a trial weekend to stay with her father. If she had used drugs before, she had not admitted it and the parents did not know about it.

On the girl's weekend at the home of the father's new family a crisis occurred: the girl left her father's house abruptly on Sunday afternoon and later arrived at her mother's house, and was "stoned" on drugs for the first time. Both parents had themselves used illicit drugs and the father was still using cocaine. Now Amy had, for the first time, seen her father and his second wife getting high together on cocaine. She had left his house and gone to some friends with whom she got stoned on drugs.

The parents each phoned the therapist immediately. The father had not seen the girl in her stoned state. His initial reaction was to be very angry at the mother for falsely accusing the girl of using drugs. Later in the day when he found out that the girl had lied to him over the phone and, in fact, had been stoned, he went over to the mother's house and struck the girl in the mouth. The next day at the end of the therapist's session with these family members, the girl dramatically threw her arms around her mother, and exclaimed, "Mommy, I love you." The mother was delighted, could hardly believe what was happening and was dancing in the hallway as she left the office. She called back to the therapist, "Did you see what she did?"

It is reasonable to assume that the father's hitting the girl may have had something to do with the dramatic turnabout in the girl's attitude toward the mother. The therapist's working with the family to lessen the impact of the girl's obsession with hating her mother might also have had an effect. It is conceivable that the therapist's authority involved in prescribing the hateful thoughts and feelings helped the mother to listen to such expressions without getting so angry and upset, and helped to release any guilt that the daughter might have experienced in connection with the hostile thoughts, and that somehow this process allowed whatever positive feelings the daughter had toward the mother to come through. In any event, such a sudden change may only have been temporary and superficial. This was suggested by the fact that the girl did not return home to her mother from school on the day of the next scheduled therapy session and missed the therapy session.

The adolescent girl had learned certain inappropriate ways to control the family situation in order to get what she felt she needed and wanted. The fact that both of her parents were emotionally immature, felt insecure in the role of parent, and related to each other to some extent as children, with sibling rivalry, laid some of the groundwork for the development of the adolescent girl's maladaptive behavior patterns. One got some impression of how the complex interplay of the motivations, needs, and problems of each family member and their relationship tendencies combined to make up the total family dysfunctional interaction system.

While the parents of the majority of adolescent drug abusers who come to treatment may not be users of illicit drugs themselves, as occurred in this particular family, or have alcohol problems, a number of the other characteristics observed in this family are seen in many of the families of adolescent drug abusers:

1. The family is split (the parents are divorced or separated).

2. The father has been abusive to the adolescent child.

3. The father has shown rejection of the adolescent.

4. The father displays impulsive and aggressive behavior.

5. The emotionally immature mother displays ambivalent feelings toward the adolescent (concerned about her, caring for her in some ways and trying to hold on to her, but resenting her and feeling inadequate as a mother and overburdened by the responsibility for her).

6. There is a lack of open, honest communication and trust between the mother and father, and between each parent and the adolescent child.

7. There is a lack of adequate understanding between the mother and child.

8. There is a breakdown of communication between the parents regarding the child, a lack of a unified approach to dealing with the child, and a lack of reasonable, consistent, and controlled discipline for the child.

As can be seen from the brief case report of family therapy above and the detailed case description to follow, the parents are likely to need a considerable amount of understanding, empathy, and support from the treatment team to help them with their difficult family situation. The following example of a family applying for treatment at a drug abuse clinic for their adolescent son is used to present a picture of the destructive impact of adolescent drug abuse on a family. It describes the personalities of the parents, their reactions to their son's drug abuse and delinquent behavior, and some of the family interrelationships. It also shows how the parents might have unwittingly contributed to the original development and to the maintenance or escalation of the adolescent member's drug abuse problem, and how their efforts to deal with it may be ineffective or counterproductive.

The following is a description of the scene at the drug abuse clinic when Bill Benson, an older adolescent polydrug abuser, arrived with his parents, who are both well-educated and have provided what appears to be a stable home in an affluent suburban community.

Bill pushed open the clinic door and let it swing behind him as he entered. His father, who followed several steps behind, caught it just before it slammed and held it for his wife, Bill's mother. Bill took one of the available seats in the waiting area and picked up a magazine as his parents approached the receptionist. No one in the lobby would have been able to discern that there was any relationship between Bill and the couple that followed him into the clinic.

It was the established practice of this clinic to see adolescent drug abusers with their families, and this was to be the family's first step into treatment for Bill's drug use.

Bill was a handsome, 17-year-old high school senior. He was neatly dressed in the "preppie" style typical of the teenagers who lived in his suburban neighborhood, which suggested both his awareness of and allegiance to an upper-middle-class youth culture. As he leafed through a magazine, he appeared determined to maintain an air of sullen indifference—as if he wanted everyone who saw him to make no mistake about his feelings—he didn't like being there, but he was resigned to it.

The attitude of being "resigned" to going to treatment was the result of several catastrophic events of ten days past: his mother's discovery of his "stash" of coke, pot, and pills; his own panicked realization later that night that someone had found his stuff and taken it; then, his sense of terror at being caught which he overcame by adolescent bravado; and his outrage that his personal property was taken from his room.

In spite of the late hour, he had barged angrily into his parent's bedroom demanding to know what had happened to his drugs. His mother acknowledged that she had taken them and stated that he could not have them back. Usually a calm, reasonable woman, now as angry as he, she threatened to call the police if Bill didn't get out of the room. The amount of drugs she had found made it clear that he was doing more than using a little pot and coke. She knew he was selling the stuff. After finally getting Bill out of their bedroom that night, the Bensons discussed what future action to take. This was not an easy discussion for Nora and Sam Benson. On one hand, Nora intuitively understood that she and Sam had to come to an agreement and to present a united front to deal with Bill; on the other hand, Sam had great difficulty accepting that Bill was abusing drugs and refused to believe that Bill was selling them—even when Nora presented the incontestable evidence. It was terribly painful for Sam to admit that Bill was disturbed enough to be involved in selling drugs and that he, his father, hadn't had the slightest idea.

For years Sam had been very involved with his teaching post at a local university and with his computer consulting work. Like a lot of fathers he spent less time with his family than he intended. It was also true that, over the years, he had completely relied on his wife's role as house manager and disciplinarian. Nora's disciplinary function with their two daughters, one older and one younger than Bill, seemed effective and appropriate to Sam. Both girls were good students and appeared to be happy and well adjusted. In contrast, Nora had been struggling with Bill's adolescence for years, and for the first time Sam realized that he had experienced the majority of this struggle indirectly, through Nora's eyes and interpretations. He seriously wondered now if he hadn't abdicated too much responsibility as far as his son was concerned.

Sam Benson also had great difficulty with the type of high-pitched emotional scene that had just transpired in their bedroom. No one ever shouted at each other in his family when he was growing up. The confrontation between Bill and his wife upset him to the point that he was paralyzed. He seemed overwhelmed by a combination of what he was actually feeling and his anxiety about the need for some authority or action on his part, and his ignorance of what to do. Unable to sort any of this out in the midst of the battle, he did nothing.

After discussing the situation at length, Sam and Nora eventually agreed that they had to make it absolutely clear to Bill that he simply could not deal drugs out of their house. They were unprepared, however, for his retaliation.

Although Bill had stolen money from the house before, the following day he tore through his parents' bedroom leaving it in disarray and took, it appeared, anything he thought he could sell; the clock radio, souvenirs, and an assortment of jewelry, which incidentally had only sentimental value.

The upshot of this was that Mrs. Benson had the house locks changed while Bill was out that evening. Naturally, he couldn't get in when he returned and started to shout and pound on the door. Nora told him through the door that if he wanted in, he would first have to tell her where the things were that were stolen from her room. "No—let me in, and I'll get them," was his reply.

Once Bill finally realized that he would get inside only by revealing where he had hidden the objects, he surrendered. The scene at the locked front door, of course, did little to ease the mounting family tensions, which exploded the following day. Mrs. Benson was baking lemon squares when Bill decided to heat some frozen fish sticks. He wanted to put them in the oven immediately; she wanted him to wait until the cookies were done to prevent them from tasting like fish. Another heated battle of words ensued. "You'll just have to wait a few minutes—they're almost done," stated Nora firmly.

Bill was not about to accept this answer. He went about removing the fish sticks from the package and placing them on a baking sheet. Nora, in disbelief, stood in front of the oven and repeated that he would have to wait.

Mustering all his grandeur Bill responded icily, "You'll have to learn that I do what I want." With that Nora, now infuriated with his behavior, knocked the tray from his hand. He grabbed at her wrist in an angry gesture and she stumbled trying to regain her balance. Remembering his martial arts training, for the first time in her life Nora was physically afraid of her son.

With the tensions at an apex, Nora shouted that she was going to call the police. Bill then adopted a karate stance, and Nora ran from her home not knowing what he would do or just how out of control he was. By that time it was late afternoon, and realizing that her husband was en route home, she waited at a neighbor's to intercept him.

The Bensons returned to their home shortly thereafter to find Bill moving the upstairs TV, shouting that he was taking it to recoup his losses from the drugs Nora had confiscated. At that point Sam Benson called the local police.

Relaying the precipitating incidents to the police, the Bensons were told that there was enough evidence to hold him; and so 17-year-old Bill Benson spent the next ten days in the county detention center.

It should be said here, after the recounting of some of Bill's problem behavior related to drug abuse, that there were also positive aspects in Bill's adjustment.

In one particular area Sam and Bill had a very good relationship. Sam had taught Bill as much general computer programming and systems analysis as Bill could absorb—which was quite a lot for a high school student. Because of Bill's skill, Sam was able to employ him on various summer projects at the university, and Bill's performance on these projects was top-notch. He earned a good salary and the money was very important to him. Not only did he do the actual work very well, he was able to interact with other staff and apparently conducted himself in a mature, responsible manner. Sam could now see how Bill's good behavior on the job stood in contrast to his unacceptable behavior in other areas.

What he did not see, however, was that Bill used his adult role at work as one way to relate to his parents inappropriately as peers, rather than as parents. Bill was able to assume this adult role, and to break the generational boundaries, in part, because of Sam's and Nora's inability to agree on clear limits for Bill.

Bill's behavior served additional functions, possibly for both of his parents. Sam had a strong need to express the anger that his upbringing and values inhibited. Tacitly, and probably out of Sam's awareness, Bill was acting as Sam's emotional proxy in giving expression to these negative feelings with Nora.

Nora also had difficulty with the expression of strong or negative emotions. Growing up in a home with an explosive, sometimes violent, father, Nora reacted against the pain of these early experiences and developed values that did not allow her to convey similar negative feelings. For Nora, Bill's behavior provided a degree of excitement which she intuitively needed and which she was not in touch with in other areas of her life. Her characteristic nonreactiveness may at times have reinforced Bill's tendency for more and more extreme behavior—until finally a heated confrontation occurred between them. During these exchanges, Sam was typically either a silent observer or absent from the scene.

There was still no conversation between Bill and his parents as they waited in the reception area. Bill's parents would have been more upset with the recent events if they had not in a sense been seasoned by and somewhat resigned to his increasingly incorrigible behavior over the last few years. His mother was willing to go another step to see if they could help him, to get to Bill in some way, but not much more than that. It certainly wasn't as if she hadn't tried—as if she hadn't, from her point of view, beaten her brains out looking at Bill's problems from every possible angle, trying to effect a solution, or at least some change. Thus the events of the past two weeks were almost, but not quite, the final straw.

At this point, we shall leave Bill as he sat mentally reviewing the details of his probation from the county, which included mandatory drug treatment. His name was then called for the intake interview and the Bensons followed Bill into the office, sat down and began to participate in developing the psycho-social history interview.

Let us now begin to explore the treatment entry terrain from the perspective of the drug counselor or therapist. The step into drug treatment is for most adolescents and their families, a pivotal and highly charged event. It is usually the result of a situation that has deteriorated progressively, often unchecked, over a period of years. Each individual new adolescent client then brings into treatment the accumulated emotional weight of all past days and nights that led him or her to this place or juncture. Typically this includes enormous pain and sorrow, the memory of drug highs and lows, the binges, the acting-out, the fights and the remorse, the family crises, violent arguments, school problems, legal problems, embarrassment, and quite often, the overwhelming sense of failure and confusion.

During their first contact with a drug treatment program adolescents are most often described by therapists as "sullen" and "closed off." The idea of entering treatment, in most cases, did not originate with the youth. Most often he or she is referred by the schools, the juvenile courts, friends or desperate, frustrated parents.

The gloomy, resentful, and resistant attitude that these young drug users initially adopt toward treatment is often seen as one manifestation of adolescent bravado which for some is their primary psychological defense against their own underlying pain and fear. Just reaching and making some genuine emotional contact with these young clients is in itself a difficult task, even for skilled and experienced drug counselors or therapists.

Many young clients are very noncommunicative at intake. Consistent with the description of Bill the adjective "sullen" captures the adolescents' response style. Since this response is so typical, therapists must develop strategies for coping with the client's silence. Regarding this point, one older therapist explained his approach in this way. "I talk about the adolescent experience directly with the kid and some of my own adolescent experiences. There's no point in denying the reality of our helplessness feelings. When the youngster sees that the treatment situation is not one of judged and blamed, he begins to talk, and things begin to happen."

A younger, more streetwise therapist may ally him or herself with the adolescent client in a variety of ways. The therapist may use humor, commiserate with the client about how "awful" it is to be taken to treatment when one doesn't want to go, or demonstrate his or her ability to speak the language of the adolescent. Once the therapist is established in the client's eyes as a non-enemy, he or she can usually be a powerful factor in helping the client to see that significant adult "others" are not enemies either.

The young client typically has great difficulty stating the problem, but most frequently, he or she may say: "I want to get my head together," or "I'm okay; my problem is that my parents are on my back." Commonly, however, the adolescent is denying a very real, serious, and acute problem.

The feelings and emotional state of the parents of a youth who is entering drug treatment are very telling for the treatment process, and therefore, must be explored, clarified, and understood. They themselves have most likely experienced a degree of emotional upheaval comparable to that of their child and have lived through the child's rebellion and antisocial and/or self-destructive acting-out behavior. Consequently, the emotional "baggage" and disturbed feelings that they carry to the first treatment session may be even heavier than those of their child, since they include the weight of their own problems as adults and often the feeling of having failed as a parents.

In describing the parents of adolescent clients at treatment entry, drug counselors report that the parents' feelings and attitudes are often muddled, confused, and in conflict within themselves. Also, conflict between the two parents is often apparent. They have been so emotionally exhausted by the events leading to treatment that they present a sense of hopelessness and willingness to give up. At the same time, they are described as overinvested emotionally in the problematic situation and as desperately seeking guidance and direction. From the therapist's viewpoint, the first task is to engage the adolescent client and the parents and attempt to establish some connection and rapport. Without such a connection (on a level of understanding, empathy, identification, or sympathy for the family) the therapist can have no real therapeutic effect. Different therapists approach the task differently. It seems natural that a young therapist would interrelate better with the adolescent client and that an older therapist would interrelate better with the parents. For this reason, if a program can afford it, it is often best to have a cotherapy team composed of an older and a younger therapist to work with the case, with the younger therapist providing the individual therapy to the adolescent client and the cotherapy team conducting family therapy sessions with the whole family. It also adds another useful dimension for the cotherapy team to be "heterosexual," and for the younger therapist who sees the adolescent client individually to be the same sex as the client. In some cases, the mother responds better to an older female counselor. The average drug treatment program, however, cannot afford to tailor the treatment team composition that is ideal for each case.

Almost all programs use the vehicle of the psychosocial history at the intake session for obtaining the necessary information, and as the first step in engaging the client and family in treatment. When this procedure includes meeting with the family members together in addition to interviewing them separately, it also allows the treatment team to obtain their first view of the nature of the family interaction and relationships.

A brief description of what the client and family will be asked during this treatment admission (intake) session follows:

The events and situations that led up to the application to treatment.

Basic demographic information about the client (age, sex, race, educational history, vocation history, hobbies and interests, living arrangements).

Reason(s) for applying for treatment.

Family background (parents' occupation, outline of structure of client's nuclear family, person(s) responsible for raising the client, siblings, birth order, a description of the quality of the client's family life, any alcohol or drug abuse history of other family members).

Information regarding the client's development and early childhood, particularly any disturbances/abnormalities in the client's birth, sleep patterns, unusual behavior, and so on.

Other notable features of the client's personal history (behavior problems, psychological problems, running away, physical or sexual abuse).

Medical history.

The history of the client's drug use and his or her perception of the effects of drug use: how it affected his or her life and functioning in school, at work, in the family, and so on.

Legal history, including the client's arrest record, details of his or her most recent brush with the law, and the client's probation/parole officer.

Previous treatment experience, if any.

In the history-taking session interactive family situations naturally emerge from the standard questions that are being asked. Some common parent-child interaction patterns noted by therapists are that a parent will identify the problem by reporting the child's bad behavior: "He's failing in school," "He breaks the rules," "He stays out all night and only comes home to shower and eat," "He's destroying the house," "She steals money," "He wrecks the cars," "She's acting out sexually."

In the face of such parent reports the adolescent will be on the defensive and will try to minimize the seriousness of the situation. Sometimes it appears that the parents, who have become tense, desperate, and angry, and worried for the future of their child, are overreacting.

While treatment philosophies, approaches and policies may vary from program to program it has become widely accepted that the family therapy approach has as good a chance as any other treatment approach to help solve the adolescent drug abuse problem.

References

Alexander, B.K. and Dibb, G.S. 1977. Interpersonal perception in addict families. *Family Process* 16:17–28.

Brooke, J.S.; Lukoff, I.F.; and Whitman, M. 1980. Initiation into adolescent marijuana use. *Journal of General Psychology* 137:133–142.

Cannon, S.R. 1976. *Social Functioning Patterns in Families of Offspring Receiving Treatment for Drug Abuse.* Roslyn Heights, New York: Libra Publications.

Friedman, A.S. 1983. High school drug abuse clients. *Clinical Research Notes,* July. Rockville, Maryland: National Institute on Drug Abuse.

Friedman, A.S.; Pomerance, E.; Sanders, R.; Santo, Y.; and Utada, A. 1980. The structure and problems of the families of adolescent drug abusers. *Contemporary Drug Problems,* Vol. IX, No. 3.

Hunt, D.G. 1974. Parental permissiveness as perceived by the offspring and the degree of marijuana usage among offspring. *Human Relations* 27: 267–285.

Jessor, R. 1975. Predicting time of onset of marijuana use: A developmental study of high school youth. In Lettieri, D., ed., *Predicting Adolescent Drug Abuse: A Review of the Issues, Methods and Correlates.* DHEW Publication No. (ADM)76–299. Washington, D.C.: U.S. Government Printing Office.

Jessor, R. and Jessor, S.L. 1977. *Problem Behavior and Psychosocial Development—A Longitudinal Study of Youth.* New York: Academic Press.

Kandel, D. 1982. Inter- and intragenerational influences on adolescent marijuana use. *Journal of the American Academy of Child Psychiatry* 21(4): 328–347.

Mead, D.E. and Campbell, S.S. 1972. Decision-making and interaction by families with and without a drug abusing child. *Family Process* 11: 487–498.

Mellinger, G.D.; Somers, R.H.; and Manheimer, D.I. 1975. Drug use research items pertaining to personality and interpersonal relations: A working paper for research investigators. In Lettieri, D.J., ed., *Predicting Adolescent Drug Abuse: A Review of Issues Methods and Correlates*. DHEW Pub. No. (ADM) 76–299. Washington, D.C.: U.S. Government Printing Office.

Streit, F.; Halsted, D.; and Pascale, P. 1974. Differences among youthful users and nonusers of drugs based on their perceptions of parental behavior. *International Journal of the Addictions* 9(5):749–755.

About the Contributors

Bruce Berg is an assistant professor in the School of Criminology at Florida State University. He served as an interviewer and data analyst on the ethnographic study reported in chapter 6.

Cheryl Carpenter is a doctoral student in the Department of Sociology at Syracuse University and has been an associate investigator on the ethnographic study reported in chapter 6.

Jerome F.X. Carroll received his Ph.D. in counseling psychology from Temple University in 1968. He has worked in the substance abuse field since 1971 and is currently the director of the Partial Hospitalization Program at Eagleville Hospital. He has published articles and chapters on addiction and has lectured on substance abuse in the United States and abroad. He developed the *Substance Abuse Problem Checklist,* a clinical assessment tool used throughout the United States and other English-speaking nations.

Leslie H. Daroff, M.Ed., is currently a family therapist/psychotherapist at Philadelphia Psychiatric Center's Drug Treatment Program. He received his certification as a family therapist from the Clinical School of Family Therapy of Family Institute of Philadelphia. Mr. Daroff was formerly director of services of Help, Inc., a crisis center and drug treatment program; and drug education specialist for the Department of Psychiatry at Thomas Jefferson Medical College. He appeared as a special witness for the U.S. Senate subcommittee on juvenile delinquency and methaqualone abuse. He coauthored the chapter "Basic Individual Counseling for Drug Abusers" in the recent NIDA publication *Treatment Services for Adolescent Substance Abusers* (edited by George M. Beschner and Alfred S. Friedman).

Harvey W. Feldman, Ph.D., the executive director of the Youth Environment Study (YES), received his doctorate degree from Brandeis University in 1970. He was a fellow of the Drug Abuse Council from 1972 to 1974 and an associate professor at St. Louis University from 1974 to 1976. He has written many articles on the subject of drug addiction and authored a book titled *Angel Dust.*

Allen Fields, Ph.D., is currently a student affairs officer at the University of California, Santa Cruz. He was previously a senior research associate for Youth Environment Study (YES). He has conducted a number of ethnographic studies in the substance abuse field and has authored numerous publications based on these studies.

Barry Glassner, Ph.D., is a professor and the chair of sociology at Syracuse University. His most recent books are *A Rationalist Methodology for the Social Sciences* and *Discourse in the Social Sciences.* A book on the study reported here is in press, *Burnouts to Straights: Drugs in Adolescent Worlds.* Glassner has published articles in journals such as *American Sociological Review, Journal of Studies on Alcohol,* and *American Journal of Psychiatry.*

James A. Inciardi, Ph.D., is a professor and the director of the Division of Criminal Justice, University of Delaware. He received his Ph.D. in sociology at New York University, and has extensive research, teaching, field, and clinical experiences in the areas of substance abuse, criminal justice, and criminology. He has done extensive consulting both nationally and internationally, and has published more than 100 articles, chapters, and books in the areas of substance abuse, history, folklore, criminology, criminal justice, medicine, and law. Dr. Inciardi was the director of the National Center for the Study of Acute Drug Reactions at the University of Miami School of Medicine, vice president of the Washington, D.C.-based Resource Planning Corporation, and associate director of research at the New York State Narcotic Addiction Control Commission and the Dade County Comprehensive Drug Abuse Treatment System. He is a former editor of *Criminology: An Interdisciplinary Journal.*

Stanley Kusnetz, M.S.Ed., is a program analyst in the Division of Clinical Research of the National Institute on Drug Abuse. He had been a commissioned officer in the U.S. Public Health Service since 1967. He received a degree in rehabilitation counseling from the City University of New York. He has produced a number of publications related to rehabilitation and to occupational health and has been active in the field of rehabilitation both as a researcher and clinician.

Jerry Mandel, Ph.D., is a social historian who has studied drug policy and treatment issues for more than twenty years. He served as a fellow of the Drug Abuse Council in Washington, D.C., during the early 1970s. He is currently working as an ethnographer for the Youth Environment Study in San Francisco.

S. Jeff Marks, M.F.A., is unit director of the Wurzel Clinic of Philadelphia Psychiatric Center Drug Treatment Program and the director of the Clinical School of Marital and Family Therapy, Family Institute of Philadelphia. He is a contributing editor of the *American Poetry Review;* author of *Lines,* poems published by the Cummington Press; and coeditor of *About Women* and *Between People;* and cotranslator of *Clouded Sky.* His poetry has also appeared in many newspapers, magazines and books. He is a coauthor of the chapter "Basic Individual Counseling for Drug Abusers" in the recent NIDA publication *Treatment Services for Adolescent Substance Abusers.*

Sidney H. Schnoll, M.D., Ph.D., is chief of the Chemical Dependence Program at Northwestern Memorial Hospital and associate professor of psychiatry and behavioral sciences and pharmacology at Northwestern University Medical School in Chicago. He is a graduate of the New Jersey College of Medicine and has a Ph.D. in pharmacology from Thomas Jefferson University in Philadelphia. Dr. Schnoll has published many articles in the field of substance abuse and is currently actively involved with basic and clinical research in addictions.

S. Kenneth Schonberg, M.D., is an associate professor in the Department of Pediatrics of Albert Einstein College of Medicine—Montefiore Medical Center in the Bronx, New York. He has authored more than a dozen articles and chapters dealing with both physiologic and behavior concommitants of adolescent drug abuse. He has served as both a member of an Executive Counsel of the Society for Adolescent Medicine and as an associate editor of their *Journal for Adolescent Health.* He is currently a member of the Task Force on Drug Abuse of the American Academy of Pediatrics.

Arlene T. Utada, M.Ed., was court psychologist and trainer of group therapy, Neuropsychiatric Division, Court of Common Pleas, Philadelphia, 1968–1972; research associate of the Philadelphia Polydrug Research Center and research psychologist at Philadelphia Psychiatric Center, 1975 to present. She is currently coordinator of the Family Therapy for Adolescent Drug Abuse Demonstration, Philadelphia Psychiatric Center. She has coauthored various journal articles including: "The Structure and Problems of the Families of Adolescent Drug Abusers" and "Characteristics of Drug Users in Urban Public High Schools."

About the Editors

George Beschner, MSW, is chief of the Technology Transfer Branch of the National Institute on Drug Abuse (NIDA). An official of the Institute since 1971, he has authored numerous articles and books on the subject of drug abuse. He began his career in the delinquency field with the New York City Youth Board in 1958. During the 1960s he directed community action programs in Washington, D.C. and Southern Maryland. He received a master's degree in social work from Columbia University and taught on the faculty of the University of Maryland.

Alfred S. Friedman, Ph.D. is director of research at the Philadelphia Psychiatric Center. He has served as president of the Family Institute of Philadelphia, chairman of the American Psychological Association's Committee on Relations with the Social Work Profession, as emeritus director of the Clinical School of Family Therapy, Family Institute of Philadelphia, honorary full professor, Department of Psychiatry, Thomas Jefferson University Medical School, and as a consultant to the Technology Transfer Branch of the National Institute on Drug Abuse. Dr. Friedman has developed and directed large-scale federally funded research projects on schizophrenia, depression, drug therapy, marital therapy, juvenile delinquency, and youth drug abuse. He has published numerous clinical research papers and books.